Date Due

JUL 15			
AUG 8			
MAY 26			
JUL 14			
8			
W			
R			

819.09 Water

Waterston, E.
Rapt in plaid.

PRICE: $45.00 (3559/go)

RAPT IN PLAID
Canadian Literature and Scottish Tradition

Rapt in Plaid

Canadian Literature and
Scottish Tradition

ELIZABETH WATERSTON

UNIVERSITY OF TORONTO PRESS
Toronto Buffalo London

© University of Toronto Press Incorporated 2001
Toronto Buffalo London

Printed in Canada

ISBN 0-8020-4785-8

Printed on acid-free paper

Canadian Cataloguing in Publication Data

Waterston, Elizabeth, 1922–
   Rapt in plaid : Canadian literature and Scottish tradition

   Includes bibliographical references and index.
   ISBN 0-8020-4785-8

   1. Canadian literature (English) – Scottish influences.* 2. Canadian
   literature (English) – History and criticism.* 3. Scottish literature –
   History and criticism. 4. English literature – Scottish authors –
   History and criticism. I. Title.

   PS8097.S36W37 2001   C810.9   C00-932193-4
   PR9185.3.W37 2001

University of Toronto Press acknowledges the financial assistance to its
publishing program of the Canada Council for the Arts and the Ontario
Arts Council.

This book has been published with the help of a grant from the Humanities and Social Sciences Federation of Canada, using funds provided by
the Social Sciences and Humanities Research Council of Canada.

Support of this publication by the Scottish Studies Foundation is gratefully acknowledged.

The University of Guelph Research Board awarded a grant in aid of
publication from the General Research Grant of the Social Sciences and
Humanities Research Council.

University of Toronto Press acknowledges the financial support for its
publishing activities of the Government of Canada through the Book
Publishing Industry Development Program (BPIDP).

Contents

Preface

In a multicultural, post-colonial age, it is not fashionable to focus attention on a single, imported strand in the national fabric. From earliest days, however, the Scottish strand has remained strong, colourful, and resilient in Canadian life. Post-colonial meditation on the development of a national identity separate from its early borrowings cannot ignore the evidence that Scottish attitudes and experiences have played a disproportionate part in developing a Canadian tang in literature and life. This book is a study of the influence on Canadian literature of certain Scottish writers. It is also a memoir of my own encounters with those writers, as a teacher, researcher, and editor.

My lifelong professional interest in Scottish-Canadian connections has been augmented by a lifetime of pleasure, as a reader, in Scottish and Canadian books. The books that enriched and sustained me when I was young remain as fresh as ever, sixty years after I entered academic life. And the fascination of watching the interconnection between two fine national literary traditions remains as great.

Acknowledgments

Over many years, my research on Canadian and Scottish literature has been supported by travel and research grants from the Canada Council and the Social Sciences and Humanities Research Council. The University of Guelph and the University of Western Ontario have furnished research funds, space, and secretarial and research assistants; again gratefully noted. In the National Archives of Canada, the National Library of Scotland, the Edinburgh University Library, the Beinecke Library of Yale, the Weldon Library at the University of Western Ontario, the McLaughlin Library at Guelph, the Fisher Library in Toronto, and the MacLennan Library at McGill University, librarians have always been very helpful. I also want to thank my husband, children, and grandchildren, and my friends, particularly Mary Rubio, for their support over a long-drawn-out process. I am grateful to Gerald Hallowell and others at the University of Toronto Press for encouraging me to go on with the manuscript, to various assessors who offered suggestions for improvement, to Jennie Litster, who provided inestimable research help in Edinburgh, and to Elizabeth Hulse for her final sensitive editing.

The work of Milton Acorn is reprinted by kind permission of Mary Hooper. *The Wars* by Timothy Findley, copyright © 1977 by Timothy Findlay, copyright © 1986 by Pebble Productions, is reprinted by permission of Penguin Books Canada Limited.

x Acknowledgments

The work of Northrop Frye is reprinted by permission of the University of Toronto Press. *The Fire Dwellers* by Margaret Laurence is used by permission of McClelland & Stewart, Inc., the Canadian Publishers. Quotations from the work of Dennis Lee are reprinted by permission of the author; from W.O. Mitchell by permission of Orm Mitchell; from L.M. Montgomery by permission of the heirs of L.M. Montgomery and the University of Guelph; from E.J. Pratt by permission of the University of Toronto Press; from Duncan Campbell Scott by permission of John G. Ayler. 'North Stream' by F.R. Scott is reprinted with permission of William Toye, Literary Executor for the Estate of F.R. Scott. *Silenced Sextet* is quoted by permission of McGill-Queen's University Press.

Part One

Auld Lang Syne

Freshman English class at McGill University. Moyse Hall holds five hundred; four hundred and ten of us are rustling and gossiping. Professor Cyrus Macmillan is about to begin his lecture to the freshmen of 1939. He is talking this morning about the ballads' 'singing strength.' (He pronounces it 'singgingg': perhaps a Prince Edward Island habit of dropping the final 'g' has been over-corrected?) Suddenly he's chanting, 'Why does yer brand sae drap wi' bluid, Edward, Edward?' And suddenly the freshman rustling stops.

Professor Macmillan is famous – perhaps not so famous as Professor Stephen Leacock, but probably just as clever and certainly considerably more sober. Professor Macmillan is from Prince Edward Island, but he was trained at Harvard as a specialist in ballads and folklore. He has published two books, *Canadian Wonder Tales* (1918) and *Canadian Fairy Tales* (1922). He tells us he finished writing the *Wonder Tales* while he was in the trenches overseas in the First World War. The *Wonder Tales* are Canadian Native legends; Macmillan had been gathering and collating them since his graduate days in the shadow of ballad collector Francis Child at Harvard. The *Fairy Tales*, published four years after the First World War ended, are Canadian folklore too.

It is Scottish folklore, in a variant picked up in Nova Scotia, that Professor Macmillan is unwrapping for us on this day as a new war is beginning. 'O, I hae killed my brother dear, Mither, Mither ...'[1] The accent is Scottish; the voice is a keening. The teacher has pulled us out of the dreadful timely tension over Hitler and Munich; he has tied us to older tragedies. It is a Scottish ballad that floods us with ancient and universal sorrow. *Lachrimae rerum*, the tears of things, Macmillan explains; a relieving function of art.

The legend at McGill is that if you want to pass freshman English, you need to know the Ballads, Burns, and the Bible. (A variant is Chaucer, Burns, and Carlyle.) Clearly, at any rate, you need to respond to British (and particularly Scottish) literature, rather than Canadian. Leon Edel, one of McGill's most distinguished graduates, remembers Cyrus Macmillan in the late 1920s as didactic, antagonistic to new ideas of poetry.[2] The bright young group around Edel – A.J.M. Smith, Frank Scott, A.M. Klein – are set on developing a Canadian voice and fitting that voice into the new chorus of complex, experimental poetry of the thirties. To them, Professor Macmillan is a fisher king, an old, repressive father figure to be challenged and killed.

But for us, in 1939, Cyrus Macmillan uses the simplicity of the old Scottish ballads to let fly the aural power of poetry. He asks us to chant with him, 'Why does your sword so drop with blood?'

Four o'clock on a summer afternoon in 1942. Mr MacCrimmon is wearing his kilt. Mr MacCrimmon is chief clerk in a big CPR office. He's also a piper in the Black Watch regimental band. All of us clerks – regular workers and summer help such as myself – know that a troop train must be due in to Bonaventure Station this afternoon. We will go later with Mr MacCrimmon; we will hand out coffee and doughnuts to the soldiers while he plays 'Wi' a Hundred Pipers an' A' an' A'.'

The soldiers disembark, form ranks in Bonaventure, and then march out to the harbour front. The pipes' skirl mixes with the cries of the French-speaking porters, shouting jokes about the *maudits anglais*, the soldiers, the war.

Montreal is built on the two peaks of an extinct volcano.

Near the crest of Westmount hulk the handsome, heavy homes built by descendants of the Scottish Victorians. The crest of Mount Royal carries a cross, placed by the earlier settlers, the French. Halfway up Mount Royal, McGill physicists unbind the atom. On the other side of the mountain, in Outremont, francophones debate socialism, elitism, feminism, and read canonized texts such as L'Appel de la race by Abbé Lionel Groulx.[3]

At the waterfront, soldiers march and porters jeer. Mr MacCrimmon is now part of a full circle of kilted 48th Highlanders, the Black Watch, pipes and drums ready to play 'Lochaber No More.' Then it's 'Will Ye No Come Back Again?' – song of farewell tied to the legend of Bonnie Prince Charlie, two hundred years ago and an ocean away.

We have been brought to these wartime docks by the romance of nationalism, the romance of history, and by the romancing of writers like Sir Walter Scott. In high school we read Scott's The Lady of the Lake and thrilled to the idea of a fiery cross calling the men of Clan-Alpine to do or die for a noble cause. We understand about loyalty. We have read about patriotic choice and destiny, about glory and fidelity. The soldiers – boys from Kamloops and Regina and Kenora, who also not so long ago read about the fiery cross – move toward the troop ship.

Tomorrow Mr MacCrimmon will be dressed in a gray business suit. The rest of us will go on tallying CPR dining-car orders. The gray troopship will have slipped away from romance to reality.

1944. Wartime night train rocketing from Montreal to Philadelphia, carrying me from undergraduate days to graduate school. As we approach the American border, a tug on the heavy green curtains of my lower berth. 'Customs and immigration. Your papers, please, and open your bags.'

I pull on my old Japanese red and gold kimono (long-ago present from a Presbyterian missionary friend). I open my suitcase: just a toothbrush – and three books in German (a brainbrush for a language-requirement exam to be written the day I arrive). Not good, says the immigration man. Also a book by Sir Walter Scott, for the course on romanticism I'll begin next week with Professor S.T. Chew. It's *The Lady of the Lake*, dug out of a trunkful of old texts from high school days. The cover of *The Lady of the Lake* features a burning cross and an unsheathed sword. Not good, says the immigration man again, and my papers now seem incomplete to him. Ferocious argument (not in Japanese or German). I must dress and get off the train at the border town to talk to the senior agent.

A ten-minute interview there with a curt but soon convinced agent; a five-hour sit in a grubby station, waiting for the next southbound train. Reading Sir Walter Scott ...

Crossing a border: very romantic. Much in the tradition of Scott's *Waverley*. And much in the mainstream of Canadian archetypes – a bemused stranger coming to an unknown land.

Being a Canadian graduate student in the United States in the last year of the Second World War offers many lessons in nationalism. I spend my week days studying romanticism and other such topics; I must choose a subject for a master of arts thesis, so as to finish the graduate year and get back home to teach Canadian servicemen, now being demobilized and flooding into college classes. My Bryn Mawr supervisor, Professor Chew, is interested in the flow of ideas from one nation to another via literature, particularly fiction. Walter Scott, says Professor Chew, as a conservative exponent of romantic ideals between 1810 and 1830, fostered a strain in American literature that treasured tradition – a Washington Irving strain of folklore, a Fenimore Cooper strain of frontier legend, a strain of southern fiction idealizing old days, old ways. A possible thesis topic here, says Professor Chew.

On weekends I go into Philadelphia and do 'war work' – conducting American servicemen on tours of historic sites. Professor Chew's notes on the pervasive influence of Walter Scott jostle in my mind with the memorized tourist-guide spiel about the Declaration of Independence, the rejection of rotten aristocratic British influences.

The weekend tours throw other lights on inter-national influence. On tour Sundays, after the memorized spiel about 'defying British might' and asserting American liberty and independence, we go back to the canteen for coffee with the soldiers. They are not interested in defying German might, but in flattening the Japanese and in arguing ferociously with each other about the unmatched glories of home regions, north and south, east and west. They dance with a freewheeling gusto amazing to a conservative Canadian.

Professor Chew suggests that a study of English influences on American literature and vice versa – Scott on Irving, Emerson on Carlyle – would be 'a good topic for a British student like you.'

'But Scott and Carlyle aren't English; they're Scottish.'

'Same thing,' says Professor Chew.

'And I'm not British; I'm Canadian.'

'Same thing,' says Professor Chew.

All that was many years ago. For over half a century since then, I have been reading and enjoying, teaching, editing, assessing, publishing, and rereading all sorts of lyrics and narrative poems and historical novels, short stories and prose of thought, magazine articles and sentimental romances and children's literature. After sixty years it's maybe 'time to draw in sails,' as Ralph Waldo Emerson says, and to quit thinking about books; but I have the opposite urge – to sail out a little farther, to skim and chart the shores of my lifelong literary horizon. Before the Gutenberg world finally merges into Nintendo land, I want to remember what reading has meant to me and to speculate about the general functions of literature. I also want to remember the way Canadian literature emerged, in my own lifetime, as a teachable subject and as an enjoyable, challenging part of reading experience.

As it happens, most of the books I have always liked have been by Scottish or Canadian writers. My grandmother made Scottish Robert Louis Stevenson's *A Child's Garden of Verses* my bedtime favourite; Canadian L.M. Montgomery led me through adolescence. I acted in Scottish J.M. Barrie's *A Kiss for Cinderella* as a student at McGill University; Canadian James Reaney's *Colours in the Dark* showed me what other dimensions theatrical work could move into. My post–Second World War college students taught me how to wrestle with the ideas of Scottish Thomas Carlyle. Margaret Laurence's Canadian novels sustained me through the years of interlacing housework and career, and John Buchan's Scots romances helped me evade their tedium. Nowadays I get new surprises from Canadian Alice Munro's short stories, and I catch myself singing Scottish songs by Robert Burns that I thought I had forgotten. Stevenson, Laurence, Buchan, Montgomery, Munro – a not-so-motley crew since all carry a strong Scottish strain, even though some of them are clearly Canadian. Sure, I have my English Trollope summers, my Austen springtimes, and my American winter evenings with Wharton or Whitman, but the once-a-year steady pleasure-givers happen to be Scots or Canadians.

Am I perpetuating a colonialism? Evading the multicultural nature of modern Canada, ignoring the modern commitment to a global internet? Forgetting that we are already living in a 'post-national' state: 'invisible to its own citizens, indistinguishable from its fellows, maintained by invisible political forces, and significant mainly through its position within the grid of world-class cities,' to quote Frank Davey?[4] I must confront and justify my Scottish and Canadian focus by demonstrating the depth and breadth of my favourites, by considering the historical significance of their sequence and, for students of Canada, the strong colour they lend to the national plaid, when woven in with other strands.

In Scottish and Canadian literatures I can feel most clearly the changing functions of poetry and fiction in my own life and in my teaching practice. The situation in each nation and in its literature seems to clarify that of the other. Here are two northern nations, ironic and sentimental, each quietly resentful of the stronger, more affluent neighbour lying south of the national border, indifferent to or unaware of the impact of its culture on others. Here are two sets of writers whose literary strategies and structures have been sharpened and maybe warped by the northernness, the doubleness, the angular spareness of their heritage, and the pressure of alien alternatives. Here are two countries where writers laid out a wide range of literary kinds, each genre developing under the pressure of time and place as well as through the freaks of individual ambitions and experiences.

When Scots immigrants came to Canada in the early nineteenth century, they brought Robert Burns's values with them, packed into their psyches, just as the volume of his poems was packed into their brass-bound sea trunks. Soon Walter Scott's swing to long, idealistic, romantic narratives found Canadian readers ready to soften and gentle the Burnsian passions. The mid-Victorian eruption of Thomas Carlyle's corrosive, metaphorical prose chimed with Canada's concern and uneasiness over a developing materialism and utilitarianism. John Buchan, one of the Scottish literary innovators to come in person to Canada, found here an already strong attachment to his kind of writing, mystery thrillers, or as he called them, 'shockers,' fit escapist reading for a war-troubled twentieth-century generation.

That historical sequence of Scottish ways of writing, from Burns through Scott, Galt, Carlyle, and Stevenson to Buchan, however, seems not merely to parallel phases in the development of Canadian culture. It also offers analogies to unchanging Canadian geographical iconography: focus on the flux of waterways, romantic reverence for the north, awareness of borders, of the lowlands of commerce and the highlands of idealism, and a yearning response to the mystique of islands, from pretty Prince Edward Island through savage Manitoulin to Victorian Vancouver Island.

My object in this book is not just to chart the sequence of Scottish and Canadian literary kinds, though the sequence is important and illuminating. Nor am I setting out just to trace the impact on Canadian literature of the Scottish tradition imported a hundred years ago, uneasily adjusted and naturalized, and surviving in disproportionate power. That is an interesting and complex story. Eager acceptance of Scottish models in the early days in Canada shifted in the nineteenth century into a sometimes unconscious reflection of a tradition perpetuated by Scottish orientation in Canadian schools and publishing houses. In modern times the influence has faded into a pale sense of affinity and recognition of the appropriateness of a comparable response to shared aspects of geography and political economy. These objectives impel me; but mostly I'm impelled to remember how particular books, Scottish and Canadian, have worked for me: to remember what fun it was to curl up on a Sunday afternoon, or to light a flashlight under the blankets, or to stand in a college library, leaning on the stacks, and give over to a book.

Out in the wider world there are still millions of readers – people who don't particularly care whether the book they are enjoying came from Scotland, Canada, or wherever. What they want is a good read: words on a page that will make them turn that page and the next and the next, until turning becomes unaware and reading a reflex. Sometimes those readers will want to slip from 'here' to the 'there' of a regional romance, or from 'now' to adventures 'then.' They may want to lurch from lassitude into violence, espionage, hunts through dark byways. Sometimes they pick up an old book of poems – a school text, maybe – to bring back school habits of attention and dreaminess; more often they read for something new. For every time, there is a genre, a special kind of book.

Perhaps our 'auld acquaintance' – literature of pleasure and stimulus, challenge, solace, ironic recognition – will soon 'be forgot.'[5] Maybe it will be video and television, movies and faxes, from this time on. But for now, on my bedside table lies an Alice Munro book, wrapped in plaid – a tartan dust jacket, adorned with a white rose and a blue teacup. Its title is *Friend of My Youth*. I'm thinking now about those books that were the friends of my youth, and I'm fingering the threads of the literary plaid woven in the past. Parts of that plaid we still need, I believe, in the cold blast of a post-literate world.

Over a hundred years ago Robert Louis Stevenson published a fine essay called 'A Gossip on Romance.'[6] I offer here a little gossip about romantic novels – and about poetry and irony and the functions of literature. Like most gossip, this one begins with people. The people are Scots writers who had an impact on Canadian literature (among other achievements). And the gossip goes from there to thoughts about the kind of things they wrote, what their impact was, why the literary forms that the Scots developed worked for a while, didn't work after a while. Then I'll call to mind how Scottish writers affected those Canadian readers who were also writers. An astonishing number, including many with no conceivable hereditary debt to Scotland, still draw strength from Scottish models, even when the Scots, in Robert Burns's phrase, may 'be forgot.'

And indeed, the first old acquaintance to be brought to mind is Robert Burns.

Chapter One

Burns, Acorn, and the Rivers of Song

This is the gossip: Robert Burns grew up in a poor time, in a thin-soiled farmland. As a boy he knew the comfort of a good home. Saturday nights in the farmers' cottages, the Presbyterian Lowland families 'took the book' and read the Bible passages.

After the older folks had gone to bed, though, the young fellows might slip out to the village, where the older lads were gathering to swagger a bit, to flirt with the girls, to watch and listen when the older cotters in the tavern raised a toast and a glass, and another glass, and another, in a toast to the lasses. The lads didn't waste too much time on the toasts – 'Come under my plaidie,' one could whisper to a girl in the dark road outside the tavern. Young Robert Burns sang the love songs for all the boys and girls:

> My love she's but a lassie yet ...
> Bonnie wee thing ...
> Ae fond kiss ...[1]

And paid the price, on Sunday, for being known as a ranting, randy lad; was pushed up to the front of the church to be shamed before the congregation for being a strong boy, over-sexed, under-occupied.

In the local taverns he sang a different song, voicing a proletarian rage against the lairds-turned-lordlings who were clutching the profits of the barley and the sheep for themselves:

> You see yon birkie ca'd, a Lord
> Wha struts, and stares, and a' that ...
> The man o' independant mind
> He looks and laughs at a' that. (K 2:762–3)

Burns paced out his poems as he worked in his father's inhospitable fields. The big visions of revolt and change alternated with small, sharp glimpses of nearer reality: the flowers at his feet, the river running near, the timid little animals startled by the coulter slicing through the sod – the small, sleek mouse scuttling out of Gulliver's way: 'Wee, sleeket, cowran, tim'rous *beastie*! / O, what a panic's in thy breastie!' (K 1:127).

Burns got drunk when 'Willie brewed a peck o' maut' (malt whiskey, that is). He disclaimed his drunkenness – 'We are na fou, we're nae that fou, / But just a drappie in our e'e ...' (K 1:476). Burns got caught when his girl got pregnant (one of his girls, that is). He swung into a sweet pride of fatherhood.

He went to Edinburgh and was recognized for the part he was playing in the renaissance of Scottish pride in local ways, local language, fifty years after the defeat of 'Bonnie Prince Charlie' seemed to seal the fate of Scotland's independence.[2] He fired up against the supercilious hand of English rule, imposed almost casually in 1707 and harshly reaffirmed in 1715 and 1745, with a ferocious cry: 'Scots, wha hae wi' WALLACE bled ...'

> Lay the proud Usurpers low!
> Tyrants fall in every foe!
> LIBERTY'S in every blow!
>   Let us DO – or DIE!!! (K 2:707–8)

Robert Burns, in other words, experienced intensely his work, his politics, his after-hours indulgence, his sex, his romance, his singing voice, and his sense of Scottish identity. That is the legend of Burns. That is the gossip that swirled around him in his lifetime and that has eddied around his memory ever since.[3]

There is an alternative view, however. Indeed, there are two alternatives. Both of them help to explain why Burns's influence was so strong, and why it lasted so long, in far-flung places such as Canada. First, and most stylish today, is the view of his power as coming, not from personal passions or a national renaissance, but from the universal tradition of carnival. The Russian cultural historian Mikhail Bakhtin, in *Rabelais and His World*, theorized that in every era, countering the official constraints of church and state, a carnival spirit erupted at dark hours.[4] According to Bakhtin, Rabelais's work reflects a disruptive proletarian revolt in France at the end of the Middle Ages. Robert Burns can be seen as releasing a later but similar revolt against propriety. He outfaced the restraints of the north, the dark cold of winter, the hard work enforced by a brief growing season, the repressive force of a generally dour Calvinism and an alien English imperialism. Blasphemous, coarse, a celebrant of drinking, laughing, coupling, eating, he pulled the eternal carnival spirit into singable, declaimable Scottish verse.

A different interpretation of Burns's poetic power has been offered by other modern scholars. Contradicting this emphasis on universal elements, literary historians such as Thomas Crawford, David Daiches, and Carol McGuirk attribute Burns's poetic powers to his particular times and the state of his nation.[5] His love songs developed, they say, out of the stylish sentimental mode of late-eighteenth-century literature. His resentment of authority rose specifically from Presbyterianism; his ingenuity in wordplay from the phenomenally fine educational system in Scotland.

The Presbyterian church that cut Burns down in public humiliation for his amorous exuberance did indeed give him two empowering gifts. The first was a tough democratic spirit. In the Presbyterian kirk, as distinct from the episcopal system of the English church, power did not flow from higher authority, from bishops and archbishops. 'Every man his own priest,' John Knox had cried as he thumped out his Scottish version of

Protestantism, and power remained vested in the ordinary members of the kirk. They elected their Board of Management for business affairs, their Session and elders for spiritual authority. They chose from among the men who preached to them and called as their minister the man of their choice. The minister preached on sin and salvation, but assumed no special power based on apostolic succession, no right to hear confessions or to dispense absolution. Minister and elders, at the national General Assembly, were chaired by a moderator, not led by an archbishop.[6] The levelling effect of Presbyterianism in church government might be countered by social hierarchies of lairds and ploughboys, or by spiritual differentiation between the elect and the damned; but a young Scot like Burns could still cry with Presbyterian assurance, 'A man's a man, for a' that!'

That cry was toughened, heightened, by the international spirit of the age. Populist revolution was in the air. There was poverty in Ayrshire, and there was the inevitable fury against the perpetrators of some of the tax bills and trade conventions and farming practices that brought the poverty. Burns's poems crystalized republican speeches and proletarian songs. In America in the 1770s, in France in the 1780s, the same revolutionary spirit was rising. Burns gave the democratic fury a song.

The words came cleverly and effectively, with apparent ease. That ease was the second part of his Presbyterian inheritance. Since Reformation days, Scots had argued that if every man was to be his own priest, then every man should have as good an education as the clerical class in a hierarchic society. The Scottish Education Act of 1694 had legislated that every child, rich or poor, male or female, had access to education. (In England a similar education act was not promulgated until 1870.)[7] After the Union with England in 1707, Scots maintained their control in the spheres of education, religion, and law. So every Scottish village had a good school.

Because his father procured a tutor for them, Robert Burns and his brother enjoyed something even better than the average village schooling. He studied grammar and rhetoric, logic and mathematics, and literature. Like Shakespeare, he had 'small Latin and less Greek,' but he was familiar with the best English writing of his own century. The language of his poems was a careful, clever blend of vernacular, archaisms, and English phrasing.[8] In many of Burns's songs, the Scottish dialect is integral. Yet the song of love in 'O my Luve's like a red red rose' is universal in appeal and in allusions: to a rose in June, a sweetly played melody, the seas, the rocks, the sands, the sun (K 2:734–5). This is poetry with the 'sing-ging strength' of folk song.

Because of the Scottish tenacity in preserving a native oral tradition, Burns was completely at home in folk songs and stories. He followed tradition in composing and declaiming mock-heroic ghost stories, low-key celebrations of peasant family life, eulogies of local heroes, political polemics. Burns was writing them all in the 1780s, forming a reservoir of popular feelings and attitudes, many of them contrary to acceptable theology and the proper sense of social hierarchy. Something disruptive, something anarchic, was set into those neatly rhymed lines. Some were recognizably in the imported aureate mode of Alexander Pope. Burns knew perfectly well the conventions of 'good' poetry. But even in long poems such as 'Tam o' Shanter. A Tale' (K 2:557–64) and 'The Cotter's Saturday Night' (K 1:145–52), he countered the Augustan elegance with folk-style phrasing and dialect. Poets like Pope had put into poetry 'what oft was *thought*, but ne'er so well expressed.' Burns chose to write 'what oft was *felt*' and to express common feelings in words that felt familiar yet roused admiration for their freshness and verve.

Soon the whole neighbourhood, the whole region, had heard of his verses. He had created and disseminated brief lyric bursts, memorable and soon memorized. He had released rivers of human song. And those rivers really were 'burns.' Not the wide Missouri, not the strong, busy Thames, not the cold continental St Lawrence, but little Scottish streams, bright and deep and swift, Burns's lyrics flowed with apparent spontaneity. But these songs flow between hard, clear banks of controlling form and management. Sometimes a familiar tune controls the lyrics: Burns's words must adjust to the patterns of a traditional melody. Sometimes it is the remembered pattern on the page of an older poem, the tight rhymed forms of Scottish traditional verses. Bird song may flow untrammelled, involuntary, and a human child may warble in the same intuitive way. But Burns, the adult song-maker, carefully channelled his songs. The first phrase might float up felicitously from his unconscious mind, but then came brain work, word work: finding the linked sounds, braiding the phrases, choosing the rhymes. He worked through deliberate repetitions, added variations, and concluded each lyric with a memorable twist, a change of tone.

Take 'Afton Water,' for example. The first line invokes the gentle movement of the river in nature: 'Flow gently, sweet Afton, among thy green braes'; the second adds a reference to that other flow, the flow of the poet's song: 'Flow gently, I'll sing thee a song in thy praise' (K 1:461–2). Third comes the addition, the variation – a thought of a girl by the river side: 'My Mary's asleep by thy murmuring stream.' Then the poet, empowered by love and by his control of words, can daringly aspire to control of the river, can boldly give it his orders: 'Flow gently, sweet Afton, disturb not her dream.' A perfect, surprising, apparently inevitable rhyme is delicately manoeuvred so as to close the thought, the rhythm, the mind play, and the momentary current of poetry.

'Afton Water' continues equally imperiously, with orders to the birds by the river:

Thou stock dove whose echo resounds thro' the glen,
Ye wild whistling blackbirds in yon thorny den,
Thou green crested lapwing thy screaming forbear,
I charge you disturb not my slumbering Fair.

The unromantic catalogue marks the difference between the instinctive sounds of nature and the sounds flowing from the poet's careful work, in which each syllable plays its inevitable, intentional part, and light rhymes echo the light rhyming of thought: stream/poem, birds/poet. This simple poem seems undemanding. But of the poet it demands a peculiar attitude to words, a sharp sense of their texture and sound and relationship to other words, that ripples along just beneath the current of meaning.

Whether Burns's poems came from an overflow of personal passion, from a voicing of a universal carnival spirit, or as a time-tied response to national peculiarities, his friends and neighbours accepted them and made them part of a rhetorical tradition. They sang or recited 'A red red rose' or 'A man's a man for a' that' or 'Scots wha hae' at community ceilidhs or convivial dinner parties. Poetry was part of a group activity that set itself against constraint, social, sexual, or political. Some of these warm-hearted gatherings were already convened specifically in Burns's honour in his own time. In midwinter carnival spirit, toasts were offered, parodying formal toasts to the king, to the bride – the revered king and the unravished bride. The three toasts at a Burns supper were Rabelaisian: to food (a toast to the pungent, inelegant haggis), to sex (a toast to the biddable, available lassies), and to Burns, uncrowner of the 'unco guid,' the lairds and the Holy Willies. That third toast, to Burns, celebrated the power of popular poetry.

With a quire of full-length narratives interlaced with passionate lyrics, love songs, and laments, Burns approached a publisher, quite rightly assuming the existence of a larger-than-local audience. In 1786 he arranged for the publication at Kilmarnock, near his home farm in Ayrshire, of a book of poetry.

The followers of Burns bought not just his book of poems. They bought his assumptions about what poetry is. For Burnsians, poetry sings; it is communal. It is heavy with central, familiar emotion. It is simple in rhythm, with repeated beat, returning refrain. Remembered as a ploughboy (his later elevation into exciseman and visiting poet in Edinburgh forgotten), Burns encouraged all the other 'ordinary people' of his time – the farmers, tailors, lumberjacks, and carpenters in Scotland and abroad – to look in their hearts and write. Not just to sing, but also to put the words of their songs on paper.

Burns's example encouraged poets to express common feelings, not in elegant abstruse aphorisms, but in 'the language
used by ordinary men.' That phrase is William Wordsworth's.
Wordsworth, an early admirer of Burns, would build his own
early poetry on the model of the older poet, although soon he
would drift into more complex poems, the reflections of a most
unordinary man.[9] Mobs of would-be poets, emboldened by the
example of Burns and the theorizing of Wordsworth, filled the
columns of local papers with their verses. Many a farmer and
weaver and housewife proved the danger of Wordsworth's
notion. Strong emotion and simple language do not suffice to
produce Burnsian songs, unless the singer has Burns's ear, his
perfect pitch, his ability to tune in to his own insights without
pretensions or condescension, his witty and poignant selection
from ordinary dialect. Burns looked in his heart and sang, but
he wrote his heart-born singings down with artistry and finesse. Soon his poems were learned 'by heart' by thousands of
his countrymen, and then by a world of readers.

   Poems, Chiefly in the Scottish Dialect, by Robert Burns was the
right thing to pack in with one's dearest belongings when the
hard times grew harder, and Robbie's neighbours and family
and girlfriends and drinking cronies faced the hardest neces-
sity: to up stakes and leave Scotland. Burns himself gave grim
consideration to the possibility of emigrating. He thought of
going to Jamaica, not to Canada, but he did not. He stayed in
Scotland and died there, still young, still enormously gifted in
song. But his works went abroad.

In Canada, in the early nineteenth century, there was hardly a
household that did not treasure a copy of Burns's poems. So
when Canadians felt the urge to write verse, many of them
found themes and meters in Burns, and a tone and a language –
poetry not intellectual, not complex, but simple, homely lyric.
Such poetry is not a frill for a leisured class. It is a good kind of
literature to keep the love of words alive in a situation where a
non-singer might be driven into perpetual, sullen silence. In
Canada, partly because of that initial appropriateness, partly

because of the continuing Scottish dominance in education and publishing, Burns's influence lasted a long time.

Scots formed an important part of the first wave of settlement in British North America. Some came to Nova Scotia in the late eighteenth and early nineteenth century involuntarily – cleared from the Highlands by landlords intent on changing from crofting to sheep-grazing. Others came by choice, dreaming of a life better than that in the impoverished countryside or the slum-slipping cities, Glasgow, Aberdeen, Edinburgh, Dundee. Some settled on the fringing isles, Cape Breton, Prince Edward Island; others spread into New Brunswick and Lower Canada, especially into the Eastern Townships south of the St Lawrence. Still others went further up the St Lawrence into the Upper Canadian counties they named Glengarry, Stormont, Dundas, Perth, Lanark, Elgin, and Bruce. Scots moving still farther west would put names such as Mackenzie, Fraser, Banff, and Selkirk on the map of Canada.[10]

The first sizeable Scottish settlements were military. Members of Highland regiments, disbanded after the Seven Years War ended in 1763, took up land grants at Murray Bay in Lower Canada and Mount Murray in Nova Scotia. Other large Highland military groups settled in New Brunswick, Nova Scotia, and Upper Canada after the end of the American Revolution around 1783.[11]

Still other groups of Scottish settlers, from both the Highlands and the Lowlands, came from 1765 on, as participants in 'proprietary schemes' run by people such as John Pagan, an entrepreneur from Glasgow who brought settlers to Pictou, Nova Scotia in 1773; Sir James Montgomery and John 'Glenaladale' MacDonald, who helped to settle Prince Edward Island; Archibald McNab, locating fifteen families up the Ottawa Valley in 1825; and the Earl of Selkirk, settling eight hundred people in Prince Edward Island in 1803 and, less fortunately, another group in Baldoon, near Lake Huron, in 1804 and disastrously in the Red River Valley in 1811–15. Later, the British American Land Company, chartered in 1834, and the New Brunswick and Nova Scotia Land Companies addressed their recruiting appeals largely to Scots. Because they came in nuclear-family groups, the Scots maintained their social and moral solidarity. Their loyalty withstood the assaults of American invaders in the War of 1812.

In the 1810s and 1820s the military and proprietary groups were augmented by 'free' settlers coming on their own, often seeking a remedy for the new ills brought on by the onset of the Industrial Revolution. Scottish ingenuity having developed machines that could replace hand labour, hand weavers and other craftsmen from the Scottish Lowlands formed a large proportion of this later wave of settlers. After the merger of the Hudson's Bay Company and the North West Company in 1821, settlement in the northwest began, consisting mostly of Scottish immigrants, administrators, clergy, and police. The far west was to have its own leadership roll-call of Scottish names: James Nisbet (1823–1874), born in Glasgow, first missionary to the Canadian west, who founded Prince Albert in 1866; James Macleod (1836–1894), commissioner of the North West Mounted Police from 1877, and A.G. Irvine (1837–1916) in command of the NWMP during the 1885 Riel Rebellion; James Douglas (1803–1877), governor of Vancouver Island from 1851 and of British Columbia in 1858–64; Matthew Begbie (1819–1894), born in Edinburgh, appointed chief justice of mainland British Columbia in 1866 and chief justice of the province of British Columbia four years later; Kenneth McKenzie (1811–1874), also born in Edinburgh, recruiter of settlers for Vancouver Island on behalf of the Puget Sound Agricultural Company; and Richard Alexander (1844–1915), yet another Edinburgh man, migrating to Canada in 1862 and becoming active in the Vancouver Board of Trade.[12]

Yet although many a Scottish-born leader was ready to conform to the establishment, from the early days, conservative administrators coming to the Canadas and the Atlantic colonies from Scotland met radical insurgents, also coming from Scotland, such as Robert Gourlay (1778–1863), a native of Fife, and William Lyon Mackenzie (1795–1861), born in Dundee.

The Scots brought their folk arts with them. Dance – not the sinuous chain of linked dancers as in Greece or Israel, but the angular solo dance of hunter or warrior, hands angled like antlers, toes pointing and shaking with the delicate strength of the stalker. And weaving – again not the motif-enriched work of Ukraine or Norway, but strong weaving of earth tones into squares and oblongs. Song – not the choir work of Wales or Russia, hundreds singing as one, but solo singing, single voice raised at the local ceilidh, single voice cherishing the words as well as the melody. And recitation – words without music, words linked in their own sequence of sound, vowels and consonants slipping into a relished alliterative sequence, as in Burns's lines, declaimed 'off by heart' at a Burns supper. The toast 'To the Immortal Memory' affirmed the worth of poetic expression, delight in language, and the possibility that plough-men and tax collectors might feel the divine afflatus, even in a very cold country.

In successive waves of immigration in 1770–5, 1790–3, 1801–3, and 1805–11, the Scots brought reverence for their native land. They also brought an assumption that Presbyterians were God's elect, that a well-woven plaid was the best provision for warmth, elegance, and durability, and that the poetry of Burns was indubitably the best literary model in the world. In Canada there was little of the contemporary American rejection of 'old country' influence; Canadian Scots took a truly colonial delight in retaining the old ways, the old language patterns, and the old arts. The Canadian poet in his bower, rapt in thought, was likely also to be wrapped in plaid.

Since most Lowland Scots immigrants, even the poorest, were probably better educated than their English counterparts, they drifted easily into teaching and into printing shops and newspaper offices. Scottish dominance in Canadian education and publishing began. The roster of early Scottish-born leaders in education includes Thomas McCulloch (1776–1843), born in Renfrewshire, migrating to Pictou in 1803, and in 1838 becoming first principal of Dalhousie College, Halifax; John Strachan (1778–1867), born in Aberdeen, migrating in 1799, first president of King's College, Toronto (1827) and founder of Trinity

College, Toronto (1851); and John Machar (1786–1863), born in Forfarshire, coming to Kingston in Upper Canada in 1827 as a Church of Scotland minister, and serving as principal of Queen's College in 1846–54.[13] Indirectly connected with education was James McGill (1744–1813), who gifted land to found McGill College in Montreal in 1827.

In *The Beginnings of the Book Trade in Canada*, George Parker writes of the army of Scots who dominated early nineteenth-century editing, bookselling, printing, and publishing, instancing early journal editors such as Alex Spark (1762–1819), who worked on the *Quebec Gazette* and edited the *Quebec Magazine* between 1792 and 1794; Glasgow-born James Brown (1776–1845), who bought the *Montreal Gazette* in 1808; and David Chisholme (1796–1842), born in Ross-shire, editor of the *Canadian Magazine and Literary Repository*, 1823–5, the *Canadian Review and Literary and Historical Journal*, 1824–6, and the *Montreal Gazette* from 1836. These editors were complemented by book publishers, including John Neilson (1776–1848), born in Kirkcudbrightshire, owner of the *Quebec Gazette* and its attached bookstore and press from 1797; James Lesslie (1802–1885), born in Dundee, who owned the *Toronto Examiner* in 1844–54; John McMillan in Saint John; Robert Armour (1781–1857) from Kilmarnock, founder of the *Montreal Almanack* in 1829 and proprietor of the *Montreal Gazette*; his son Andrew and partner Hew Ramsay, who became the leading booksellers in Canada in the 1830s; George Renny Young (1802–1853), born in Falkirk, founder of the *Nova Scotian* (1824) in Halifax; Hugh Thomson (1791–1834), immigrant in Upper Canada by 1812, founder of the *Upper Canada Herald* in 1819, who later joined forces with James Macfarlane in running the *Kingston Chronicle* and in the 1830s the *Brockville Gazette*. A plethora of well-known editors and publishers maintained the Scottish qualities in Canadian books and journals.[14]

In early anthologies of Canadian poetry, such as E.H. Dewart's *Selections from Canadian Poets* (Montreal: Lovell, 1864), the names of the poets read like the roll-call of the clans or like a digest of the Glasgow phone book. McCarroll, McIntosh, Murray, Ramsay,

Wallace – they are all there, major makers of a nineteenth-century Canadian poetic tradition.[15] In the Maritimes, Andrew Shiels (1793–1879), farmer, magistrate, and prolific poet of Dartmouth, Nova Scotia; Moses Nickerson (1846–1943) and David Little (d. 1881) of Nova Scotia, and William Murdoch of Partridge Island (1823–1887) are cited by Fred Cogswell in his chapter in the *Literary History of Canada* as followers of Burns in form and language, witness a verse by Murdoch quoted by Cogswell:

> God pity, then, the poor blue-noses,
> Their cheeks like flour, their nebs like roses;
> They puff they grue, and swallow doses
>   To heat their wame,
> Till oft when night their business closes
>   They hiccup hame.[16]

Other pre-Confederation poets, not necessarily Scottish in heritage, wrote in Burns's short lines, with his strong rhymes and rhythms; they sang like him of elemental emotions – love, patriotism, amusement at neighbours' pretensions – and appropriated his sentiment and his response to nature's details (though one poet might substitute 'To a Dandelion' for 'To a Daisy,' and others might find inspiration in pretty Canadian streams in lieu of 'The Banks o' Doon').

Central among these early poets was Alexander McLachlan (1817–1896), who gloried in being called 'the Burns of Canada.' In the 1840s this big, rough-bearded tailor settled just west of Toronto, there to raise a big family and a big reputation as a poet. Born in Renfrewshire, Scotland, twenty-two years after Burns's death, McLachlan had learned from his reading of Burns how to value and express the warmth of his own feelings for his 'cotter' home, the tenderness of his first love, the sympathetic delicacy of his response to small things in nature. Contemporary poets in the United States – the young Walt Whitman, for example – might wrestle words into a new expansive rhythm, a democratic swinging length of line, a republican idiosyncrasy of language. Alexander McLachlan blithely lifted from Burns the rhyme schemes and rhythmic patterns of established tradition.

Far from being anxious about the danger of imitation, he was delighted to let Burns's ideas flow through his own poems.[17] Writing a poem to a Canadian hummingbird ('Circled in a radiant ring'), McLachlan swings, Burns-fashion, from a fond and tender response to the small creature into a sad and rueful and humorous recognition of human realities: 'But, like pleasure, lovely thing, / Thou art ever on the wing.'[18] He was proud that in *Sketches of Celebrated Canadians* (Quebec: Hunter Rose, 1862), the contemporary critic-historian Henry J. Morgan saw him as being to Canada 'what Burns was to Scotland.'[19] McLachlan addressed Burns in one of several poems as 'thou glory of our race' (95).

His debts never included picking up Burns's bawdiness. Nor were his love songs (to his wife, mother of his eleven children) as passionate or haunting as the earlier poet's. But he did well with other Burnsian themes. In his newly chosen country, McLachlan, tailor, cobbler, unsuccessful farmer, taunted the would-be aristocrats – 'my lordly fellow-worm,' he called one of them. 'Are ye o' Robin Burns's line?' he scolded a submissive fellow who was prepared to take off his cap in deference to Canadian authority:

> Gie honour to the brave and good,
> To them, and them alone;
> E'en tho' inspired by gratitude,
> Man, keep your bonnet on. (363)

Good stuff to learn by heart and to recite at a farmers' gathering, a Mechanics' Institute meeting, or a Burns Night supper. Mocking pretension, disrespectful, McLachlan remembered Burns's 'A man's a man for a' that.' He added the Canadian proof that 'Jack's as good as his master':

Here's to the land of lakes and pines,
On which the sun of Freedom shines,
Because we meet on all our lines
The man who rose from nothing. (204)

It was the carnival cry of reversal, the celebration of a break-up of order and stasis, fixed in the New World by a 'Family Compact' of the high-culture establishment.[20] Yet McLachlan countered that utopianism with a bitter proletarian protest:

We live in a rickety house,
In a dirty dismal street ...
And pious folks with their tracts
When our dens they enter in,
They point to our shirtless backs,
As the fruits of beer and gin.[21]

This is not simple imitation. Notably, the Scots dialect has been washed out by the new local content. 'Shirtless' and 'rickety' have a New World ring. Yet, as in all his best poems, McLachlan here retains the auditory appeal of Burns. The art of song is there, the crafting of short lines so that they set up a little melody in the mind.

McLachlan published his first volume of verse in 1846, when he was twenty-eight years old. A later and better volume followed in 1856, and in 1859, when he spoke in Toronto at the hundredth anniversary of Burns's birth, he was hailed as 'at the head of the literature of the working classes.'[22]

His longest, and most discussed, poem, 'The Emigrant,' presents a puzzle. It capped seven strong sections on early settlement life with a promise to go on to write about modern changes in the hands

[o]f the swarms of public robbers
Speculators and land jobbers –
Of the sorry set of teachers,
Of the bogus tribe of preachers,

Of the host of herb physicians,
And of cunning politicians. (256)

But the promise was never fulfilled. In his fine edition of 'The
Emigrant,' David Bentley suggests a reason for that discontinu-
ance. McLachlan in 1862 was appointed emigration agent, to
encourage Scottish workers to come to Canada. It would hardly
be appropriate, Bentley argues, for an official spokesman for
Canada to expose its contemporary troubles.[23] McLachlan hardly
dared go on with an indictment of the Canadian lordlings, the
capitalists, the Holy Willies of Toronto.

His failure to finish 'The Emigrant' may also stem from two
other causes. The poem shows a weakening of original power,
as the poet depends less on Burns and more on Longfellow and
Wordsworth. As high Victorianism suffused Canadian publications, every reader (and writer) felt increasingly the constraints
of 'Parnassian' taste for propriety and decorum. 'The Emigrant'
remains unfinished because the old farmer-cobbler-tailor, like
poetry itself, had lost his early energy. Something had happened to the poet (namely, age) and something had happened
to poetry (namely, prettiness). Second, the running-down of
energy may have stemmed from the fact that McLachlan remained an emigrant, not an immigrant. He was too tied to his
native range of awareness to be able to move on and adjust as
poet to his new homeland. It was a mark of his limitation as
well as of his achievement that he was always called 'the Burns
of Canada.'

In *Tradition in Exile* (1962), John Matthews paid tribute to
other Burnsian poets, Scottish-born versifiers, contemporaries
of McLachlan: Alexander Glendinning and Robert Boyd.[24] Their
popularity reflected the nostalgia of many Canadians who might
still cry with McLachlan, 'When I hear the sweet lilt of o' some
auld Scottish sang, / Oh, how my bluid leaps as it coorses
alang!' (103). Long after his 'bluid' stopped leaping, McLachlan's
verses remained in Canadian school readers and in anthologies
of poetry, maintaining Burnsian metre, tone, and language. His
collected works were published in 1900, four years after his

death, and eight of his poems appeared in *Selections from Scottish Canadian Poets*, published in Toronto (under the auspices of the Caledonian Society of Toronto) by Imrie, Graham, and Company, in the same year. Thirty-six other poets of Scottish descent were also featured in this neat little volume, including Alexander Muir, author of 'The Maple Leaf Forever,' A.J. Lockhart, and Evan MacColl, Gaelic bard of Lochfyne and of Kingston, Ontario. Burns was still strong among these poets.

Many native-born Canadian poets at the turn of the twentieth century still bore Scottish names – witness William Wilfred Campbell, Isabel Ecclestone Macpherson MacKay, and Duncan Campbell Scott – but indebtedness to the old tradition was becoming diluted. Where Burns always linked details of nature with human passion, 'Sweet Afton' with 'my Mary,' 'Bonie Doon' with a once-'lightsome heart,' a Canadian post-Confederation poet such as Wilfred Campbell (1860–1918) in 'Indian Summer' used a Burnsian verse form to paint a world without a human presence:

> Now by the brook the maple leans
>   With all his glory spread ...,
> Now by great marshes wrapt in mist,
>   Or past some river's mouth,
> Throughout the long, still autumn day
>   Wild birds are flying south.[25]

Of course there was also less and less use of dialect. Writing in Scottish vernacular might constitute a stubborn patriotism in the old country, but in the new melting pot, Scots was less and less 'the language used by ordinary men.'

As elsewhere in the English-speaking world, new lyric strains fed into the Canadian poetic tradition, from Tennyson, Longfellow, and others. Lonely poets – Emily Dickinson in America, Gerard Manley Hopkins in England – had begun experimenting with new, difficult styles. Verse-making was becoming more private, more complex, more philosophic, than it had been for Burns and the Burnsians. The audience for poetry throughout the English-speaking world was becoming less general, more sophisticated, and considerably smaller.

Working in forms closer to Burns than to the experimental verse of Dickinson or Hopkins, however, at least four Canadian poets found worldwide popular audiences at the turn of the twentieth century: Robert Service (1874–1958), Bliss Carman (1861–1929), William Henry Drummond (1854–1907), and Pauline Johnson (1861–1913). All produced strong vernacular verse and carried it from the pages of little magazines out onto public platforms, both urban and rural. All four used swinging rhythms, folk language, and clicking refrains for aural force.

William Henry Drummond picked up the French-Canadian patois during his youthful summers as a telegrapher in Bord-à-Plouffe and his subsequent time (after graduating in medicine from McGill and Bishop's University) in the bilingual townships south of the St Lawrence River. An amateur elocutionist, he began incorporating his own 'habitant' verses into his performances and, from 1893 on, publishing them in Montreal newspapers. In the broken English of his Quebec patients, Drummond memorialized a peasant way of life, a simple religious faith, and a sturdy acceptance of hardship, in the same tone as Burns's 'The Cotter's Saturday Night.' Like Burns, he used a dialect that was an abstraction rather than a recording of actual speech. Some Québécois resented the touch of patronage in Drummond's comic dialect – a 'bastard idiom,' as La Patrie dubbed it. Other compatriots, such as Louis Fréchette, hailed his achievement as accurate and loving portraiture. A more modern view is that 'Drummond unconsciously "loosened the straitjacket of literary puritanism."'[26] At any rate, from the 1890s on, schoolchildren learned 'Leetle Bateese,' and elocutionists intoned,

For de win' she blow lak hurricane,
Bimeby she blow some more,
An' de scow bus' up on Lac St. Pierre
Wan arpent from de shore.[27]

Pauline Johnson, splendid in white doeskin, feathers, beads, and moccasins, disdained such thumping comedy. Daughter of a Mohawk chief and an English mother, she hypnotized audiences with the pounding force of the corn-dance song, lulled them with the hesitant rhythm, the linked similes of wind, trees, winging birds, and canoe in 'The Song My Paddle Sings,' chilled them with 'As Red Men Die.' From 1894 on, wide audiences in Europe and the United States, as well as in Canada, found value in Johnson's poetic celebration of endurance and resistance to wrongful discrimination:

> By right, by birth we Indians own these lands,
> Though starved, crushed, plundered, lies our nation low ...
> Perhaps the white man's God has willed it so.[28]

Pauline Johnson's two performance costumes, the Native dress and the satin elegance of a court lady, signified the same blend of authorized and counter-cultural forms that appeared in Burns's language, where vernacular was stitched to elegance. Pithy like Burns, she added to these Burns themes something else: a woman's sensibilities, her awareness of delicacies of opal-tinted skies, bubbles, and ferns, her memories of lullabies. And it must be said that she also added precious phrasings such as 'The velvet air, stirred by some elfin wings,' in 'Under Canvas, in Muskoka' (49). Such genteel delicacy meshed strangely with her harsher notes of social protest.

The blend of Burnsian love of liberty with *fin de siècle* delicacy had appeared also, since 1893, in the poetry of Bliss Carman. Carman struck many of Burns's familiar poses: passionate lover, ardent observer of natural detail, rebel against the 'unco guid' burghers and pushers of propriety. He had found a second Scottish model in Robert Louis Stevenson, and he appeared in public like RLS, extravagant in flowing clothes, conspicuous in his wild shock of hair, self-consciously a vagabond and a bohemian rebel. Fairly late in life, Carman began reciting in public halls and theatres all across Canada, half-chanting his short-lined rhymes about love, freedom, nature:

'The scarlet of the maples can shake me like a cry / Of bugles going by ...'[29] Or maritime ballads about the 'shambling sea,' pounding with a folk-song quality:

God, who sent him a thousand ships,
Will send him a thousand more;
But some he'll save for a bleaching grave,
And shoulder them in to shore –
Shoulder them in, shoulder them in,
Shoulder them in to shore. (51)

Singable, memorable – the audiences loved it, and him, and his lyric poems. He is remembered, nearly a century later, by Canadian men and women who learned the Carman verses when they were in school. Some of Carman they happily forgot, such as the lovesick twilight stuff written in the Celtic mode of the 1890s; but much they remembered because of its singing strength. For he too was 'o' Robin Burns's line' in his tight verse forms, his humour and naturalism, simplicity of diction and rhyme – and more important, in his concept of what poetry is, how essential is its performed presence.

But the real Burnsian in this turn-of-the-century group of popularizers of poetry was Robert Service. Service spent part of his childhood in Ayrshire. He claimed Burns as a remote cousin, 'savoured him at his saltiest,' and boasted in his autobiography, *Ploughman of the Moon* (1945), 'in my earthiness I have followed my kinsman Burns.'[30] As a youth in Glasgow, Service became a 'proletarian prig,' inciting his fellows to socialism, working for Keir Hardie's election in 1892, and only reluctantly beginning an unpoetic, unpolitical career in banking. Vagabonding westward over a six-year period (in a variety of stages, including a brief time as student for admission to McGill), he eventually wound up as a bank clerk again, in the post-gold-rush Yukon. Himself by this time abstemious, chaste, conservative, Service nevertheless gave voice to the uproarious, promiscuous, obstreperous folk 'up north.' No doubt his apprenticeship to Burns[31] had left him open to the carnival world that he celebrated, the world of 'Dangerous Dan McGrew' and 'The lady that's known as Lou.'[32] Certainly, he found his rhythms in Burns. He acknowledged, of course, the debt to his contemporary Kipling, but Kipling's *Barrack-Room Ballads* never included the coarse stuff that Service packed into his *Bar-Room Ballads*. The locale was a strange land under northern lights; the tales were ridiculous, unpredictable, eruptive, bumptious, disruptive; but the form and the function were still those of Burns: simple, accessible, singable, memorable. Retired in quiet affluence on the Riviera, Service wryly noted his long-lasting popularity:

> I wrote a verse of vulgar trend,
> Spiced with an oath or two;
> I tacked a snapper at the end
> And called it *Dan McGrew*
> I spouted it to bar-room boys,
> Full fifty years away
> Yet still with rude and ribald noise
>   It lives today. [33]

That last short line is what Scottish scholars call a 'bob,' the traditional concentrating click at the end of a stanza, quite the reverse effect from the English drawing-out effect of Spenserian lines. It seems to undercut sentimentality and 'poesy,' like the sharp wind of the north that epitomized Canada to non-Canadian readers. Like Burns, Service in his tight, controlled, and rhyming forms caught the wild folk response to the dark: the tavern life, the roaring drunken parties, the rowdy womanizing. *Ploughman of the Moon*, the title of the last volume of his autobiography, signals the Burnsian affiliation: in earlier volumes he presented himself as 'Sourdough,' 'Cheechako,' 'Rolling Stone,' 'Red Cross Man,' and 'Bohemian,' but in the end he adopted Burns's image.

His poems did indeed live, however much academic critics might belittle them.[34] As his Scottish biographer James Mackay says, 'No other poet, save Burns, enjoyed such a wide appeal with the common man.'[35] As for the common, and uncommon, woman, all, from Agatha Christie to Elizabeth the Queen Mother, were fans of Service in his own time. Sales of his books reached the millions. Over five million copies of *Songs of a Sourdough* had sold by 1958, when he died, long after his north Canadian days were over.

Drummond had died in 1907, Johnson in 1913, and Carman in 1929. In their work, Burns's compulsive rhythms, his gusto, his fun, his rebellious honesty, survived in Canada through the First World War. In the United States in the early part of the twentieth century, comparable performances by Carl Sandburg and Vachel Lindsay added the beat of machinery and of Afro-American music to the sound of popular poetry. Like Drummond, Carman, and Johnson, they drew thousands to their melodious readings. The third great American poet of the new century, Robert Frost, laconic, deliberately unmelodious, lowered the temperature, but he too brought poetry to a popular audience as well as to a learned one, from the time of the publication of his first book until his death in 1963. Canadians, however, paid little attention to these Americans. In the 1920s and 1930s our poetic affiliations were still basically British.

When I was a little girl (I was born in 1922), *The Empire Song Book* was our musical text, from grade three, when we could hardly read the words, to grade seven, when we were learning to 'sing in parts,' reading both the words and the musical notes. Our music teacher was a Scot. So were many, many teachers in Canadian city and country schools. Remember 'Mr. MacPherson' in Mordecai Richler's *The Apprenticeship of Duddy Kravitz* (1959) and 'Miss MacDonald' in W.O. Mitchell's *Who Has Seen the Wind* (1947)? In Montreal West elementary school in the 1920s we had Miss McLeod in grade two, Miss Carr in grade six, Miss MacCammon in grade seven, all Scottish in name though Canadian by birth. But our music teacher was fresh come from Scotland, and he led our little voices through Burns, Burns, and more Burns as we moved from grade to grade. In grade three we sang 'Ye banks and braes o' bonie Doon' when we were too young to know that 'braes' and 'bonnie' were not words in common usage in our native land. In grade seven, we thundered 'Scots wha hae,' from 'Robert Bruce's March to Bannockburn,'

Wha will be a traitor-knave?
Wha can fill a coward's grave?
Wha sae base as be a slave?
– Let him turn and flie. (K 2:707)

It was 1933; Mussolini was spreading tyranny and Hitler was inciting terrorism. Our fathers, survivors all of the First World War, were shedding their hope that their war had ended all wars and beginning to ask the same old questions: 'Who would be a coward knave? Who would lie, his life to save?' In peace and in the shadow of conflict, in happiness and sadness, Burns's songs supplied expression for us children in inter-war Canada.

Unnoticed by us, poetry, as accepted by new critics, was moving into a different mode. In Canada, in the States, and in Great Britain too, academics were slowly accepting the cerebral influence of T.S. Eliot. His erudite, abstruse poetry was concentrated in hidden chains of metaphor, subtle gradations of sound, half-rhymes, and deliberately faltering rhythm. A new conception about poetry – or at least a revival of the metaphysical kind of poetry written in the seventeenth century by John Donne. In Canada, at McGill University, a group of young writers were already changing their assumptions about what poetry is, how it works, and what sort of readers can appreciate it.

Frank Scott, A.J.M. Smith, A.M. Klein, and Leo Kennedy were diverting the stream of lyric poetry into new channels. Beginning in the English Department once dominated by Cyrus Macmillan, these young Montrealers (one Scottish in ancestry, one Jewish, two English) encouraged each other in the creation of difficult, lonely music – 'a beauty of dissonance' (to quote A.J.M. Smith); 'a moving / with no note' (F.R. Scott); 'purities / curdling upon themselves' (A.M. Klein). Such a music seemed to the poets appropriate not only in general for the modern age

but also in particular for Canada. After all, the rivers of Canada
– the northern and western rivers like the Mackenzie and the
Fraser – are not friendly burns for fly-fishing but channels to
penetrate a strange continent. In the new imagist way, Frank
Scott gave voice to a 'North Stream,' far different from 'Sweet
Afton':

> Ice mothers me
> My bed is rock
> Over sand I move silently ...
> Foam runs from the rapid
> To rest on my dark pools.[36]

No Mary, asleep, in this clear, cold poem; no bird song. Like the
Group of Seven paintings, which are cognate to poetry of this
kind, this is 'landscape without a face.'[37]

This difficult Canadian poetry moved away from the vernacular. It moved also from populism into elitism. By the 1930s,
students at McGill and the University of Toronto, and 'down
east' at Dalhousie and 'out west' in Manitoba and 'on the west
coast' at British Columbia, began to bypass the easy-reading
poems of Sandburg and Frost, Service and Carman, in favour
of 'lonely, difficult music.' Old, widely accessible poems such
as Burns's got even shorter shrift. His smoothness, rhyme,
singing rhythm, and neat stanza forms were all rejected. Taut,
complex, metaphysical poems led sophisticated teachers (and
hopefully, students) into rarefied analysis and image-chasing.[38]

By the late 1940s and early 1950s Burns's poems appeared
on college reading lists, if at all, as negative examples: illustrations of the absence of wit, of wordplay, of intellectual challenge. The occasional student would raise a protest, 'But I *like*
Burns better than Donne and T.S. Eliot.' A would-be-stylish
teacher had to pray for patience.

It took considerable schooling and willingness for readers to
follow and enjoy the delicate dance of images, metaphors, sound
chains, and play of thought so complex that an attendance of
footnotes was necessary for comprehension. This poetry led

into a Wasteland very different from Burns's country. Poetry readings became increasingly rarefied and sparsely attended. In 'Portrait of the Poet as Landscape' (1948), A.M. Klein soberly admitted, 'from our real society / he has disappeared ... / incognito, lost, lacunal.'[39] Most students assumed that poetry is all complex, compacted, with rhythms subtle to the point of being imperceptible. Even in grade schools, children were confronted with tiny imagist poems, the intention being to stir them to their own tiny imagist imitations. Small wonder that young people did not associate poetry with aural pleasure or with accessible, singable wording. The traditional joy in simple public poetry diminished.

One exception to this diminution was in the lingering popularity of Burns Night suppers – occasions, mostly in rural areas in Canada as in Scotland, when traditional toasts led to a recital of Burns's poems, usually followed by original verse, composed to Burnsian models and greeted with great appreciation by the devotees. These occasions validated the enduring popular feeling that anyone – not just an aesthete or a professor – could make verses to commemorate a special occasion or to honour a local hero. Thus Scottish tradition contributed strongly to the continuance of 'people's poetry' throughout Canada.

In *True Poetry: Traditional and Popular Verse in Ontario*, folklorist Pauline Greenhill documents the regional persistence of a tradition of folk poetry. She notes the objections raised by her professors in Texas that her research 'had located an unusually poetic community and/or a unique group of poets rather than a pervasive and highly significant Ontario cultural phenomenon.'[40] Her research, however, proves that verses created for and performed at gatherings such as Women's Institute meetings, wedding showers, and other celebrations do in fact connect with something 'highly significant.' The performances she records link with a phenomenon observable not just in Ontario but throughout the nation. Poets throughout Canada continue to express the aspirations and fears of a rural but literate population. I believe that a lingering memory of the 'ploughman poet' contributed to this unusual persistence of confident versemaking in rural communities.

Furthermore, these Canadian folk poets were not naive in their appropriation of poetic traditions. Scottish insistence on universal schooling, implemented in nineteenth-century Canada thanks to the support of people such as John Strachan, James McGill, and William Macdonald, among other influential, successful Scots, had meant that 'backwoods' villages in Canada were not backward.

Enter Milton Acorn, 'the people's poet.' Acorn (1923–1986) grew up in Prince Edward Island. Son of a military martinet who had been shell-shocked in the First World War, he joined up in the Second World War at the age of eighteen and was permanently damaged when a torpedo blasted his war-bound ship, HMS *Cameronian*. He came home to Charlottetown, and 'The Island' made him a socialist, a drinker, a carpenter, and a poet – a poet 'o' Robin Burns's line.'

Acorn had started for overseas with a Highland regiment: 'Down Great George Street, up to the station, / The skirl of the pipes the very thrill of your nerves.'[41] War confirmed him in political protest, summed up in 'Rabbie still be with us':

Canucks wha hae bled beside Mackenzie
– last man to retreat from Montgomery's tavern
– haven't we got a Scottish situation?
Much more in common than good whiskey ...
On a hundred foreign fields crosses and shattered corpses
Commemorate our pointless victories. (*MPP*, 12)

Burns *was* with Acorn, often in intensified form. Burns sang of love; Milton Acorn cried, 'I shout love even though it might deafen you' and 'My heart's a furred, sharp-tongued thing' (*ISL*, 12). Burns wrote affectionately of the simple bareness of the cotter's Saturday night; Acorn moved through to a fiercer attitude to poverty: 'I've tasted my blood too much to love what I was born to' (*DUMH*, 130). Some of Acorn's little elegies for his mates flood us with the same deep sadness as Burns's line, 'Man was made to mourn.'

If Burns wrote of a river, so did Acorn – 'Jack and the River,' a poem truly in Canadian dialect – about a river when 'The thaw's come down and she goes with a roar':

> 'Bet you it's nice on the river Jack?'
> 'I'll say she is ...
> That river keeps flowing!' (*IMM*, 40)

Not a burn this, but a Canadian river; but also not a Group of Seven river, like Scott's 'North Stream.' It is a river 'where young fellas swim,' 'fishermen dawdle and dream.' It is also a river changed by the Canadian climate and mirroring the deprivations and depravities of the country:

> 'What's it like now with the river Jack?'
> 'You wouldn't call it a river at all:
> It's a glassy plain where the slow drifts crawl
> In a bitter wind that freezes your brain.
> There's cracks 'cross the ice like drunk men's scrawls,
> And icicles hang from its waterfalls,
> But underneath in the pearly dim
> Where the fat fish poke in their lazy swim –
> She's still flowing!' (*IMM*, 40)

Like Burns, the poet slips into the apparently effortless rhymes, and like Burns, Acorn recognizes and admits the analogue to his own concerns. He moves beyond clever play with the image of scrawled surface and still-flowing life in the depths to a necessary comfort, and he demonstrates the old, possible fit between fine poetry and common needs and experiences.

Like Alexander McLachlan, in a new localized echo of Burns's cool catalogue of birds by 'Afton Water,' Acorn concentrates on the Canadian hummingbird:

> I saw one with wings
> a pipesmoke blur
> shaped like half a kiss
> and its raspberry-stone
> heart winked fast in
> a thumbnail of a breast.[42]

Acorn's images in this poem do not end with their own cleverness. They lead to a ferocious bit of advice to the 'charming little being': 'Grow stings!' 'Honesty's the first and main tool of a poet,' he said.

Milton Acorn visited Montreal in 1949, moved there in 1953. Unlike Burns in his visits to Edinburgh, he found in the centrifugal city a group of like-minded poets: Al Purdy, eking out a living in a mattress factory while polishing his early poems; Irving Layton, teaching part-time, writing full-time in Rabelaisian eruption ('What luck, what luck to be loved / by the one girl / in this Presbyterian country / who knows how to give / a man pleasure'[43]); Frank Scott, battling authoritarianism and Duplessis's fascism both in poetry and in legal and political action. When I was teaching at Sir George Williams College (later Concordia University) in the 1950s, Milton Acorn was one of a group of poets who moved in and out of classrooms there, haranguing the students, selling mimeographed poems, surviving.

With publications in chapbooks, in the Marxist publication *New Frontiers*, in Montreal and Toronto 'little mags' such as Louis Dudek's *Delta* and his own little mag *Moment* to his credit, Acorn prepared to move in more disputatious mood to Toronto.

By this time, a younger poet was beginning to sing in Montreal in the 1960s. Leonard Cohen (born in 1934) lived a life that was the polar opposite of Burns's or Acorn's. He was urban, child of a wealthy Jewish family, living in Westmount, university educated. Once again, McGill University had something to do with the emergence of the new, popular poetry. In Moyse Hall and then in all the comparable assembly rooms in Canadian colleges, Leonard Cohen raised his unmistakable voice. The new rivers of song were dark like that chanting voice. 'Flow gently, sweet Afton, among thy green braes ... / My Mary's asleep by thy murmuring stream' rasped into 'Suzanne takes you down / to her place by the river ...'[44] Cohen brought from his own ethnic background the plangent melancholy of Jewish music and the randy brashness of music-hall comics, but much of the lyric tension in his poems came from the straining of one kind of heritage and sensibility through another. After all, he went to school in a Montreal system still dominated by descendants of the Scots and still inclined to beat out the old tunes in *The Empire Song Book*. Maybe a memory of 'Annie Laurie' impels the new song: 'With Annie gone / who's to compare?' (68). Like Burns, like Acorn, Cohen knew how to raise a primal song, to lift poetry off the page and bring it to the people.

Leonard Cohen moved on to recordings, films, television, and public appearances. Milton Acorn, in the 1960s in Toronto, found a different medium. He read at new counter-culture groups, both at poetry readings in taverns and at political rallies for Marxist protests. It was at the Burns's memorial in Toronto's Allan Gardens that he fought for the poet's right to read in public.[45] The public enjoyed the spectacle of poets challenging policemen. The poetry, however, proved not as accessible as Burns's had been because the stream of poetry had moved on, through modernist, imagist loops.

If gossip swirled around Robert Burns, it churned in the wake of Milton Acorn. Torontonians gasped at his marriage to mystic, *soignée* Gwen MacEwen – he himself pictured it as the short-lived marriage of Beauty and the Beast. Schoolteachers shuddered when it turned out that, at 'Canada Days' convened to introduce real live poets to their classes, Milton Acorn, half-drunk and thoroughly disorderly, emerged as the most real, the most live, and the most popular of the visiting writers. And the academic establishment that had been garnering governor general's medals for poetry shuddered when a congregation of poets put on a roaring parody of the governor general's ceremonies, awarding a new medal to Milton Acorn as the 'People's Poet.' His award was presented in a Toronto tavern.

Milton Acorn's taut, vernacular verse was paralleled in Scotland in the verse of Hugh MacDiarmid. But because the two traditions, Scottish and Canadian, had now lost their connectedness, Acorn never named, probably never knew, and certainly never echoed his powerful Scottish contemporary. The dialect that had endeared Burns to their great-grandfathers was now a bar to the generation in Canada that might have relished MacDiarmid's *A Drunk Man Looks at the Thistle* (1926).

After Acorn's heyday, poetry dimmed and dwindled again in popularity. Poetry readings in the 1980s again became esoteric, apolitical, an in thing for sophisticates. On the radio and on CDs and records, however, poet-singers, survivors from the seventies, continued to reach huge audiences. Gordon Lightfoot still celebrated, like Burns in the 1780s or like Alexander McLachlan in the 1850s, the small beauties of 'Pussywillows and Cat-tails' or 'The early mornin' rain.'[46] Stompin' Tom Connors, who came, like Milton Acorn, from Prince Edward Island, where old ways lingered, to central Canada, still thumped out a new version of Burns's drinking songs: 'The men are gettin' stink-o, / And there ain't no time for Inco / On a Sudbury Saturday night!'[47] The truck driver pushed his rhymes beyond the confines of elitism, like the carpenter, the tailor, and the ploughman before him.

As for the 1990s, the lyrics of popular songs owe more to the revival of wordplay in American rap music than to any lingering memories of Burns. The serious poetry currently being 'critiqued' at workshops, the poems I listen to now at poetry readings, are nervous, introspective, clever, complex, but they lack the 'singing strength' of Burns. Folk in the modern city never go along to the Burns Night suppers that pull rural communities together in the coldest week of January. Maybe Canadians no longer need Burns to keep the river of song flowing in the chilly night. But his poems served Canada well in the past. People working in the 'cauld blast' of northern winds and northern irony found in him a much-needed warmth. His sweetness, his vigour, his laughter, his bawdiness, his obstinacy, and his honest anatomizing of a hard, ordinary life helped our first poets to release their singing power, and helped more modern balladeers to find their own voices. Burns's values – the Scottish emphasis on independence and universal education and his scorn of pomposity – remained woven into Canadian culture long after his poems were commonly heard or read.

Mouré, Moritz, Michaels, Reibetanz, Tregebov – the names of these significant newly published poets in Canada now trail no Scottish echoes. But neither do their publications flow, for me at least, with the singing strength of the past. In nostalgia I turn on my car radio. The Rankin Family of Cape Breton are singing an old ballad: 'My heart's in the Highlands.' They sing without attribution to Robert Burns, who wrote the song (K 2:527), let alone to Walter Scott, who once gave the dream of the Highlands a universal currency.

Chapter Two

Scott, Crawford, and the Highlands of Romance

When Walter Scott was a youth, he met and revered Robert Burns. There is a charming picture of Scott as a boy in silk breeches gazing up in awe at burly Burns, briefly the darling of Edinburgh drawing rooms. Burns was a freakish visitor to Edinburgh; Walter Scott had been born there in 1771, privileged son of a lawyer (indeed, a writer to the Signet) and of the daughter of a university professor of medicine. But Scott, like Burns, was to spend childhood years in the countryside. Lamed as a baby by a form of polio, he was sent to his grandparents in Tweeddale, and there he absorbed the love of nature that would suffuse his early poetry. This passion for nature was to be one of Walter Scott's gifts to the romantic revolution which characterized poetry at the turn of the nineteenth century.

Soon he would be moved back to George Square in Edinburgh, to tutors and school and college, but he was already poised to offset the urbane rationality of the Enlightenment period, now in its amber evening. He lived in a city of peaceful propriety, in a nation that had weathered nearly a hundred years of union with England. Edinburgh was called (and not just by its own citizens) 'the Athens of the North.' The city of Scott's youth still glowed with intellectual activity in philosophy, economics, theology, and historiography.[1] Edinburgh's New Town offered clear vistas, symmetrical rows of houses and gardens decorated in the style of Robert Adam, delicate, well balanced. The revolutionary ardour that had ignited Burns had been doused by the horrible excesses in post-1791 revolutionary France. But Walter Scott would lead a revolution of a different sort – a literary shift in values. In place of a taste for balance, authority, and control, he would help to instill a passion for shadows and intensities. 'Romantic,' he called it later, 'that delightful feeling for the beauties of natural objects ... romantic feelings which ... gave to my admiration a sort of intense impression of reverence ... an insatiable passion.'[2]

It is not gossip that hovers over the life of Scott but a misty romantic glamorizing. His biography, piously composed by his son-in-law, John Gibson Lockhart, codifies that warm legend.[3] The legend is faded now, but the influence of the warm-hearted, energetic, furiously productive writer remains, both in the tradition of idealistic nature poetry and in the more ambiguous historical novels of his later days.

From childhood, Walter Scott had absorbed the tales of lords and ladies, chieftains and clansmen of olden days in Scotland, remembered by country folk and passed along to a little boy limping in from his pony rides to listen. As a schoolboy antiquarian, Scott busied himself in retrieving physical memorials of a feudal age, as well as the Scottish folk ballads of old-time love and war. (Eventually he would publish collections as *Minstrelsy of the Scottish Border* in 1802 and 1803.) In his own early compositions he celebrated the life and belief system of that older time of fierce loyalties and heroic pride. He also enjoyed the poems of two older fellow Scots – James Thomson's 'Winter,' from *The Seasons*, and James Macpherson's Ossianic fragment – both celebrating the wild appeal of Highland places. In the newer work of his English correspondents, William Wordsworth and S.T. Coleridge, he found poetic excursions into mysterious seas, romantic chasms, and ruined abbeys. Like all romantics, he was 'amorous of the far.' He delighted in long-ago deeds, faraway places, passions and values of classes no longer powerful – anything a long way from the humdrum of modern urbanism.

He married rather less than romantically. Stealing time from his growing young family, Walter Scott began to ride out again to his own wild places: Loch Katrine in the Trossach hills; forests where 'the stag at eve' still reared his head when hunters approached; remote crofts and clachans where clan loyalty still lingered. Beyond the Lowlands he coursed, beyond Edinburgh and Stirling and into the Highlands, along the wild road to the isles and glens north of Loch Lomond. Scott came to revere the 'aboriginal races' of Scotland: the Gaelic-speaking Highlanders, whose values provided a striking contrast to those of his everyday world.[4] In his daily life as a young barrister he might espouse Lowland utilitarianism, material progress, and conformity to a comfortable marriage; in his poems he would celebrate opposite values, Highland values: unquestioning loyalty, fierce love, vigorous action.[5]

The idea that there was something empowering in the northern hills was in the air. Scottish scholars shared with Scandinavians an interest in old sagas.[6] 'Nordicity' was a buzz word, with a connotation of aboriginal power. Perhaps the notion of nordicity represented the inevitable pendulum swing against the pull of the great temperate-zone cities, London and Paris. Scottish historians view the Enlightenment as 'attuned to the ideas of North Europe: Germany, Scandinavia, partly in stubborn resistance to England.'[7]

Scott felt that his country was emerging from an age of barbaric heroic strength; but he believed that the new age needed to find ideals for life in the strength and mystery of Highland scenery. Encouraged by friends who had admired his *Minstrelsy* collections, he began composing long narrative poems idealizing the northern past. *The Lay of the Last Minstrel* (1805) opens with the image of an old harpist, 'wizard of the north,' celebrant of fierce feuds and battles. The first lines of *Marmion* (1806), where 'A northern harper rude / Chanted a rhyme of deadly feud,' suggest Scott's continuing desire to join the league of epic bards as celebrant of ancient Scottish life in the Highland realms. 'Harp of the North ... / O wake once more!' was the cry which sounded early in *The Lady of the Lake* (1810), best loved and longest remembered of all his poems (I.i.1, 19).[8]

But Scott was not a northern harper rude; he was a nineteenth-century romancer. His dreams of the past carried him not to barbaric brutalities but to an image of life ennobled by the beauties of nature, and to an idealization of courtly love and chivalric combat. *The Lady of the Lake* begins with a sweeping vision of precipice, lake, glen, and dale – 'the deep Trosachs' wildest nook' – as a majestic stag flies from huntsmen's pursuit (I.viii.15). The stag draws the hunters into a mysterious Highland landscape. The hunt ends; the 'antler'd monarch' escapes, and Scott swings his attention, first, to the kingly lead-huntsman, in terms emphasizing his kinship with the stag,[9] and then into a vivid description of a Highland sunset. The huntsman views the beauty of Loch Katrine, 'raptured and amazed' (I.xv.2). He maintains his sense of reverence and awe when he sees, within this setting, the beautiful young woman who is the 'Lady of the Lake.' The opening of Scott's long poem is 'nature poetry' of a kind intensely admired in its own time.

Ecocritics might well see in the opening of *The Lady of the Lake* an example of reverence, awe, and love for nature typical of the early nineteenth century. Scott and his fellow romantics began a century of poetry filled with wonder and admiration for landscape beauty. Scott's landscape writing released powerful emotions and ideas in the period before the world began to drift toward environmental consumption and destruction. This text, with its notion of northern place as cultural community as well as landscape, played its part in the development of ecological wisdom. Subsequently, modernist critics might decry 'landscape poems' and urge poets to focus on social issues; now, however, Scott's use of poetry to direct attention to the beauties of nature is being revalidated, as 'ecocriticism' seeks to rectify the erosion of human sense of relatedness to and responsibility for the non-human environment.[10]

Scott's description of the Scottish huntsman's response to the wild, strong beauty of the Trossachs implied a vision of the interface between individuals, nation, race, and place. Edward Said, in *The World, the Text, and the Critic*, writes of works like Scott's that 'texts are events,'[11] and he emphasizes 'the priority of a great work' in creating the sense for a reader of being 'at home in a place,' participating in a national-cultural community (154). More recent ecocritics explore the impact of landscape writing on the sense of responsibility for the environment. For Scott himself as an emerging author, describing nature was a conscious device for expressing the romance of his Scottish homeland.

The Lady of the Lake is also a 'romance' in the common sense of focusing on courtship. Two great heroes clash as suitors of Ellen Douglas, the lady of Loch Katrine. But their wooing is gentle, restrained to speeches and glances, sighs and sentimental songs. Scott was freshening fiction after a half-century of stories of physical seduction of the *Tom Jones* and *Pamela* variety. Deferential love surrounds Ellen on her romantic island. Fearless and high-spirited, graceful and gay, she holds an influential place among women characters of nineteenth-century love stories.

Away from the island of love, in the equally romantic world of manly warriors, Roderick Dhu and James Fitz-James, the two mighty leaders, lock in a political power struggle. Roderick McAlpin ('Roderigh Vich-Alpine Dhu,' as his Gaelic clansmen call him) is dark, rough, and strong, like the pine tree that is his natural emblem. His is the absolute power of the past. He is threatened by the subtler power of the present: the huntsman from the Lowlands, James Fitz-James, king of Scotland, in disguise. Fitz-James is a suave and sophisticated nationalist set on weakening the old clan system. The rivalry of fierce Highlander and supple Lowlander will culminate in the historic battle of Beal' An Duine.

First, however, the heroes clash in hand-to-hand combat. Meeting Fitz-James travelling alone through the heather, Roderick Dhu whistles up a terrifying circle of men:

> From crag to crag the signal flew.
> Instant, through copse and heath, arose
> Bonnets and spears and bended bows ... (V.ix.4–6)

> And every tuft of broom gives life
> To plaided warrior arm'd for strife. (V.ix.13–14)

Roderick whistles his Highlanders away again, but the image

of those ferocious kilted fighters, springing from the heather, fired by unquestioning fealty to their chieftain, would stay with generations of readers as an image of the romantic heritage of Scots.

A 'fiery cross' is sent by Roderick to rouse his clansmen. The final battle is glamorized by poetic metaphors of tempest and oceanic tides. This is romanticized war without any sense of agony or desolating aftermath. After the battle, in the court of the king, comes a romantic closure. Neither of the two great heroes has won Ellen Douglas's heart. She loves a young Highlander, Malcolm Graeme, quiet and strong but imprisoned by Lowland foes. King James magnanimously releases him into the golden chains of Ellen's love. In Malcolm Graeme, Walter Scott perhaps mythologized his deep belief in the resurgent power of a unique national ethos. The lady – the nation – may reject the brutal force of Roderick Dhu, but she need not bow to the blandishments of the King's southern sophistication. Malcolm Graeme offers a quiet Highland alternative to both the past and the present.

The new vision in the poem is matched by novelty of form. The story surges forward from line to rhymed completing line through a series of Spenserian 'cantos.' Scott had tightened his lines from the classical five beats to four, quickening the movement. Then he enriched his driving narrative with short earthy songs: the boatmen's paean that begins, 'Hail to the Chief who in triumph advances!' (II.xix) – the song that still greets an American president on state occasions; the rowdy drinking song of the soldiers: 'Yet whoop! bully-boys! off with your liquor!' (VI.v.17); the coronach of mourning: 'He is gone on the mountain, / He is lost to the forest' (III.xvi.1–2). Scott uses these ballads to reinforce his belief in the lyric power of the Gaelic singers, the 'aboriginal races.'

This idealizing of the Highlanders was happily accepted by readers throughout the Western world. Tartans became high fashion in France; Highland shields adorned hunting lodges in Germany; kilts flared on little Yankee lads; Highland bonnets were the rage in Regency London. Everyone was 'Scottified.' Scott's metrical romances started a long-lived fashion, followed in Europe and America as well as in Britain, bringing fame and wealth to the new 'Wizard of the North.'[12] Around the world, Scott's poems were read for vicarious adventure. They offered relief from the worries of the Napoleonic times, dreams of high-minded valour as alternative to the reality of commercial enterprise, and for the young lady readers, fantasies of an open-air freedom remote from chaperoned sitting rooms.

Walter Scott, stretching from law into a second career as a writer, had also inadvertently launched a tourist trade. Specific references to Glen Fruin, Bannochar, Glen Luss, Ross-dhu, and Loch Lomond (II.xx.1–4), criticized in the first reviews of *The Lady of the Lake* as too 'geographical,' have kept tourist curiosity still unslaked, even after a century and a half of trips to Ben Leven and Loch Katrine.

For Scots, Walter Scott's poems may have fed subliminal national aspirations and confirmed a stubborn northern resistance to the apparent takeover of the nation by British imperialism. Like the epic poets of the past, Scott had discerned and transmitted essential elements of the ethos of his own nation. But his poems function also in a more universal way, as 'secular scripture,' to use Northrop Frye's phrase.[13] Later critics mostly focus on Wordsworth and Coleridge as originators and popularizers of the romantic enthusiasms in poetry. But in their time and his, Scott was considered the major force in bringing readers 'back to nature' and back to the belief in nature as moral and aesthetic teacher. Indeed, in his early poems, natural setting, characterization, and plot development all suggest what to believe and how to behave. Scott carried readers not only to the Highlands of his native country but also to the universal high lands of romance. He gave readers an imaginary world in which nature charms and enriches, where a man fights heroic battles for the values he clings to and loves with reverence an innocent and beautiful woman. It was an unreal realm, but one that brought joy and uplift to those who moved into it in imagination.

Scott's values first came across the ocean to Canada, not as escapist dreams but as viable codes of behaviour. The romance of clan loyalty bolstered mutual support in new settlements. It was easy to import into Canada the idea that the north had special virtues and that the wild, cold places were to be valued for their testing of courage. Careful delineation of the details of natural beauty was part of sensitive realization of the nature of nature in the New World; and the natural world encountered had much in common with the northern lights and shadows, forms and movements, of Scottish scenery.

Easy also to import into Canada Scott's vision of two radically opposed peoples living within one country. *The Lady of the Lake* dramatized the antithesis between the anglicized Scots of the Lowlands and the Highlanders, that group which Scott himself, in the 'Introduction' to the 1830 edition of his poem, had called 'the aboriginal race.' Canada harboured an 'aboriginal race' in the more common sense of that term. In Scotland a poet could glamorize the dark and ragged Highlanders, with their strange, poetic language and their set of enigmatic values; Canadian writers could romanticize the Native people, a different 'dark other' but with the same glamorous appeal in poetry (if not in life). Nineteenth-century Canadians found in the native Amerindians and Inuit many parallels to the Highlanders' mores, ethos, appearance, language, and rituals.

Scott's vision of epic conflict also fitted Canadian actuality. Like dark and powerful Roderick Dhu, the strength of the wilderness rode through the consciousness of early settlers. Like Fitz-James, imported sophistication and garrison civility offered one kind of challenge to that wilderness force. The alternative was still in chains, like Malcolm Graeme – native Canadian strength, beginning to stretch and grow as the nineteenth century progressed. Deferential treatment of women was fostered, perhaps, by garrison life and by the preponderance of genteel youths, the 'remittance men' and the younger sons sent from good homes to the colonies, a part of the social mix different from that in the United States.

In colonial Canada, Scott's idea that poetry should revive and continue an old strain, the song of the bardic harp, was also easily accepted. Colonial reverence for old cultural modes persisted. Canadians happily imitated an 'old country' poet. In comparison to the intricate variations of Edgar Allan Poe, for instance, Canadian poets of the mid-nineteenth century maintained the tightness of Scott's four-beat line, his rhymed couplets, his division of the long heroic poem into cantos interspersed with lyrics and ballads.

Long and loving exposure to Scott's narratives left its mark on early Canadian poetry. He had hymned the beauty and significance of a wild Highland part of the realm, the colour of the northern aboriginal race, its language and rituals. Second, he had stressed the importance of the relations between men and women and the need to conduct transactions between them with dignity and gentleness. Third, he had emphasized the possibility of compromise and a resolution of antagonisms. All these elements transported well to nineteenth-century Canada, not only because of their intrinsic appropriateness but also because of Scott's beautiful and effective presentation of them in his narrative poems.

One did not need to be Scottish to admire and emulate Scott. Isabella Valancy Crawford was of Irish extraction, but this much-admired poet of the 1870s and 1880s is the best example of a writer who drew heavily, in much of her best work, from Scott. There is no full biography of Crawford, nothing like the scrupulous day-by-day recording of Scott's life by Lockhart and later scholars. The subtitle of the fullest account of her life is telling: *Isabella Valancy Crawford: The Life and the Legends.*[14] A mix of family traditions, research, and conjectures covers a short life, not an easy one.

Born in Dublin in 1850, Isabella Valancy Crawford was brought to Canada as an eight-year-old child. Her father became the doctor of the village of Paisley, at the confluence of Willow Creek and the Saugeen River in southwestern Ontario, an unpicturesque region we would now call 'Alice Munro Country.' North of Paisley the Niagara Escarpment moves through the Bruce Peninsula, as a kind of Ontario Highland reaching toward Manitoulin Island. In Paisley, an observant child could eye hard-working settlers, some of them Gaelic-speaking Highlanders, and also the 'aboriginal race' fringing the settlement, a 'dark other' harbouring a different language, different legends.

She studied the books that Dr Crawford had brought from the old country: French and Latin grammars, translations of Horace and Dante, poems by Tennyson, rising star of the 1850s, and of course, the works of Scott, still the grand master of British literature, even thirty years after his death. The doctor's bookishness was not matched by practical probity: he left Paisley in disgrace, convicted of misappropriating public funds. To add to the tragedy, by the time the family left, nine of the twelve Crawford children had died, leaving only Isabella, one brother, and one sister.

From Paisley, the remnant of the family moved to Lakefield, an older settled area northeast of Toronto. This brought Isabella in her teenaged years near to the sophisticated and sympathetic literary circle consisting of the Strickland sisters (Susanna Moodie and Catharine Parr Traill) and the Stewarts and the Langdons. Did they encourage her to write, help her find publishers? Probably; possibly; but not provably. A family tradition suggests that she remained a friend of Catharine's daughter Kate Traill, even after a further move, to nearby Peterborough.[15] Crawford began sending poems and stories to Toronto papers, first finding a publisher in 1873, when she was twenty-three. Dr Crawford died in 1875, the surviving sister died the next year, and Isabella's brother had already left home for the north. She remained, at the age of twenty-five, as the only source of support for her mother.

They moved to Toronto in the early 1880s, to a series of boarding houses in the Adelaide-King Street area downtown, close to the Toronto newspaper offices. Crawford sold whatever she could, to the *Globe*, the *Evening Telegram*, and the *Star*, and to American publications such as the *Fireside Monthly*. She tried her hand at American dialect poems, Irish lilts, and idylls in the delicate English style of Tennyson. A large number of her poems, however – 'My Ain Bonnie Lass o' the Glen,' for instance – show the weight of the Scottish tradition for a young

woman trying to sell her work to contemporary markets, even
if that young woman happened to be Irish by birth.[16]

In 1884, some seventy-five years after *The Lady of the Lake* was
published, Crawford titled her most ambitious work *Malcolm's
Katie*.[17] Scott-conscious readers of 1884 would no doubt notice
that the Katie in Crawford's poem is the daughter of Malcolm
Graem, a man with essentially the same name as the impoverished and imprisoned young suitor in *The Lady of the Lake*.
Crawford also borrowed Scott's general story line and his dig-
nified tone, using blank verse rather than his rhyme to further
heighten the sense of significant action. Though echoing his
romantic epic form, however, she adapted his themes of wilderness power, aboriginal value, and chivalric courtship to the
emerging realities of a Canadian community. Crawford does
not go back to a time of lords and ladies, chieftains and clansmen (except in her imagery and allusions). Scott's Malcolm
Graeme, as a young chieftain in Scotland, held the hereditary
power of his clansmen's fealty. Crawford presented *her* Malcolm
Graem as a prosperous, middle-aged Canadian farmer, proud
of the New World acres he has acquired by his own efforts. In
one of those metaphors obliquely ringing in the high aristocratic tradition, Malcolm is said to be rich in fields and barns,
'full of ingots shaped like grains of wheat / His flocks have
golden fleeces, and his herds / Have monarchs' (195).

Scott began his narrative with a romantic vision of the
noble huntsman and the equally kingly stag; Crawford, in her
opening, recalls Malcolm Graem in youth, he and his brother
yoked like humble oxen to the plough as they break up new
land. 'Swords into ploughshares': in the Canadian poem a
new ideal of work ethic replaces the chivalric ideal of hunt ·
and battle.

For a man like this new Malcolm Graem, the marriage of his
only child, Katie, is crucially important in economic terms as
well as social ones. Crawford echoes Scott's focus on a young
woman's choice of suitors, but adds a reflection of the realities
of Canadian farm life. Importing and naturalizing Scott's work,
she also twists the story into a feminine perspective. She em-

phasizes the wit, sensitivity, and intelligence of her Katie, rather than her physical beauty or her appeal to men.

Malcolm's Katie lives, not on an isle in Loch Katrine (though perhaps that Scottish memory accounts for her name), but on a Canadian river. Here she can canoe, pick water lilies, sing, and dream of her suitors. One of these is a young woodsman named Max Gordon. (One Canadian critic, Kenneth Hughes, suggests that 'Max' stands for all the 'Macs,' all the Scots whose values live on in Canadian descendants.)[18] Max is engaged, not in Highland feuds, but in hard work as an axeman. For him, the great trees are not valued emblems of strength, like Roderick Dhu's pine; they are antagonists to be dominated. 'Bite deep and wide, O axe, the tree!' he cries, in a new version of slaughter (215). He battles the Canadian forest in his effort to acquire wealth and convince Katie's father of his worth. (It is a battle we can admire as poetry, though with ecological hindsight we may deplore it.)

Scott followed the opening scenes of *The Lady of the Lake* with a first sight of the Lady, Ellen, in her 'little skiff,' moving across the mirroring bay. Crawford presents an echoing lyric, the song of the light canoe, floating between rosy sky and star-filled water. The Canadian lyric emphasizes harmony and the trusting love between man and woman rather than Scott's suggestion of distance and alarm.

His second canto introduced Roderick Dhu, the Lady's fierce and frightening suitor. There is no Roderick Dhu in Crawford's poem. The wild and powerful traits associated with the Highland chief, however, are flung into *Malcolm's Katie* at the parallel point of development. The warrior's power and ferocity are ascribed to the winds in the northern forests, imaged in Native metaphors. Proud Roderick, first seen as his clansmen flash him across the lake, reappears in the still hunter,

> His form as stirless as the brooding air,
> His dusky eyes two fixed, unwinking fires,
> His bow-string tightened , till it subtly sang
> To the long throbs and leaping pulse that rolled
> And beat within his knotted, naked breast. (200)

Such mythic passages have roused the admiration of Canadian critics such as James Reaney and Catherine Ross, have inspired writers like L.M. Montgomery, and have stirred generations of Canadian students to response and respect. In their original placement, however, they also deserve interest as a successful example of importation of models. Walter Scott had absorbed and expressed the ethos of his compatriot Gaels; Isabella Valancy Crawford was moved to absorb and express Canadian aboriginal vision when she sought for a parallel to the power figure of Roderick Dhu.

In *The Lady of the Lake*, Roderick stirs the drama of the wild conflagration of clan warfare, when runners carry a fiery cross through the Highlands. The fiery cross is echoed, transposed into Canadian terms – aboriginal terms – as Crawford describes the flames of autumn colour:

> ... the scouts of Winter ran
> From the ice-belted North, and whistling shafts
> Struck maple and struck sumach, and a blaze
> Ran swift from leaf to leaf, from bough to bough,
> Till round the forest flashed a belt of flame. (199)

Comparable 'Indian' passages evoking the forest's power introduce each canto in *Malcolm's Katie*. They lift the poem to an epic plane, and at the same time they invoke and imitate the Native poetic tradition of personification of natural elements.[19] Crawford suggests a vision of the north as articulated in aboriginal orations, angular but also rich and beautiful.

Malcolm's Katie has a second suitor, modelled in part on the stranger, James Fitz-James. The wooer, with 'Saxon-gilded locks' (207), bears the kingly name of Alfred. Fitz-James disguises his identity when he comes to the Highlands to hunt; Alfred disguises his self-serving intentions when he woos Katie, when he follows Max into the north to destroy his faith in Katie, and when he returns to bring equally false news to Katie that Max has taken a Native wife. Less truly noble than Scott's Fitz-James, Alfred fights Max not with arms but with insinuations. Fitz-James wanders, lost, in glens and mountains; Alfred is more dangerously lost in self-justification and self-deception. He is implacably set against romance and sentimentality. In the conclusion, when Fitz-James realizes Ellen's unswerving love for Malcolm, he nobly relinquishes his suit. Alfred, at a parallel revelation, tries to kill Katie and himself. At every point the power of Scott as model is strong, but Crawford's extraordinary power appears in the original ways in which she adapts and embroiders on her model.

But the true battle in the Canadian poem is not between man and man, Max and Alfred, but between man and nature. It is the half-hewn tree, not Alfred, that fells Max, presumably leaving him to be killed by the 'white, traitorous frost' (222). The world of nature is locked and interlocked in its own battles, season against season, as the opening chant here and in other sections of the poem suggests. Max, fighting the forest so that 'nation strong shall lift his head' (216), tempts Alfred to sneer, 'Nations are not immortal' (216). And Max's answering cry of love and faith calls a response from the winter forest, as the dying tree beats him to the earth, 'And the dead tree upon its slayer lay' (222). Katie, too, almost is conquered by nature. Drawn to the river by the beauty of water lilies, she steps on the logs cut from her father's wealth of forest; the last great log turns and plunges her under the water. Alfred rescues her; later, in his suicidal desperate jump, he will leap into the 'knot / Of frantic waters,' where 'the white / Wild waters pluck the crocus of [her] hair'(233). Throughout Crawford's poem, the power of nature threatens the lives of men, even of conquerors like Max and Malcolm Graem and the new men whose mills and steamers and iron tracks augment the songs of the axemen with 'the steel tongue of the present' (205). This is a complexity of vision different from Scott's, a surprising conception of the consequences of human pushing of nature beyond the limit of sustainable development. Crawford foreshadows the erosion of nature and of human society that can reduce the smiling land of her time to the erosion, human and natural, which Alice Munro portrays.

In the romantic poem, however, Max will survive and return,

'gaunt as prairie wolves in famine time' (233), to save Katie from the dastardly Alfred. The poem will end, as Scott's did, with the lovers reunited and all evil denied. Crawford adds to Scott's six cantos a sentimental seventh, with a domestic idyll celebrating the new Eden in a pioneer farm home. Like Scott, she concludes her narrative in a mood of adjustment. She returns from the high lands of struggle, loyalty, cruelty, faith, jealousy, and fierce beauty to the gentle binding chains of marriage. Like Scott, she presents love as gentle, sentimental, and deferential, but she domesticates romance. Her poem ends not in court but in a cottage, with babies, and with the once-villainous Alfred received as a welcome visitor.

The poem lifts, however, through metaphor, to a paradisal, erotic vision of nature couched in Canadian terms:

> ... Eden bloomed
> Deep in the heart of tall, green maple groves,
> With sudden scents of pine from mountain sides,
> And prairies with their breasts against the skies. (235)

Crawford's lines epitomize Canadian poets' struggle to nationalize traditional nature poetry, to use language as a medium for mediating nature. From the first days of European settlement in Canada, writers had pushed their way into Canadian groves and mountains and prairies with words. Crawford's mythopoeic power, recognized by Frye and others as central to the development of Canadian literature, is appropriately fitted into a narrative derived from the early idealist, Walter Scott.

Isabella Valancy Crawford died, lonely and poor, in a Toronto flat, brought down by the desperate effort to support herself and her mother. She was thirty-seven, Scott's age when he published his first narrative poems, younger than he was at the time he wrote *The Lady of the Lake*, and much younger than he was when he started on his second great adventure of novel writing. But she had produced at least one romance as revelatory of its time and place as Scott's poetry had been in his.

After Crawford's death, friends collected and published her

poems. John Garvin, a doyen of Canadian critics at the century's end, prefaced his 1905 edition of her work with a significant question: 'What other epic of its kind excels "Malcolm's Katie" in picturesque description, in brave-hearted purpose, and in tender, constant passion?'[20] Ethelwyn Wetherald added her praise to that 1905 edition, extolling Crawford as 'affluent in the possession of a high heart, an intrepid spirit, and ... unfailing joy in the music and beauty of nature' (15). Her life was celebrated in surveys such as Thomas O'Hagan's *Canada: An Encyclopedia of the Country* (1891) and H.J. Morgan's *Types of Canadian Women* (1903), and her work discussed in studies such as Archibald MacMurchy's *Handbook of Canadian Literature* (1906). L.M. Montgomery (who, incidentally, was a friend of the MacMurchy family) gave many talks on Crawford's poetry to literary groups in the 1920s and capped her admiration of the poet by giving the name Valancy to the heroine of her adult romance, *The Blue Castle* (1926).[21] The admiration of early writers foreshadowed the almost idolatrous respect for Crawford among such later authors as James Reaney and Dorothy Livesay.[22]

Isabella Valancy Crawford remained in the consciousness of Canadians, but with little emphasis on the link between her work and Walter Scott's. She was valued primarily as a poet of nature, of romance, of high ideals – by generations forgetful of the literary source of many of those qualities. Crawford's poems continued to appear in readers used in Canadian schools. There they stood, from 1900 until around 1940, alongside 'The stag at eve had drunk his fill,' 'Oh, to be in England / Now that April's there,' 'The splendour falls on castle walls,' and 'Read this Song of Hiawatha!' – a modest gesture to Canadian nationalism.[23]

In 1935, when my classmates and I ascended from public school to high school, we were ready to move beyond *The Empire Song Book*, ready for something more complicated than the simple bursts of feeling that Burns had stirred. We were moving from childhood emotion to adolescent sentiment. We were moving toward romance. Our teachers launched us into *The Lady of the Lake*. A century and a quarter had passed since Scott had set aside his 'minstrel's harp,' but his poem was still treasured by our parents and grandparents – and also by the school board of Montreal.

We drifted from our high school English classes to the mists of Loch Katrine, from the presence of gauche boys our own age to the charms of James Fitz-James and Roderick Dhu and Malcolm Graeme, and from the rumours of ugly modern troubles in Ethiopia and Spain to dreams of more chivalric wars of ancient times. Our conductor was a pretty grade nine teacher (rumoured to be flirting with the school principal); our conveyor was Walter Scott. My high school classmates and I could rattle off line after line:

> A chieftain's daughter seem'd the maid:
> Her satin snood, her silken plaid
> Her golden brooch, such birth betrayed. (I. xix.1–3)

Or we could chant the fierce curse raised against the clansman who failed to rally to his chieftain's call: 'Woe to the clansman ...':

> Deserter of his Chieftain's trust
> He ne'er shall mingle with their dust,
> But, from his sires and kindred thrust
> Each clansman's execration just
> Shall doom him wrath and woe! (III. ix.6–10)

We enjoyed raising the answering Highland yell: 'Woe to the traitor, woe!'

For us in 1935, as we entered high school, Walter Scott's story slipped easily into current adolescent life. The tale of Ellen's suitors fitted in with our shy courtship rituals. We were not feminists: we were young ladies, and although we knew that the world was much more open to us than it had been to our mothers, we were ready to sigh over chivalric courtesy directed toward a modest young woman. Scott's work subtly taught us to enjoy stories that were correlative to our own lives, and to relish the heightening of those lives into romantic elegance and chivalric stateliness. The tale of battle and confrontation could be assimilated into awareness of fierce rivalries in the classrooms and on the football fields. We were living in the afterglow of the First World War, when no one believed that Armageddon could loom again; we saw no reason why we should not glory in the fighting loyalty of romantic Highlanders.

Did we read 'Malcolm's Katie'? I have no memory of it, although research shows me that it was in our school reader. But for us 1935 was more attuned to 1810 than to 1884. It, however, happened to be the year when 'At Gull Lake: August 1810,' by Canadian poet Duncan Campbell Scott, appeared in print. It had taken that long for a metamorphosis in poetry to occur. Poets of the twentieth century had shifted slowly from long, musical lines to taut, thin, vortical verse, and from ambling, rambling narrative to vortical poems, condensed to the point of being cryptic.

It had also taken that long for adult Canadian sentiment to shift from the romantic idealization of the wilderness and its inhabitants, and from a reverential relation between the sexes. There was now a breach in the old assumption that Scottish and Scottish-Canadian morals were higher and nobler than those of Americans or Europeans. These shifts appeared in 'At Gull Lake,' a poem experimental in form and deeply anti-romantic. It was not a poem recommended to high school students in 1935.

In Duncan Campbell Scott's poem, romantic Loch Katrine is replaced by Gull Lake in the wasteland of the alkaline prairies. Keejigo, a Native girl, is the 'lady of the lake' here. Duncan Campbell Scott sparely sketches her distressing story. Like James Fitz-James, the alien Nairne of the Orkneys has crossed an ethnic border into her world. The dark Roderick Dhu of this story is a powerful chieftain, a Native of the plains, who holds claim to Keejigo as one of his wives. Unlike Ellen in her velvet snood, her silken plaid, her golden brooch, Keejigo is barbaric in her beauty:

> Clad in the skins of antelopes
> Broidered with porcupine quills
> Coloured with vivid dyes.
> Vermilion here and there
> In the roots of her hair.
> A half-moon of powder-blue
> On her brow, her cheeks
> Scored with light ochre streaks.[24]

Where Walter Scott's story focused on romantic love, Duncan Campbell Scott presents male protagonists untouched by tenderness for Keejigo. She loves Nairne, the alien trader, but her love is expediently and coarsely rejected. The ending of 'At Gull Lake,' unlike the romantic closure of *The Lady of the Lake* or *Malcolm's Katie*, is savage. Nairne throws Keejigo back to her husband, the ugly old Native chief, leaving her to be mocked by the other women, blinded, and flung over a cliff to the ravening dogs.

This story of terror reflects the knowledge of prairie life in primitive times that was part of the professional equipment of Duncan Campbell Scott, a deputy superintendent in the Department of Indian Affairs. He was sharply aware of the tensions that had been built up through the years when the two cultures came into conflict. As George Johnston says, 'he had an irreconcilably double attitude towards [the Native peoples], and confronted it constantly: the official, rational, structured approach which categorized and judged them, comprehended tensions and reduced everything to One answer (in their case, assimilation), and the other approach which experienced the people as individuals, personally, with sympathy and regret.'[25] Memories of the confrontation of white and Native drew Duncan Campbell Scott away from Walter Scott's high land of loyalty and love to a starker vision of terror and cruelty and abandonment.

Certainly, Walter Scott's gentle romanticizing of woman's

role and Isabella Valancy Crawford's focusing of interest on that role have both disappeared in 'At Gull Lake.' If Ellen represents Scotland in Walter Scott's mythic vision, Keejigo, as positioned by Duncan Campbell Scott, suggests a Canada to whose needs and passions both the alien trader and the aboriginal chieftain are indifferent.

A cruel, beautiful poem, in modernist, minimal verse – not easy to memorize or recite. And not a good conveyance for idealistic adolescent pre-war dreams. We did not read 'At Gull Lake' when I was in high school. We stuck with Walter Scott and Tennyson and Longfellow, even after a new barbarism engulfed our world, bringing us simultaneously to college age and to the opening phase of the Second World War.

After the war was over, the older expansive form of long cantos and full exposition resurfaced in the work of E.J. Pratt. This Newfoundlander, not brought up on porridge, heather, Burns Night, or the ceilidh, saw his work as an extension of that older tradition of the true bards, epic creators such as Homer and Virgil. Like Walter Scott, however, Pratt perceived himself as in an age emerging from barbarism and needing to remember a national past, before the gloss of civility sheened over manners and mores. Furthermore, he was sufficiently aware of Scott as a model that he called the second section of his epic *Towards the Last Spike* 'The Gathering,' drawing the title from that of Scott's third canto in *The Lady of the Lake*.[26]

Pratt's epic poem, completed in 1952, celebrated a Canada bound not by golden chains of love but by the iron bands of the railway-building enterprise. This is a poem of heroes – not heroes of clan loyalty and of battles between opposed idealisms, but economic and technological heroes, fighting to conquer the land itself. The northern wilderness, especially the country north of Lake Superior, is mythologized as a female thing, a continental dragon stretching to oppose male effort. No human female, either white or Native, plays a significant part in *Towards the Last Spike*. Pratt's bardic treatment carried Canadian readers to the high land of myth, but without any 'romance' in the sense of a love story. His heroes are Strathcona, Van Horne, and the other railroad barons, financiers, and engineers.

Yet there are several echoes of *The Lady of the Lake* in *Towards the Last Spike*. That silent central moment in the Highland glens when Roderick Dhu's men spring from the heather looms behind Pratt's description of the nameless non-epic warriors springing to their places along the railway line:

> Oatmeal was in their blood and in their names.
> Thrift was the title of their catechism.
> It governed all things but their mess of porridge ...
> Foreheads grew into cliffs, jaws into juts ...
> Eyebrows came out as gorse, the beards as thistles.[27]

Thrusting up like the clansmen in *The Lady of the Lake*, Pratt's ordinary people echo Scott's sense of the true pattern of history: unhistoric people caught up in and affecting national events. Of the chiefs who direct their assault against the mountains, the swamps, and the forests, one is the American Van Horne. The others are Scots.

> Their names were like a battle-muster – Angus
> (He of the Shops) and Fleming (of the Transit)
> Hector (of the Kicking Horse), Dawson,
> 'Cromarty' Ross, and Beatty (Ulster Scot),
> Bruce, Allan, Galt and Douglas, and the 'twa' –
> Stephen (Craigellachie) and Smith (Strathcona) –
> Who would one day climb from their Gaelic hide-outs,
> Take off their plaids and wrap them round the mountains. (5)

The battle-cry that runs, not by fiery cross but by telegraphy, across the country is a Highland yell: 'Stand Fast, Craigellachie!' Pratt explains in a footnote that this 'war-cry of the Clan Grant, named after a rock in the Spey Valley,' was used as a cable message to the directors in Montreal at a crucial moment (6). He echoes the sense of urgency, unity, and ferocity of the Highland warriors that Walter Scott had immortalized.

But the day of Scott's direct influence was over. Pratt's epic was not romance-centred, not enhanced by loving response to natural beauty, not filled with high ideals, ancient or modern.[28] Scott's influence trickled on in prose romance: his motifs recur, for instance, in Harlequin romances, where handsome, courtly strangers approach remote and beautiful venues and find golden-haired girls waiting in the mists, taunted by wild, dark power figures like Roderick Dhu.[29] Although without Scott's poetic medium, and also without the savour of his wisdom and his antiquarian grounding, formulaic romance proves the continuing hunger for a literature functioning on the plane of his values: a reading resource that can reinforce idealistic dreams.

The Lady of the Lake is also echoed still by more serious writers of prose romance. For example, Thomas Raddall read The Lady of the Lake in grade nine at Chebucto School in Halifax, Nova Scotia, in 1917. When he wrote Hangman's Beach (1966), he gave his heroine, a young orphan from the Highlands, the name of Ellen. She lives on an island – McNab's Island in Halifax harbour. Like Scott's Lady, this Ellen must choose between an old power figure (Rory – i.e., Roderick – MacDougall) and a younger, more romantic man. The young warrior, a bonny fighter, is bound by loyalty to his race and his leader, echoing again Scott's chivalric ideals. Coincidentally, Raddall begins his story in 1805, the year that Scott came into prominence with the publication of the first of his long narrative poems.

The echoes of The Lady of the Lake in modern prose romance are dying. Yet even though differences of place and time, politics and economics, have loosened the strands tying the colonial culture to its originating influences, the high romantic dreams poetically presented by Scott persist obliquely. His epic urge to glorify his own northern nation long found a response in Canadian writers, moved to differentiate their own north. John Matthews notes in Tradition in Exile that nordicity was part of the mystique of the Canada First movement (82–9). In 'The North in Canadian History,' Professor W.L. Morton says, 'What makes the difference is the North, the fact that Canada is a northern country with a northern economy, a northern way of life, and a northern destiny.' He adds, 'It is no wonder Scots and Icelanders have played so large a part in Canadian life.'[30] Perhaps Scott's theory of nordicity, his belief that there is something noble in northern life, some valour in outfacing a wild climate, and that northern race and place correlate with moral – and poetic – elevation, underpins the illusion that because of Canada's position in the true north, Canadian ethical standards are higher than those in the United States in public politics, higher than in England in private morality.

For Scott himself, the high lands came, over time, to seem too romantic to be real. He moved in his mature years beyond the idealism of the narrative poems into the richer, rather reductive realism of his later fiction. Yet when he set aside his minstrel's harp and began writing prose fiction, many readers raised a cry of loss for the genre he had first popularized. Literary romance seemed, sadly,

> ... gone on the mountain,
> ... lost to the forest,
> Like a summer-dried fountain,
> When our need was the sorest. (III. xvi)

Chapter Three

Scott, Findley, and the Borders of War

Walter Scott, at forty, faced the possible bankruptcy of the printing company in which his fortune was invested. Ever sanguine rather than prudent, he flung himself at this critical moment into a new and expensive venture and bought an undeveloped piece of property in the Tweed valley, between the ancient ruins of Melrose Abbey and the bright stream of Tweed. Defying economics, he began to build a handsome manor house there and to fill it with expensive antiquarian oddments, mementoes of the history of the Border site he had chosen for his home.

Scott was a borderer. In his mature years he chose to live, not in the Highlands and not in Scotland's capital city of Edinburgh, but in the shires that border on England. He might sing Burns's song 'My heart's in the Highlands, my heart is not here', but his talk, his practical business, and his prose writing were positioned in the borderlands in human experience – the crossroads between high ideals and practical compromise.

As the house and grounds developed at Abbotsford, Scott worked on the last of his Scottish romance poems, *Rokeby* (1813) and *The Lord of the Isles* (1815). But young Lord Byron was beginning to outpace him in gothic thrills and sensual love stories and to steal readers away from him by coarsening storylines and sophisticating verse forms. Sales of the new Scott poems were hardly good enough to ward off bankruptcy.

Twice, in 1805 and 1810, Scott had dabbled at a prose story about Bonnie Prince Charlie and the Rebellion of 1745. In 1813, in effect crying, 'Harp of the North, farewell!' he crossed the border from romantic poetry into realistic prose fiction. He moved from the mists of the distant past to a time within memory. As he dashed off the pages of a new manuscript in his neat advocate's handwriting, he also crossed from the poetic view of history as a matter of clear-cut oppositions, final choices, and visible results into a view of human wants and actions and motivations confused and blurred. Scott's attitude to the furious commitments, the wild zeal, and the battles of the recent past, like that of many Scots, was rueful rather than chauvinistic.

Of course, he had not been alive in the days of Bonnie Prince Charlie. He had never had to choose between the glamour of the young prince, born heir to the throne of Scotland and England, and the legal claims of a Hanoverian George, held on that throne by parliamentary acceptance. But memorials of the Rebellion of 1745 remained throughout Scotland: songs and stories, old bits of plaid that had been hidden because the wearing of the tartan was proscribed until the 1770s, dances that covertly reasserted allegiance to the lost cause by 'shaking the trews,' the plaid trousers, at the arrogant pro-British bureaucrats. Walter Scott, who had grown up in the whispering aftermath of 'the '45,' added another, very different memorial in *Waverley; or, 'Tis Sixty Years Since*,[1] published in 1814.

As he began writing, a new war was raging. Scottish and English regiments joined to face the threat of continental invasion by the indomitable Napoleon. Readers were ready for a story of war at a safe distance of time; women readers (who formed a large part of Scott's audience) grasped at the chance to experience vicariously the soldiering that they would never share with their menfolk in real life. Scott himself had never experienced war, had never slept cold and hungry in the bracken waiting for dawn to bring the sight of a battlefield strewn with dead bodies and crawling with scavengers robbing the dead. He had not shivered in terror of wild, Gaelic-speaking clansmen. But he could move in imagination from the relatively comfortable modernity of Abbotsford to those discomforts and deprivations.

To focus his vision on the reality of the past, he created a peaceable, un-Byronic young hero called Waverley. The novel follows this half-hearted English soldier when he crosses the border from England to Scotland in 1745, as part of the force sent to dispose of the rebellious Prince Charles Edward Stuart. Edward Waverley's story neither begins nor ends in the Highlands. But after dallying briefly in the Lowlands with pretty Rose Bradwardine, he moves north. He has crossed a border between English certainty, wealth, and rationality and Scottish mystery, poverty, and obsession.

Beyond this border Waverley encounters Fergus Mac-Ivor, one of the Highland chieftains totally committed to the Stuart prince's cause. Fergus (properly called Fergus Vich Ian Vohr) and his ardent sister, Flora, bedazzle young Waverley. Their high call to arms sweeps him toward the great battle of Prestonpans. He is tempted to join the fight at Culloden, against the very army in which he holds a commission and to which he has sworn allegiance. In the crisis, Waverley turns back, disenchanted with Prince Charles and his cause, and disgusted with war-making in general. Dropping out, he drifts back to his Lowland Rose. The hopeful young traveller subsides into an inglorious escapee, saved by a farm girl, rescued by his patron, Colonel Talbot, bundled back to Rose Bradwardine with society's blessing. At the end of the novel, the defeated Scottish survivors of the battle of Culloden repair to the Highlands; but Waverley returns to his own estate in England. There he can contemplate the fierce Jacobite battle as merely a picture on the wall.

Waverley's war remains in the stock of imagined experiences that have enlarged and subtilized readers. Scott had spread out his war story to include the prologue and aftermath of battles and power plays, alliances and antagonisms. He had added psychological dissections of momentary states of feelings in war, finely discriminated from normal responses away from the battlefield. He had recreated military campaigns and individual battle scenes with classic vigour. Scott was no longer the minstrel glamorizing chivalric deeds; he was now a quiet story-teller, chatting and leisurely, recognizing the complexity of human needs and desires, the self-delusions, and the mixed motivations.

Almost as soon as it was published, anonymously, in 1814, readers warmed to *Waverley; or, 'Tis Sixty Years Since*. For Scots, this novel rang with national obsessions. *Waverley* helped Scottish readers to refocus their national pride, their sense of what was gained and lost in the past battles between Jacobites and the established regime of the United Kingdom, between centralism and its opponents. In a preface written years after *Waverley*'s first publication, Scott admitted his nationalistic ambition: 'I felt that something might be attempted for my own country.'[2] This man from the Scottish Borders knew where the border of his country ran, what it meant, and who was on the other side of it. For readers outside Scotland, the battles over the Stuart cause and the battles in the mind of Waverley symbolized conflicts beyond the national limits and the emergence from conflict into adjustment. Scott taught his readers to dream that a hero could ride into the horrors of war and safely return to the consolations of home. James Kerr, in *Fiction against History: Scott as Story-Teller*, suggests, 'History enters the novel but in a retextualized form, only as ideology.'[3]

As his literary reputation and sales flourished, however, Scott lavished sums exceeding his royalties on his home and his hobbies. More serious money problems rose from the financial troubles of his printers and publishers, Constable and Ballantyne. Worries about finances began to coincide with bouts of terrible pain and illness. Walter Scott's life story ends with the drama of his efforts to bear the burden of his debts, pay them off without hurting his creditors, and retain Abbotsford for his family. He alternated fierce rushes of writing with brief visits to Edinburgh, on rare occasions joining fellow writers for good drink and good talk ('*Noctes Ambrosianae*,' as Blackwood called these sessions when he published parodies of them in his *Edinburgh Magazine*).

A vast public continued to devour Scott's final novels, written in intervals between a series of financial disasters, followed by several strokes, from 1830 on. Whatever his health, whatever his financial and family distresses, he continued to satisfy the hunger for big-scale stories, crammed with surprising and believable people, presented in a prose rich and steady. He battled bravely to defend his code of generosity and courage up to the moment when he crossed the final border into death in 1832.

Scott had led a conversion of fiction. In the years before *Waverley*, novelists had given readers the joy of entering either into an imagined world very close to the familiar one or else into realms obviously fantastic. Eighteenth-century readers of Smollett, Richardson, and Fielding had found a little vicarious travel, a little vicarious flirtation, in stories of fight, flight, tumble, and escape. Closer to Scott's time, readers of Radcliffe and other gothic fantasists had enjoyed the frisson of a shadow world. Readers of *Waverley* and successive Scott novels, however, entered a world neither entirely familiar nor strange, not clearly tragic or comic, sentimental or practical – a world of mixed motives, moods, moral choices, and results.[4]

Georg Lukács, the leading critic of historical fiction, saw Walter Scott as the prime architect of the genre.[5] Scott's great nineteenth-century successors in historical fiction, from Fenimore Cooper to Tolstoy and Stephen Crane, acknowledged him as literary progenitor. Each in his own country followed Scott in using local details to establish a peculiar spirit of place; each also transcended these particularities. They followed him in the creation of complex characters who could appear as participants, victims, and to some extent changers of actual events – characters who misunderstand and endure pressures of the time and finally wield a modicum of choice and will to partly control their own destinies.

With urbane and benign composure, Scott had crossed a number of borders in his historical fiction, national borders and also personal ones. He established emotional borders around the Scottish sense of national identity, but he also broke through the boundary of time. He conveyed the sense of past as past and emphasized differences between ages.

Philosophies of space emphasize the importance of borders, edges, 'critical junctions,' whether between ecosystems or economies or ethnic groups, or on the verge between human habitation and the natural landscape.[6] Philosophers of time must place similar emphasis on the junction between remembered time and time out of mind. Historical fiction is at a critical junction between two time systems, and it has vitality comparable to that of a spatial borderland where unique species flourish. Travelling in a fictional border country both spatial and temporal, Walter Scott touched a nerve particularly sensitive to his countrymen, the Scots. His exploration of a conflict at the edges of time and space was to stir strong resonances in many other lands, not least in Canada.[7]

When they first appeared between 1814 and 1832, Scott's novels crossed the ocean to leap into the eager hands of homesick Scots. They immediately appealed to a great many readers in Canada, not as a fillip for jaded interests but as part of a report on reality. Edinburgh burghers, complacently reading Scott's novels safe in their new city, might relish a second-hand terror in reading about wild deeds in wilderness places; terror was a first-hand experience for contemporary Canadians, in a land of bears, mosquitoes, Irishmen, and Yankees. Picturesque and sublime views of crags, moors, and cascades, offered in fiction to readers in the United Kingdom as a substitute for travel outside city limits, were for Canadians a description of everyday scenery. Torture and tribulation, trial and temptation, subdued in Scott's real world and therefore offered in his fiction as a means of dispersing the clouds of ennui and boredom, were far from subdued in backwoods life.

Nowadays, critics belittle the part of Scott that has to do with the gentry, the 'silver fork' elements in his novels, preferring the gutsy accounts of farmers, fishermen, and gypsies; preferring also the rich vernacular of the humbler of his speakers to the formal dialogue imputed to the gentry. For readers in the backwoods of North America, the pleasure in the highfalutin parts was very great, a clutched reminder of elegant ways, careful speech, and conventional manners, all the dearer for their having been perforce abandoned in the bush.

Scott's heroes – especially Waverley, but this is true also of Guy in *Guy Mannering* (1815), Lovel in *The Antiquary* (1816), and Francis Osbaldistone in *Rob Roy* (1817) – are travellers, unpretentious in a loquacious, strange land; watching smuggling and gypsy raids and prison breaks and terrifying fights. The protagonists find offers of friendship, are rescued from tides and crags and storms, and yet manage to do business, deliver letters, collect debts, and thus connect the wild, uncertain hinterland with ordinary reality.[8] That fictive hinterland riddled with uncertainties about law and duty represents one more example of the closeness between Canadian reality and Scott's fantasies. Having a literary prototype probably soothed real travellers' feelings, as they identified with Scott's fictional 'young man, of genteel appearance, journeying ...'

From his fictional Scotland, Canadian readers, young and old, imported a sanguine readiness for surprise and change, and an ability to be amused as well as enlightened by honest contemplation of the past. In 1832, the year that Scott died, a young Canadian named John Richardson produced a historical novel largely in the Scott mode. He pulled from his experience of the Canadian-American borderland the memorable *Wacousta; or, The Prophecy: A Tale of the Canadas*. Like Scott in *Waverley*, Richardson went back to some 'sixty years since' – back, in this case, to the 1760s, just after the British conquest of Canada. Richardson's grandmother, remembering those times, had recounted tales of the massacre at Michilimackinac, on the border between fortressed civilization and forested savagery.

Richardson's *Wacousta* dramatizes the 1763 stand of the Fort Detroit garrison against the Natives under Pontiac. The really sinister person, however, the dark and terrifying Wacousta, though disguised as a Native, is in fact a renegade Cornishman who has spent time as a soldier in the Highlands of Scotland. He shares the ferocity and pride of Scott's Fergus Mac-Ivor.

Like Fergus, he is a zealot. But Wacousta is a maverick, without clan focus and without a cause other than personal revenge. His antagonist, Colonel de Haldimar, is an older version of young Waverley in his conventional behaviour and his patriarchal protectiveness toward women. An antiquarian like Scott, Richardson carefully details the Native artefacts that decorate the drawing room of two young ladies in this frontier fort. These young white women match Rose Bradwardine in gentility, while the Native maiden, Oucanasta, plays something of Flora Mac-Ivor's role of fanatic, self-sacrificing sister. The violence of Scott's battle scenes is concentrated by Richardson into memorable vignettes: a dog licking the brains spilled from a shot-down soldier; a parlay with Pontiac, ending when a curtain drops to display the naked guns of the redcoat British.

Cloaks within cloaks, daggers without number, sometimes disguised as tomahawks – Richardson's work is almost a travesty of the historical novel as initiated by Scott. Yet it holds a convincing sense of past realities, sets sudden shocks of action into the slowly unfolding plot, and enriches with the dialects and folkways that readers expected from Scott's genre.[9] Richardson had appropriated the atmosphere of mystery and the sense of movement through unknown, dangerous borderlands that had made *Waverley* so powerful a model, and so capable of being translated into Canadian terms.

But he drew his readers beyond the borders of his own young nation, and beyond the borders of his own times. He took them to the border between rationality and neurosis, the border between fiction and fantasy. *The Borders of Nightmare* is the title of a modern study of Richardson's fiction.[10] In it Michael Hurley postulates a Canadian quality in Richardson's localization of oppositions: civilization/savagery, command/chaos, order/anarchy, fixity/flux, sobriety/romance on the Canadian-American border (15). Most critics, from the early reviewers chosen by Carl Ballstadt for inclusion in his retrospective selection[11] to those who contributed to the John Richardson conference in 1983, would confirm Robert Lecker's emphasis on the novelist's 'intermingled vision' of the 'civilized' and the 'savage.'[12]

For the North American setting, Richardson probably drew from James Fenimore Cooper's *The Last of the Mohicans* (1826). But as Dennis Duffy points out in his study of the historical novel in Canada, 'The novel's events have their origin in two historical facts. Pontiac's uprising in 1763 is the proximate cause of what happens, but the defeat of the Scottish Jacobite rebels in 1715 is the first cause.'[13] By drawing Scott's material into his own wilder fiction, Richardson implied his own intention: to do for Canada's memories of border wars what Scott had done for his country in *Waverley*.

Richardson used, as Scott did, the 'intense compressional force of the borderland.'[14] Like Scott, he fused the vision of a border as a breaking place where identities blur, with a vision of war where norms of human action go into abeyance. That focus on war as a deeply disturbing and distressing human boundary would motivate many writers who in succeeding years tried to establish in fiction a sense of Canadian identity, of separateness from other nationalities. Between the frontier skirmishes that Richardson fictionalized and the world wars of the twentieth century stretched a Canadian cavalcade mostly consisting (at least in the eyes of traditional historians) of battles, ambushes, sieges, and military raids. The Conquest, the War of 1812, the Rebellion of 1837, the Fenian raids by American guerrillas in the 1860s, the Northwest Rebellions involving Louis Riel and the Metis – for each of these, novelists eventually appeared. Many of them were ready to suggest, in Scott's fashion, the unheroic inner conflicts underlying the armed struggles. Long after the early wars faded from readers' minds, the predominant novels in Canada were still positioned in a primitive war-torn past and still modelled on Scott.

Perhaps the strangest result of this influence was the appearance of *Les anciens Canadiens* (1863), a major French-Canadian novel about the battles for Quebec by Philippe Aubert de Gaspé. The dashing and noble hero of this bicultural novel is a Scot, Arché Cameron de Locheill. Aubert de Gaspé, a seminal figure in the early development of Canadian literature in French, acknowledged a loving debt to Scott in many ways. He recognized in Waverley, according to John Lennox, 'a template of remembrance and reconciliation.'[15] Aubert de Gaspé also demonstrated that Scott's qualities could appropriately be absorbed into the Canadian tradition, and not only by Canadians of Scottish descent. Another illustration of this fact appeared in the publication of The Manor House of de Villerai (1860)[16] by Rosanna Mullins Leprohon, an Irish-Canadian Montrealer married to a French Canadian. Again, the period of the conquest of Quebec is presented, this time with the loving antiquarian detail that Scott had popularized. In this novel, however, a female protagonist dominates the story, a strong-minded young woman like Flora Mac-Ivor. There is a Rose in the story too, gentle and beautiful like Rose Bradwardine. The female focus drains strength away from the military thread in the story, but it leads to an unusual ending as Blanche de Villerai gallantly faces a solitary life in the old manoir.[17]

While the novel in America and England became dense with self- and social consciousness, Canadian fiction remained backward-looking rather than inward-looking, perhaps a lingering colonial trade mark. Some historical novels, such as English-born William Kirby's The Golden Dog, published by the big Montreal firm of Lovell in 1877, reached a wide audience; some a small one. Scottish-born Robert Sellar's Hemlock: A Tale of the War of 1812, published in Montreal by Grafton, a minor firm, in 1890, and his Morven: The Highland United Empire Loyalist, published in his home village of Huntingdon, Quebec, in 1910 by his own newspaper, the Gleaner, had at best a local popularity, although Sellar's sense of war was close to reality.

The Canadian novelist who rivalled Sir Walter Scott in popularity, however, was Sir Gilbert Parker (1862–1932). His father had come to Quebec as a soldier reinforcing the British garrison during the Rebellion of 1837. Gilbert, born near Kingston in 1862, taught at Belleville and then at Trinity College, Toronto. He was working at Queen's University in 1885 when his younger brother joined the forces sent west to quell the Riel Rebellion.

He himself travelled the world before returning to Canada, making friends with Duncan Campbell Scott, Bliss Carman, and Pauline Johnson, as well as with the mighty in their seats in New York and Ottawa – including powerful ex-Scots such as Andrew Carnegie and Lord Aberdeen. In the 1890s, reading Aubert de Gaspé's work, translated by C.G.D. Roberts as *The Canadians of Old* (1890), and rereading Scott's, he set out on his own literary foray into the borderlands of war. Like Aubert de Gaspé's hero, Robert Moray, who is Parker's protagonist in *The Seats of the Mighty*, plays a part in the battle of the Plains of Abraham and at the conquest of Quebec. As in Scott, Parker's battle scenes blend the sour realism of common soldiers with the romance of high strategy. Like Scott, Parker introduces native folklore, in his case the legends and the dialect of the Québécois. Melodramatic elements had crept into historical fiction since Scott's day: Parker presented a more swashbuckling hero, a more sentimental and teasing romance, and a plot based on unlikely coincidence. Nevertheless there are many direct and indirect echoes of Scott in Parker, echoes that helped sweep Canadian history onto an international stage. Parker's *The Seats of the Mighty* became an international best-seller in 1896, one of the first Canadian books to catch a world audience.[18] I regret to say that in the burst of Canadian nationalism of the 1970s, I excised these Scottish elements from my New Canadian Library edition of *The Seats of the Mighty*.[19] In reducing the novel to the length required for the paperback format, I cut out the hero's reminiscences about his Scottish boyhood: his memories of a Jacobite patron who died on the day of Culloden without knowing that his prince had been defeated; of compromising letters from a lover of Bonnie Prince Charlie; of an old religious fanatic, like the Covenanters of old, preaching and prophesying 'darksome prisons' and defeat in war. I see now that those were all important marks of the continuing influence of the Scottish tradition in this Canadian best-seller.

It was in its original full form, however, that Parker's novel remained on Canadian school reading lists throughout the early years of the twentieth century, keeping the traces of Scott fresh in children's minds. As the world moved again toward war in the 1930s, many new historical novels began to appear. American writer Kenneth Roberts's *Arundel* (1930) and *Northwest Passage* (1937) proved that Canada's past could still be recreated in best-selling form, almost matching Hervey Allen's *Anthony Adverse* (1933) and Margaret Mitchell's *Gone with the Wind* (1936) in popularity. Thomas B. Costain (1885–1965), Canadian-turned-American writer and editor, sustained the trend. It was Costain who encouraged Thomas Raddall to write his stories of the troubled border between Canadian and American loyalties.

Raddall's father, like Gilbert Parker's, came to Canada from England as a soldier; young Thomas, though born in England, grew up in the shadow of the Halifax Citadel.[20] His earliest stories were published in *Blackwood's*, and John Buchan, then a leading Scottish writer, responded with praise of writing of 'a type which has had many distinguished exponents from Sir Walter Scott through Stevenson and Maupassant to Kipling and Conrad. To this school Mr. Raddall belongs, and he is worthy of a great succession.'[21] In his novels, beginning with *His Majesty's Yankees* (1942), Raddall focused on the kind of divided loyalty that had bedevilled Waverley.[22]

In 1942, with the Second World War under way, I read *Waverley* for the first time when I was in university. Scott's popularity had dwindled. *Waverley* and its fellows lingered only on grandparents' bookshelves – and in university courses on fiction. Faced with selecting the most significant works in the major modern genre, our McGill professor chose *Waverley*, *War and Peace*, and *The Red Badge of Courage*. It was rather a heavy dose of war novels in a single course. But the war was on, and Professor Files no doubt felt its pressure.

For us students, war novels opened a path to empathy with the young men and women overseas, our classmates no longer in class with us. The young hero in each war novel rode through decisions about loyalty, courage, and also romance, such as the young men in our generation were already making. Most of the boys in my high school class had joined the Royal Canadian Air

Force, the Royal Canadian Engineers, the Royal Canadian Navy, or the Royal Canadian Signal Corps. For us girls, reading *Waverley* carried us over the border of gender into male life. War novels carried us beyond our safety to a sense of ultimate perils, threat, and terror. They also acted as antidote to some of the pro-war sentiments which blurred the borderline between Christian peace and patriotic killing. Such fiction made us bold to question, to confront, to change. I remember leaning against the stacks in the McGill library, drawn by young Edward Waverley, if only momentarily, from my war to his.

It was easy for all of us in 1942 to imagine a world of kilted warriors. Soldiers marched down Montreal streets just outside the gates of the university. Many of the regiments were Highland ones: the 'SD and Gs' from Stormont, Dundas, and Glengarry counties near the Quebec-Ontario border; and from Montreal itself the famous Black Watch, the 48th Canadian Highlanders.

In spite of the kilts and the 'Royal' tags, these were Canadian soldiers. For us, as for the Scots, war had defined borders. First the Boer War and then the First World War had set our sense of nationhood. Our parents and grandparents had rallied to the call of the 'mother country' in 1914–18, but we had shifted from Empire to Commonwealth in the 1930s, and our participation in the 1939–45 war against fascism followed a national, not a colonial, decision. People in our generation were going overseas voluntarily, drawn as sharers of an ideal of freedom and peace. We were not Brits, and certainly not Americans, those tardy participants in the war. Our borders had indeed been set, as our arts had been inspired, by war. *Waverley* now offered a thoughtful correlative for the moment of being drawn beyond those familiar borders into a real world of war.

In 1944–5, the year that the Second World War ended, I reread *Waverley* in a postgraduate course, having myself crossed the border to an American college. In that course, Scott's fiction became a documentary resource. We studied it as part of the history of romantic ideas. In the critical style of our day, we examined the origins and development of romantic views of love and nature, peace and war. But *Waverley* shrugged off that dry burden and re-emerged, still exciting and involving. The story of an intense young man who chose to turn his back on war, not fiercely, not cynically, not ideologically, but in a mood of quiet rejection, was very moving in that time when the war was over but too many young men would never come home. Historical fiction, romantic or otherwise, furnished sad and rich perspectives on present reality.

Then, the war being over, we stopped reading historical romances for some twenty years. We were cutting away from the past, cutting away from British literary models (and hopefully, from American ones) as a Canadian literature gathered force. Historiography was changing. Even novels for children veered into a counter-establishment reconstruction, as in James Reaney's *The Boy with an R in His Hand* (1965).[23] Such novels emphasized the difference between Canadian memories and American ones. No bombastic glorying in the flag, the *Mayflower*, and the westward wagons, but rueful awareness of less-noble incidents: Laura Secord pushing a cow through the War of 1812; Montgomery's Tavern becoming the nexus of the Rebellion of 1837. Not very glorious, but very satisfying for readers determined to 'read Canadian.'

For adult readers, new writers in the nationalistic post-war decades, 're-membering' (as they would put it) the Canadian past, produced more-iconoclastic fictional constructs.[24] Our sense of the past was wavering, waverleying, ironic and reductive. Revisionist historical novels like Rudy Wiebe's *The Temptations of Big Bear* (1973) or *The Scorched-Wood People* (1977), postmodern in technique, offered new interpretations of past events as alternatives to official history texts or traditional loyalist novels. The Riel Rebellion, the Boer War, the First World War, the Second World War, the Cold War of the 1950s, Korea, FLQ terrorism, the wars in the 1970s between generations, sexes, races, classes, and the wars within the self, all became stuff for variant versions in memory, in history textbooks, and also in fiction and poetry.

Crossing the boundaries between war and peace, present and

past, epitomized the border crossing that increasingly obsessed postmodern novelists. Linda Hutcheon, in *The Canadian Postmodern*, sees the margin or border as the postmodern space par excellence, the proper site for fictional probing. In their focus on boundaries or margins, Hutcheon says, Canadian writers, including Robert Kroetsch, Margaret Atwood, Susan Swan, Rudy Wiebe, Michael Ondaatje, and Timothy Findley, explore the way Canadian protagonists reach boundaries, points of reversal generating a paradoxical blurring or exchanging of identity.[25] Of these postmodern Canadians, the one who seems closest to Scott in his vision of the borderlands of war is Timothy Findley.

For a young Canadian in the mid-1970s, 'the war' meant Vietnam. Not essentially our war, but a war that seeped across the American border, bringing despair, disillusionment, escapes of various kinds into our dismayed society. But Findley, like Walter Scott, turned back from the war of his own day to another war, within living memory, still felt as a national scar. Findley's *The Wars* (1977) might have carried Walter Scott's subtitle, "'Tis Sixty Years Since.' Sixty years after the First World War, Findley promulgated a new view of that agonizing experience.

Like Scott, Findley grew up in a nation fixated on wars of the past. During his boyhood in the 1930s, in most Canadian towns and villages, the only public art was a monument to the dead of the First War – a youth in khaki, sometimes raising a rifle against the village heaven, sometimes held in the arms of the angel of death. The Peace Tower in Ottawa was a national symbol of the manhood that had been lost in the First World War. Virtually every Canadian schoolchild could and did recite one poem: John McCrae's 'In Flanders Fields.' The whole nation stopped on 11 November for a two-minute silence to commemorate 'the' armistice. Findley, born in 1930, saw new names added to those commemorations, in tribute to the dead of the Second World War. After that second war, the fixation seemed dormant. A modern critic, Gordon Martel, says, 'The first war inspired little fresh enthusiasm or imagination in historians until an apparently meaningless struggle in southeast Asia revived it.'[26] By the mid-seventies, everyone was pondering war, talking about Paul Fussell's *The Great War in Modern Memory*, reading the fulminations of American novelists such as Norman Mailer and Joseph Heller. Anglo-Canadians, in that determinedly bicultural decade, were reading Roch Carrier's *La Guerre, Yes, Sir!* published in 1968, translated in 1970. Readers were ready for Findley's *The Wars*.

A new life and a new literature had emerged in Canada in the 1970s, remote in many ways from Scottish traditions. Yet in many ways, Findley followed Walter Scott as he slipped over the borders of time, self, and nation. It is highly unlikely that he had Scott in the foreground of his mind when he created *The Wars*. His choice of names – Ross for the surname of his hero, Stuart for the brother, Rowena for the sister, Heather for the friend of Robert Ross, even Meg for the pony – is appropriate for a story fixed in a well-established Canadian family. These names certainly encode social meanings for Canadian readers. But nevertheless that choice of names brings strong echoes not just of Scottish-oriented Canadians but also, specifically, of Walter Scott. Rowena, for instance, whose sudden death catapults her brother into a decision to become a soldier, bears the strange, distinctive name of the queenly Anglo-Saxon love of Ivanhoe: a dark irony, since Findley's Rowena is hydrocephalic, a crippled innocent. In rejecting romantic glorification of war, Findley works, even if only partly consciously, in the lingering shadow of Scott's gentler irony.[27]

Waverley meandered across the border into war in a mild mood of romance. Findley's protagonist, nineteen-year-old Robert Ross, not only crosses the border from peace to war; he also moves from innocence to a kind of mature experience darker than anything that Scott included in his historical fiction. In Robert Ross, Findley retooled the traditional figure of reluctant questor, circuit traveller, disillusioned and readjusting soldier, and keyed it into the exponentially worse experiences of 1914–18.

For the Canadian soldier, the geographical border to be crossed is the Atlantic ocean. Robert's crossing is an experience of horror, in the hell-hold of a ship where artillery horses, tethered and suffering, pound and scream while the young man must use his gun for the first time.

In no man's land, in the plash of muddy trenches, Robert finds comradeship, the old *comitas* relationship of the classic sagas. But he is not seduced by any ferocious Fergus Mac-Ivor into even temporary battle fury. Instead he experiences the ugly side of male life in a world without women: Findley forces us to watch the gang rape of this innocent young soldier by his brutish fellows. The gentle Rodwell, who creates a small circle of art and tenderness with his ministrations to helpless animals, adds something of the quiet refuge that Rose Bradwardine offered in *Waverley*, but his sensitivity does not survive the war. He kills himself. In this story there is no Flora to energize and inspire; Lady Barbara d'Orsey chills the heart even while she inflames the sexuality of Robert.

The Wars resets and fixes national qualities through the same devices that Scott used. Details of flora and fauna, furnishings, clothes, and mannerisms of speech and thought specified in the sections of the novel set in Canada are matched by specification of attitudes and allusions of the Canadians overseas. All the male characters in the book are Canadian, and Findley is as adept as Scott at catching the idiom and cadence of their speech:

> Devlin turned the dome of his countenance on Levitt.
> 'What's in *your* sack?' he asked.
> 'Yes,' Bonnycastle echoed Devlin's evident expectancy. He poked at the sack with his wet fingers. 'Uhm? Eh? Uhm ...?'
> 'Books,' said Levitt.
> 'Oh,' said Bonnycastle, 'Books, eh? What a waste of knapsack.'
> ... Levitt picked up the sack protectively. 'Well,' he said, 'someone has to know what he's doing.' (88–9)

Yet the impact of *The Wars* is also like Scott's novel in being strong enough to carry it across the borders of Canada to an international audience.

For its climactic scene, however, *The Wars* produces something for which there is no possible comparison to Scott. A young German soldier, responding to a bird call, almost restores Robert's sensitivity and sympathy; but as soldier, the Canadian ignores the song and becomes slayer. That climactic moment carries us beyond and behind romance to the stark cry of the old ballads, '*Why* does your brand sae drap wi' bluid?' The answer is still as terrible: 'I hae killed my brother dear.'

Findley added to the portrait of war a specification of its squalor and horror and its consequent trauma.[28] The nightmare quality of *The Wars* reflects his conviction that, in spite of the reminders of art, reason and compassion have failed in our time, and that our inner nature has remained undeveloped because of our acts of war, national or personal.

In the end of Scott's novel, Waverley leaves the field of battle ignominiously. Disillusioned, he withdraws from battle and rides back to Bradwardine Manor, to 'seek for his happiness in Rose's heart and hand.' There he allies himself with the chivalry of the past. Findley's Robert Ross bursts away from the war in a terrible blaze of action. He kills his superior officer; he frees the horses doomed to die in the service of war; he survives his own torching into a terrible post-war death-in-life. Perhaps this is another, more realistic view of Waverley's ultimate peacetime fate.

The ending, as befits a postmodern book, is open. Findley modifies Scott's straightforward closure, augmenting the authorial voice with comments in the voices of a nurse, an archivist, and the elderly Englishwoman who as a girl loved the young soldier, Robert Ross. The novel ends with an enigmatic cry, reacting to a snapshot of Robert and Rowena and Meg, the pony – a cry that has aroused much critical comment about the power of literature to reinstate the life of the past: ' "Look! you can see our breath!" And you can' (226).

Findley's work carries the same power as Scott's and Tolstoy's and Crane's. He moves his readers to examine the force of time and place and uncontrollable events upon the development of self. Transactional theorists suggest that readers transform the stuff they read to fit their own therapeutic needs. Like all great historical novels, *The Wars* may permit a reordering of psychic chaos by forcing an imaginative endurance of analogous historical sufferings and terrors.[29]

The Wars, like *Waverley*, swept up an international readership. In and out of Canada it won awards and rewards, and was translated into French, German, Norwegian, Dutch, and Spanish. Moving-picture and television versions extended its reach. In later novels, such as *Famous Last Words* (1981) and *Not Wanted on the Voyage* (1984), Findley, like Scott, continued to probe the past. He remained, like Scott, a potent force in the literature of his nation and beyond. And like Scott, coincidentally, he escaped from the city to his own version of Abbotsford, filling his country home with 'collectibles' the new version of 'antiquities.' But these life connections are indeed coincidental; the literary links are not. Findley was building on parallels in politics, geography, and economics, on a still-pervasive, half-conscious memory of Scottish involvement in war, and on awareness of a literary tradition traceable to Scott, a tradition that confronted war as a viable topic for realistic fiction.

A Cup o' Kindness

It is easy to understand the response to Scottish tradition in early Canadian writers – McLachlan imitating Burns, Richardson echoing Scott. There were personal reasons: McLachlan was emigrant, not immigrant, and Burns wrote in his native tongue; Richardson was poor and ambitious, and he aimed for the sales that a novel inculcating the stylish frisson of Scott's Highland romance would enjoy. Furthermore, the idea of imitation was respectable. Readers remembered the influence of Chaucer on Spenser, of Marlowe on Shakespeare, and accepted as a truism that creative people are stirred by earlier creations and are moved to imitate them. In the early nineteenth century there was general acceptance of what a modern American scholar calls 'the aesthetics of emulation.'[1]

As objects for imitation, both Burns and Scott were affable, reasonable writers, not likely to stir anxiety or hostility or to arouse resistance to imitation. It was fortunate that two such amiable, undaunting authors should have appeared at the very moment when Canada was opening up. Burns's lyrics set up tight, melodic word-funnels that could release the pent-up feelings of elated, impoverished, emotionally powerful men and women in early Canada. Scott's poetry bequeathed to Canada a myth of Highland virtue, and his novels added a mystique of unaggressive self and turbulent other. The audience in British

North America, the editors, and the publishers all were very open to Scottish turns of phrase and turns of thought, being to such a surprising extent Scottish themselves.

By the time of Scott's death, however, immigration patterns had changed. The influx in general was slowing, and the proportion of Scots to Irish and English was shifting. All numbers would bulge again during the years of the potato blight in the 1840s, climaxing in the famine years of 1848–9. By 1860, however, the numbers of all British immigrants were down, relative to Europeans. The proportion of Scots, in comparison to what it had been at the beginning of the century, diminished steadily. The accompanying table shows statistics on immigrants entering Canada at the port of Quebec. One could draw up similar charts for other ports of entry. The Maritimes, Ontario, and the west all felt the thinning of direct connections between Scotland and Canada.[2]

Numbers of arrivals at the port of Quebec from the British Isles, Europe, and the Maritimes, 1829–1859

Year	England	Ireland	Scotland	Europe	Maritimes	Total
1829	3,565	9,614	2,634	–	123	15,945
1830	6,799	18,300	2,450	–	451	28,000
1831	10,343	34,133	5,354	–	424	50,254
1832	17,481	28,204	5,500	15	546	51,746
1833	5,198	12,013	4,196	–	345	21,752
1834	6,799	19,206	4,591	–	339	30,935
1835	3,067	7,108	2,127	–	225	12,527
1836	12,188	12,590	2,224	485	235	27,722
1837	5,580	14,538	1,509	–	274	21,901
1838	990	1,456	547	–	273	3,266
1839	1,586	5,113	485	–	255	7,439
1849	8,980	23,126	4,984	436	968	38,494
1859	4,846	417	793	2,722	–	8,778

As Burns's old song goes,

> We twa hae paidl'd in the burn
> Frae morning sun till dine;

But seas between us braid hae roared
Sin auld lang syne (K, 1.443–4).

Demographic 'seas' and economic and political ones increasingly stretched between Scotland and Canada.

Attitudes toward literary 'emulation' would change also, as the confederation of British North American colonies enhanced a belief that a unique national voice and native themes were possible and desirable. Elsewhere other colonies began straining to throw off the styles imported from Britain, the trappings of royalty, and the forms of imperial caste systems. British writing seemed increasingly inappropriate in new zones, new economies, new ethnic mixes. Post-colonial resentment foreshadowed the emergence of Australian, Indian, and African literatures. In Canada, however, the Scottish part of the imperial inheritance remained acceptable. Perhaps the long-continued force of Scottish models was due to the fact that Scotland, as a fellow colony politically and economically, did not rouse the anxieties that imperialism usually stirs. In Canada, post-colonial nativizing showed few traces of struggle or fear of Scottish influences.

The leading scholar in post-colonial studies, Edward Said, in *Culture and Imperialism*, emphasizes the dangers in the persistence of imported elements in a colonized country, 'continuities of long traditions, sustained habitations, national languages and cultural geographies.'[3] Outside the literary sphere, Scottish values indeed led to radical changes in the Canadian environment, of the kind that imperializing nations always impose. According to ecologist Alfred Crosby, a colonizing force always enforces changes in crops, animals, kinds of experience, plants, and farming methods, as well as in housing and urban planning.[4] The phenomenon of Scottish persistence, even in such subtle forms, might seem dangerous, invidious, in a country moving away from colonialism. Yet even when trying to recover a more indigenous ecology and a nativist and continental patterning, Canadians evinced a persistent feeling of fondness for the Scottish colonizers.

Theorists such as Said and Aijaz Ahmad, who emphasize the

hostility surrounding most nativist movements and the ravag-
ing effects on the nativists as they abandon history, underline
in particular the struggle of writers in emerging nations as they
work to become fully empowered and integrated, and prepare
to fully celebrate a post-colonial community.[5] In other parts of
the British Empire, that post-colonial resistance to Eurocentric
infiltration parallels or perhaps reinforces the anxiety that, as
the American scholar Harold Bloom suggests, haunts many
writers. The basic premise in Bloom's *The Anxiety of Influence* is
that although a great precursor stands behind the work of each
new poet, empowering the articulation of a new creative
vision, the young writer struggles anxiously to find a way
through, around, and beyond the precursor. Denis Donoghue
(who calls Bloom an 'Oedipal terrorist') gives a condensed
definition of Bloom's terms for the tropes of resistance: *askesis*
(self-purgation) separates into solitude; *daemonization* exploits
what the predecessor was unconscious of; *tessera* retains terms
but uses them differently; *clinamen* swerves, makes a corrective gesture; *aprophades* opens self to precursor's spirit; *kenosis*
breaks away in spirit of self-abasement.[6] Pounding away
beneath Bloom's complex discrimination of the kinds of response to influence runs the essential theory that poets are
anarchists, dreading authority, feeling stress and anxiety over
the impact of others' ways, dreading the repression of the
new, individual voice.

There is, however, a Canadian counter-thesis, based partly
on observation of Canadian writers, and it is articulated in part
by Northrop Frye. Poets, he says, come alive in a universe of
poetry.[7] Each young poet is indeed aware of some influencing
models, but the result of that awareness is not so much anxiety
as delight. Responding, borrowing, slyly sidestepping, invert-
ing, selecting, reinforcing, the new poet happily stakes out a
new claim in a recognizably rich universe. And if the claim lies
in the shadow of a particular predecessor, well, shade and
shadowing are among the subtle glories of poetry. The Frye
thesis seems to apply to Scottish writers following in the wake
of Burns and Scott, as well as to their Canadian successors.

Maybe this Canadian thesis reflects deep colonialism and reports a timid (but perhaps appropriate) humility. Maybe, however, it reflects a proper self-assurance of workers in a tough terrain and reports their sustaining sense of sequence and connectedness.

In an essay in *In Theory: Classes, Nations, Literatures*, Julia Kristeva decries the way post-colonial institutions – the university, the literary conference, the professional journal – continue to authorize certain discourses and repress alternatives.[8] My own feeling is that Canadian history validated a non-confrontational attitude. Confederation, rather than civil war, would exemplify the tendency toward accommodation, compromise, and peaceable negotiation. Canada's story is one of decolonizing without violence. (Quebec, one hopes, would throw off what is seen there as imperialism in the same peaceful, if compromising, way.) Canadian literature emerged powerfully from the early period of imitating Scottish models without demonstrating a phase of anxiety or mockery perceptible in other post-colonial parts of any empire, whether British, French, German, or Russian. This was an anomaly in an era building toward the overthrow of old imperialisms and the setting of national borders. Canada and Scotland were indeed both infused with a new border-setting spirit.

Increasingly separate in all obvious ways, Canada maintained, amiably rather than anxiously, subtle ties to Scottish traditions. In spite of demographic developments, Scottish strands would still be threaded into Canadian life by the postwar weavers of Canada's literary, educational, and social fabric. Toward each other there remained (partly a legacy of the shared wars) a bond, a readiness to 'tak a cup o' kindness yet, / For auld lang syne.' Legacies of early settlement by Scots remained as assumptions about race, culture, and nation. Canadian writers continued to create works in which Scottish echoes reverberated – echoes of Burns as late as in the ranting poems of Milton Acorn; shades of Scott's *Waverley* in Timothy Findley's decision to do a sixty-years-since perspective when he created a war novel.

Scottish lyrics had taken root in Canadian literature, hybridizing easily in New World soil, bringing joy and strength, needed as much in Canada as in Scotland, grey countries where oral power exceeds visibility. Scots and Canadians sang to disperse the mist, the foggy haar, the veil of snow. They read with continuing delight the words that traced the song, even when the melody had died away. The mystique of the high lands, bracing, value-enhancing, spirit-strengthening, brought reassurance as to the persistent strength of courage, hope, self-sacrifice, and responsibility, even in softer days, without the tribal setting or the peat-fire flame. Tales of past conflict and courage kept the nation (Scotland or Canada) moving to the chilly ground of tough decisions. Readers slipped back to examine historical roots, like children pulling up a seedling for reassurance as to the presence of earth-grasping tendrils.

The first eager openness to Scottish influences among early Canadian writers might have ended, but Scottish attitudes continued to be reflected in Canadian writing, thanks to the disproportionate power of Scots in publishing, editing, and education. Traces of tartan remained, even when a new nation was re-membering in experimental ways or (in W.H. New's phrase) was articulating West.[9]

Part Two

Signs of the Times

Twelfth of July 1957. I'm on a train again, hurtling westward this time. My husband and I are travelling with the Ontario Crop Improvement Association, a group of elderly farmers so prosperous they can afford to leave their home farms in the height of summer and go on tour to see changes in agriculture on the prairies, in the foothills, and on the west coast of Canada.

My husband, as an editor of a farm paper, is going along, to write a series of articles on the revolution in post-war agriculture. Pre-war Canada – a string of rural communities, basically agricultural, basically British, with a French fringe and faint Native markings – is gone. Like every Western country, Canada is straining to move into the ways of urban, industrial, international technology.

I too am writing in our railway-car roomette – lecture notes for my first teaching job, back in Montreal at Sir George Williams College. In my world as well there is a sense of revolutionary change. The courses laid down by my old mentors, from Dean Macmillan to Professor Chew, fail to interest my students in the late 1950s. For them, Burns writes in a foreign dialect; Scott is slow and misty and long-winded. How about a course in Canadian literature? But there was no such thing at McGill or Toronto in my training days. I am straining to change. In university education, as in agriculture, we are (in Matthew Arnold's phrase) 'between two worlds, one dead, one powerless to be born.'[1]

A bang on our roomette door. Lurching down the train car comes a wiry old farmer playing a fife. It's 'The Campbells Are Coming!' – song of the 'Glorious Twelfth,'[2] battle song of the Lowland militiamen, pibroch of Presbyterian prejudice. Behind him a taller and older farmer with a small drum. And behind them the whole gang, spoiling to take part in a parade. Train or no train, they are Scots Canadians who have always paraded on the twelfth of July. They are going to maintain their own tradition.

As soon as we pull into a station, they pour off the cars, muster up, and strut proudly up and down the platform, aging cocks o' the north. The people at this railway station in Saskatchewan are Mennonites, Ukrainians, Natives, post–Second World War Englishmen, Hungarian-born Jews, American travelling salesmen, and backpacking students. They briefly watch this old and alien ritual, then turn away. They have no common song with which to counter the imported tune. Their toes don't tap to the high pitch of the fife and drum.

Our farmers look a bit disconsolate. This is not the community they expect, out here in the west.

'All aboard!' cries the conductor, and the train chuffs into motion. With something less than a hundred pipers and a' and a,' the old boys scramble to the steep train-car steps.

The Canadian train rocks westward.

Springtime, 1962. We have moved our family west – not boldly west to the prairies or the Pacific coast but to London, Ontario, and that is a long way from Montreal, where we were both born.

On this spring evening we are at the Reaneys' house in London, stuffing envelopes with copies of a little magazine called *Alphabet*. Poet-professor-editor James Reaney has recently moved to London too, back from the University of Manitoba to live and work in his own home region. He is writing poetry, 'Twelve Letters to a Small Town,' about his home base in Stratford, Ontario. As teacher, Reaney exhorts his students to dig into their own regional life. 'Sit at the cross-roads of Huron

Avenue and Richmond Street,' he says. 'Look north, south, east, west. Study what is – and was – here.'

His students, looking out from their London base, have found gothic John Richardson and rollicking 'Tiger' Dunlop to the west; pallid William Wilfred Campbell to the north; mystic, prophetic Dr Bucke, friend of Walt Whitman, and witty realist Sara Jeannette Duncan to the south. Colourless Toronto looms in the east, where Isabella Valancy Crawford once toiled at poetry and at journalistic hack work. Like Carl Klinck, our senior mentor at the University of Western Ontario, James Reaney is leading students more deeply into Canadian facts and helping them discern the shape of Canadian myths.

It is the third part of Reaney's work that absorbs us, however, in this spring night of 1962. Here we are, students and colleagues and friends, joining Jamie and his wife, poet Colleen Thibodeau, ready to mail out copies of the little magazine he has founded. The list of young contributors to *Alphabet* includes some Scottish-sounding names: Jay Macpherson, Stuart MacKinnon, Gwen MacEwen. But they interlace with non-Scottish names like Keewatin Dewdney and Don Gutteridge. Writings interleaf again with art work by Tony Urquhart and Greg Curnoe and Jack Chambers, in a new mélange of documentary and iconography.

We hear rumblings of similar little mags: *Laurentian Review* to the north in Sudbury, *Windsor Magazine* to the south near the American border, *Fiddlehead* to the east in New Brunswick, *Tish* on the west coast of British Columbia. The same kind of publication is probably springing up in Scotland and England and the United States, but we are not interested in them. We are working at our own local crossroads.

1966, and we are moving toward the Centennial year in Canada. Our children are already singing the song that will celebrate a hundred years of Confederation since 1867: 'Ca-na-da! We love you! ... North, south, east, west – it's a happy time!' We have moved our family to Guelph, following Murdo MacKinnon, to help build a new university, one among many

in this expansive decade. The new University of Guelph incor-
porates three older Ontario colleges. We take part, nervously, in
preparations for the university's first convocation.

John Kenneth Galbraith, great, gaunt man, adviser to presi-
dents, ex-ambassador to India for the United States, is a graduate of the Ontario Agricultural College in Guelph (having been
in the 1920s an ungreat, gaunt farm boy from southwestern
Ontario). Now he is accepting an honorary degree from his
newly expanded alma mater. He tells us wryly in his convocation address that the only good part of his education at the
agricultural college came from the Department of English, which
taught him to write well. The agriculturalists are not pleased.

Nor do they enjoy hearing J.K. Galbraith make fun of his
home region. Most of the local people know, even if the Ameri-
can-born academics on the Guelph faculty don't, Galbraith's
recently published book *The Scotch* (1964) – know it, and resent
his chuckling, reductive memories of his own early days in
nearby Dutton, Ontario. (My own father, who also went to
school in Dutton, came as close to seething as a peaceable man
could when he read *The Scotch*.) Galbraith as ironist, realist, big-
time operator, looked back on his Dutton days with amusement and amazement. He remembered his boyhood neighbours
as small-minded. So set in old ways. So grumpy. So – so Scotch.

In a local café, after the pomp of the convocation ceremony is
over, Galbraith is pounced on, trounced verbally for portraying
his home turf so sardonically. He exclaims, 'But all I did was
tell the truth!'

'Who the hell wants to hear the truth about a place like this
here?' comes the irate answer.

Though the local people see what a local boy can make of
himself, given brilliance, wit, luck, and a postgraduate degree
from Harvard, they won't read *The Scotch*, even if the rest of the
world chuckles and enjoys. Who wants to hear home truths
when they read a book? Not the local audience.

Galbraith's irony fits neatly into a Guelph tradition. It links
him with another great, though not so gaunt, writer who once
lived here. This grey stone city was founded in 1826 by Scottish

novelist-cum-settlement agent John Galt. He too wrote sardonically about the reality of life in pioneer days, in his *Autobiography* (1833) and in his sour novel *Bogle Corbet; or, The Emigrants*, published in 1831.

Guelph people are proud of their Scottish heritage, their Burns Night suppers, Highland dancing, curling, kirking the kilts at the Presbyterian church. They enjoy celebrating the anniversary of the day that John Galt cut down a maple tree to start the building of his little settlement and then joined his friend Tiger Dunlop in pouring a triple libation of Scotch whisky: one dram on the stump, two drams down their throats.

Guelph, however, doesn't particularly care for the ironic novel Galt wrote about his experiences here on the banks of the Speed River. For one thing, his work is too Scottish, in language and mores. Guelph is rather American in both, these days, although being anti-American is part of the received piety here as in most Canadian small towns. Furthermore, *Bogle Corbet* is a little too factual for them. Facts about poverty, bad weather, recalcitrant settlers, sullen drunkenness, fires – this is not the kind of writing they want to read about the past in their own place. Who wants to read such a story? Not Guelph. People prefer the colourful legend. They will celebrate their founder, but they won't buy his books.

So Galt's literary influence seems dead in Canada, even in the city he founded.

John Galt left Guelph in 1829 in disarray, recalled by his supervisors in the English Canada Company. Professor Galbraith sails away in 1966, returning to Harvard and further glories. Inadvertently (we presume) he carries off with him his alma mater's one and only ceremonial gown. We trust the great, gaunt man wears his Guelph gown in the morning when he is putting salt on his porridge.

'Carlyle weather!' Ian Campbell says as we work our way up the crag that looms above St John's, Newfoundland. Dr Campbell teaches at the University of Edinburgh and is working on a new edition of Thomas Carlyle's *Reminiscences*. 'Carlyle weather,' he says as storm clouds build over Signal Hill. It's a good metaphor, and since we have just spent four days at an international conference at Memorial University, we are suffused with symbolism.

We look down at the steely harbour. Here British and Canadian battleships once slipped in for wartime refitting. Now again, on this June day in 1975, the harbour is filling up. The storm has driven a motley fleet of fishermen into safe waters. Not the grey ships of war, but bright painted boats, Portuguese, Norwegian, West Indian – all are beating their way into Canadian anchorage. Symbols again: signs of the times.

Forty-some years ago, almost by chance, responding to literature became my profession as well as my recreation. At graduate school at the University of Toronto I had settled into a study of travel literature – books on Great Britain by nineteenth-century Americans, books on the United States by British travellers. As a sideline, I glanced at some British accounts of life in Canada (outside the scope of my thesis but surprisingly interesting). That was when I first met the work of John Galt, who travelled to Upper Canada in 1826.

Soon I was reading books (no microfilm) at a research pace: faster than reading poetry, slower than when skimming through novels. On little index cards I carefully wrote notes, copying apt and memorable passages verbatim (there were no Xerox copiers of course and no laptop processors). Graduate students in those days carried around note boxes called 'spotted coffins.' Marbled grey on the outside, with the dead weight of index cards on the inside, our coffins moved with us from one library to the next. Gloriously, my first intensive research reading took place in the British Museum. My coffin and I sat in the wonderful old reading room, accumulating information about travel books.

Back home in the other London, I added a growing pack of note cards dealing with Canadian travel literature. I had become one of the handful of academic workers charting Canada's literary history. I began publishing articles in Canadian

critical journals, editing out-of-print texts, reviewing new studies of early Canadian writers, producing items for the *Dictionary of Canadian Biography* and other cyclopedias.

On the side, I had become one of the hundreds of thousands
of readers rejoicing in the flood of strong Canadian writers –
Margaret Laurence and W.O. Mitchell, and all those other clus-
tering names – Hugh MacLennan, Hugh Hood, Hugh Garner;
Ethel Wilson, Sheila Watson, Adele Wiseman; Alden Nowlan,
Al Purdy ... and on and on. This was also of course the era of
Northrop Frye and Marshall McLuhan. It was possible to feel
that we were in a period like that of the Scottish Enlightenment
of the late eighteenth century, when creativity and analysis
flowed together.

In schools and colleges, Canadian studies were burgeoning,
and a Canadian canon was emerging – a list of books appearing on the reading lists of the new Canadian courses. Non-
academic Canadians were reading Canadian books. Canadian
publishers were flourishing. Throughout the 1970s, Canada
Day was celebrated in many schools with visits by real live
Canadian authors. (Milton Acorn and Farley Mowat were
most enthusiastically welcomed because most deliciously outrageous.)

Confident that they would understand and appreciate the
Canadian macrocosm if they conscientiously mapped a regional
microcosm, writers were gleefully delineating local mores and
manners. Every town and village seemed to have its annalist,
documenting regional idioms, accents, ceremonies, daily routines. (The local people were rarely pleased to undergo such
documentation. Who wants to see the truth about the home
town blazoned abroad?) Then, ready for more than facts, writers picked up those grains of reality at local crossroads, put
them into the lens of poetic vision, absorbed their mythic significance, and emerged not with 'just the facts' but with significance and meaning, facts transmuted into visions of national
portent.

Yet self-discovery in Canada might include rediscovery of
the surviving Scottish strain. There was still a disproportionate

presence of Scots and Scottish Canadians in intellectual institutions. Scottish professors continued to set curricula. Scottish-educated Canadians had dominated late-nineteenth-century education, including William Dawson (1820–1899), principal of McGill University, 1855–93, and George Munro Grant (1835–1902), principal of Queen's University, 1877–1902.[3] Scottish-born and educated editors approved manuscripts for publication and selected material for anthologies. Scottish-trained public school officials chose school texts, all with a bias toward their imported favourites. As to the philosophical position backgrounding these biases, the relevant chapter in the *Literary History of Canada* affirms the force of Scottish Enlightenment ideas imported into Canadian universities in the late nineteenth century, at McGill by John Clark Murray (son of the provost of Paisley, educated at the universities of Edinburgh and Glasgow); at Queen's by John Watson (born in Kilmarnock, graduate of the University of Glasgow); at the University of Toronto by George Paxton Young (educated at the University of Edinburgh). It concludes, '[T]he philosophical literature of nineteenth-century Canada was almost exclusively characterized by a positive religious orientation and devotion to Scottish Common Sense philosophy or some variety of Idealism.'[4] So in the period of burgeoning nationalism, many of the notes struck by our strongest and best writers in the 1960s and early 1970s echoed modes of writing established by Scottish writers of the early nineteenth century and adopted by Victorian Canadians. John Galt, writing in the 1830s in ironic specification of detail, had taught writers to hunker down to unpicturesque truth. In the 1840s Thomas Carlyle, younger than Galt by sixteen years, had evolved a rhetoric for dark winters of bleak despair, a code of work and effort to counter darkness, and an allusive method that could swing from Galtian realism into symbolic vision.

In their day, John Galt and Thomas Carlyle redirected Scottish literature into post-romantic channels. Though they differed radically in tone, technique, and themes, both were set on telling the truth in their literary work, rather than on providing reading pleasure and escape. They led the way beyond Burns and Scott, Galt turning the fashion toward documentary prose,

Carlyle experimenting with consciousness-raising rhetoric. Both produced prose on the borderline between fiction and non-fiction. So doing, they established modes of writing peculiarly appropriate for the major development of Canadian writing in the 1960s and 1970s.

Desire to anatomize and chuckle at hard, ordinary life had once linked Canadian writers to Robert Burns; regional irony in later Canadian work would persist, but it would be more close in tone and manner to the less well known and less obviously influential John Galt. Readiness to consider the high lands of idealism and to move across the borders of time and place, once consciously modelled on Walter Scott, would still mark new Canadian novelists. Their rhetoric, however, would sound notes comparable to the fierce symbolic rhetoric of Thomas Carlyle, rather than to the more affable easy style of urbane Scott.

But although Canadian authors might work in the Galt or Carlyle manner, interest in both these writers was minimal. Burns's songs were still sung in Canada; Scott's novels were resurrected in movies and radio specials; but neither Galt's *Annals of the Parish* nor Carlyle's *Sartor Resartus* seemed accessible and relevant in the 1960s and 1970s.

For me, however, their work remained a central part of the material I used for research and for teaching. As I swung into research on the origins and development of Canadian literature, I became more and more convinced of a continuity of development from tentative, imitative colonial writings to the present assured and assertive ones. Scottish literary genres and mannerisms still seemed appropriate. A rugged north, a long dark winter, a stubborn soil, whether in Scotland or in Canada, had privileged certain ways of observing and reporting life. The influence of Thomas Carlyle and John Galt on Canadian literature might be oblique, but it nevertheless seemed strong and significant.

So I propose now to break open my old spotted coffin of notes on the work of John Galt and Thomas Carlyle and take another look at their lives and works, and to theorize about that lingering influence.

Chapter Four

Galt, Ross, and the Lowlands of Irony

Although born in Burns country, west-coast Ayrshire, in 1779, John Galt had no farm-field boyhood. No pony rides through romantic hills either – son of a seafaring man and a hard-working, sharp-tongued woman in Irvine, Galt was apprenticed as a boy to a business in Greenock, a busy town where Glasgow shipping moved toward the Firth of Clyde. At school in Irvine he learned to write clearly, compute and calculate accurately; in Greenock he ran messages to warehouses and dockyards, and in those same apprentice years he gobbled his way through the Greenock Subscription Library.

He was at a crossroad in time. All around him Galt could see the effects of a new spirit of pragmatic enterprise, energy pistoning in the west-coast Lowlands, building on the engineering genius of Watt of Greenock, burgeoning into ship-building and the India trade. Burns's plough was being replaced by a mechanized cultivator – invented by a Scot. His scythe would soon be supplanted by Bell's Automated Reaper – product of the another Scot's ingenuity. The same practical energy was leading to new genres in writing, different from the romantic narratives being written by Scott and the singing poetry of Galt's west-coast countryman Burns. It was to be a time for more-prosaic, down-to-earth writing, a time for realistic accounts of practical life. Never since the Doomsday Book had there been such efforts at tabulating facts – facts about soil,

seeds, schools, population trends, ailments, social organiza-
tions. The whole country seemed bent on compiling 'statistical
accounts': measuring and summarizing the life of man and
nature in each shire.[1] With a curious prescience, John Galt
joined the fashion with an early publication, his 'Statistical
Account of Upper Canada' (based on information supplied by
a cousin and published in the *Philosophical Magazine* in 1807).

Ambitious, creative, Galt directed his early energies into business schemes, lobbying, for instance, to further the development of a canal between Glasgow and Edinburgh. Unlike Burns,
he could travel from one city to the other along smooth roads,
soon to be 'macadamized' thanks to another Scot's experimental bent. In Edinburgh he found another, older, more elitist
culture, the Enlightenment world that emphasized philosophy
and tradition rather than profits and progress. Galt stood at the
crossroad between the old and the new Scotland, and he found
the clash of ideologies amusing. Soon he began to travel in the
late-Napoleonic years, far from Scotland. With Lord Byron, he
engaged in anti-embargo activities (aka smuggling) in European outposts and wrote of his adventures in *Voyages and Travels, in the Years 1809, 1810, and 1811*. When peace came, Galt
travelled back and forth between Scotland and England, dab-
bling in business management, investments, and politics.

He was a big, healthy man, John Galt, with a big, healthy
sense of his own potential. Rightly so: in his fortieth year he
entered a new field and challenged the current taste in fiction.
Walter Scott, of course, was the star of the dominant romantic
style; although Galt had written some early romantic poems,
he staked out a territory different from Scott's. Before *Waverley*
was published, he began writing, not romantic history, but
accounts of prosaic life, 'annals' of the Lowlands. Local manners, the small ceremonies of community life, attitudes to pos-
sessions and status, the adaptation of theology to mercantile
hard-headedness, local politics in their deviance from stated
ideals – these were the topics Galt enjoyed and covered in
thirteen novels published between 1821 and 1826. Each narrative centred around the life of an individual, characterized by

his profession or social role: the Provost, the Radical, the Member, the Last of the Lairds, the Presbyterian minister in *Annals of the Parish*. Each of these people tells his own story, marking the tiny changes that time brings.[2]

This is low mimetic prose (in Northrop Frye's phrase) in the ironic mode.[3] Galt's work is sour, autumnal, ironic, anti-romantic, lacking a love story. His heroines are mostly bad-tempered, good-hearted, middle-aged women, maybe easier to live with in the long run than Flora Mac-Ivor or Rose Bradwardine but not so good to read about. Nathaniel Hawthorne, whose *The Scarlet Letter* (1850) was deeply influenced by Galt's best-seller *Lawrie Todd* (1830), offered the definitive discrimination between novels (like Galt's) and romances (like Scott's). The novel, says Hawthorne, eschews the charm and mystery of moonlight; it weaves stories so close to daytime reality that readers may believe that they are reading the very truth about a particular locale and its people.[4] Galt's work opened the way for the great regional realists of the mid-nineteenth century: Anthony Trollope, George Eliot, George Meredith. Eliot's *Middlemarch* and Trollope's Barchester are limned from an ironic point of view established in Galt's Lowland parish of Dalmailing.

In *Annals of the Parish* (1821), the hero, the Reverend Micah Balwhidder, makes no wild dashes over the border or into a Highland fastness. He rides carefully around the small parish to which he ministers, observing his parishioners: poor workers, a gentle widow trying to bring up obstreperous grandchildren, an arrogant patroness, a nabob back from India with enormous riches and equally enormous self-satisfaction. The annals begin with the year 1760, which makes this novel also, curiously, a tale of 'sixty years since,' but Galt brings his story up to his own day. Ugly violence as well as amusing folly appear as the years pass in the village of Dalmailing. For example, when wild and wicked soldiers are stationed in the village, one of them, pestered by a discarded camp follower, 'put an end to her, with a hasty knock on the head with his firelock, and marched on after his comrades,'[5] leaving a battered body to be discovered by school children. Mr Balwhidder naively reports life in Dalmailing – a clachan developing into a town by the end of the fifty years he chronicles – interspersing local romances, comedies, and tragedies with world events unfolding year by year, decade by decade.[6] His self-assurance is rarely ruffled, and his goodness of heart never subtilized by the darkness of the times.

In a Presbyterian parish like this, in spite of democratic church structure, the minister would normally be set apart, idealized as more spiritual, better educated, more righteous than ordinary men. In his fictional minister, however, John Galt creates a man who maintains the façade of power and righteousness, but is ultimately revealed by his own words as puffed up with a petty vanity. Moving through a succession of years and friendships, marriages and practical theological adjustments, he emerges as an anti-hero. Not an ugly one though: Galt invites us as readers to be tolerant and amused by the self-deceiving minister.

With rueful self-recognition we acknowledge our ties to Mr Balwhidder, or to Mr Pawkie, the provost in Galt's book of that title, as they claim to give 'just the facts.'[7] They develop our scepticism about factuality. So to the pleasure of story is added the pleasure of ironic expansion of awareness, part of the wealth of the emerging great novelists of the nineteenth century. In a witty book titled *Splitting Images*, Linda Hutcheon splits irony into its component parts: 'irony rhetorical, irony humourous, irony critical or corrosive, irony self-deprecating, self-critical, self-mocking; irony elitist, irony demystifying, irony destabilizing, irony corrective.'[8] Galt's work runs the gamut of these, except for 'irony corrosive.'

The success of his early novels brought Galt a place in the inner circle of Blackwood's authors. These Edinburgh luminaries recorded some of their meetings in farcical dialogues published as *Noctes Ambrosianae*.[9] In that uproarious group, he met Dr William 'Tiger' Dunlop (1792–1848), a young ex-army surgeon just back from India, where he had earned his nickname by rounding up all the tigers on an island in the Bay of Bengal, throwing snuff in their faces, and then shooting them point-blank. (So he said.)

While Dunlop was throwing snuff at tigers, Galt had begun politicking. In 1820 he lobbied for a group of Canadian Loyalists, who claimed that they had never been compensated for damages done to their properties by Americans during the War of 1812. The connection led to the job of secretary of the Canada Company in 1824, commissioner to Canada in 1825, and finally manager. Galt talked his friend the Tiger into accepting the position of 'Warden of the Woods and Forests' and joining him in a venture to Canada.

They were an awesome twosome, John Galt and Tiger Dunlop. The Tiger was red-faced and red-headed and fiery-tempered. John Galt stood ready to use his six-foot-two presence to establish and defend his opinions. Together in 1826 they pushed their way up the St Lawrence, past Kingston, past York, and on to a spot where the shallow Speed River looped around a little hill. Here Galt proposed to build a New World metropolis.

On the site selected to be the headquarters of the Canada Company, he cut down a maple tree in 1827 and spread out his hand on the stump, fanning out his fingers to indicate where five main thoroughfares would be laid out. Then came the mock ceremonial, with Tiger Dunlop donning a Native blanket kilt-style and doing a Highland fling. Galt the ironist relished this comic reductive touch, even in the moment of launching his most cherished enterprise.[10]

Despite their flamboyant manners, both Galt and Dunlop brought practical skills to a new country encumbered by the inefficiency and melancholy of exiles, on the one hand, and the impractical enthusiasms of American-style projectors, on the other. But in 1829 Galt fell out with the Canada Company; he was recalled (tricked out of his job, in his version of the story). Dunlop stayed on, becoming general superintendent of the Huron Tract, hunting, drinking, roaring out on road-building expeditions, becoming part of the political manoeuvring of Upper Canada.

Galt, alas, found a dimmer life back in England. He was arrested for debt and sent to prison. There, to buy his freedom, he furiously scribbled non-fiction articles and also two novels set partly in North America. He had travelled through the United States en route to Upper Canada. *Lawrie Todd*, which he set partially in the northern United States, became a best-seller in 1830. *Bogle Corbet*, about a Canadian settlement (again in part),[11] was not as well received when it appeared a year later. The dash and vigour of Galt's Canadian adventures are toned down in the novel into an autumnal note. Much of the detail in *Bogle Corbet* is unpleasant: quarrelling neighbours, scolding wives, drunken ministers, malcontents setting off from Canada to the greener United States.

There is no consequential pattern in *Bogle Corbet*; chapter headings suggest the fragmentary structure, almost like a series of sketches or essays: 'Emigrants,' 'Visitors,' 'Evasions,' 'Depression,' for example. The one tiny plot line, a story of secret identity revealed, involves minor characters and has no bearing on the main drive of the book – to reveal the reality of settlement in an unromantic New World. There is no hermeneutic pleasure of a significant unfolding of plot.

In Canada, once again, Galt was at a crossroad of ideologies. The New World parish stood where British imperial expansion met United States business enterprise. In the novel, as in reality, the five roads fanning from the founding point of the settlement lead toward the west: three roads to the three church properties, Presbyterian, Anglican, and Roman Catholic; one road toward the community meeting-ground and market place; and one toward a mill site. The layout of the town suggests the fragmentation of society, very different from the homogeneity of Dalmailing. Promptly an American settler argues that 'bons' should be sold so that settlers could finance the mill as a speculative venture. 'This is a new country,' says the American, Zebede L. Bacon, '... [s]o the gentleman, I guess, should make his calculations for the spec of that there mill, not on what the settlement is, but by what, with the nourishmentality of God's blessing, it may be.'[12] God's blessing, presumably, did not nourish Galt's efforts to combine American and British ways in his Guelph settlement.

Three years after Galt's ignominious departure from Canada, Tiger Dunlop published what is arguably one of the first Canadian classics, *Statistical Sketches of Upper Canada, for the Use of Emigrants. By a Backwoodsman* (1832). The title seems to promise an accountant's sober reckoning. The Tiger's pungent account does indeed include accurate information on everything under the Upper Canadian sun, but he also flips the facts around in deft, ironic, zestful style. 'The wild turkey ... you can only distinguish him from his civilized cousin by a quick, firm, light infantry step in his gait, and his independent watchful look.'[13] Far from being folk art of a frontier, Dunlop's ironies and enthusiasms, turbulent and complex, launched a series of sophisticated records of the region.

Meantime Galt in London, released from debtors' prison, turned out another nine novels, pseudo-autobiographies, biting, detailed, irreverent, and two 'non-fiction' accounts of the myriad adventures of his life, *The Autobiography of John Galt* (1833) and *Literary Life and Miscellanies* (1834). His non-fiction, like his novels, emphasizes the slow accretion of change and specifies in detail the economic, political, social, and theological pressures shaping the life of the individual. His style is warmed by wry juxtaposing of a wider world perspective with the humdrum details of daily life.

When he wrote the *Autobiography*, Galt had already suffered a first stroke. The rest of his life was plagued with illness, yet he managed to produce novels, dramas, short stories, and essays up to the moment of his death, at home in Scotland, in 1839. Tiger Dunlop eventually died in Canada in 1848. Little interest in his writing outlasted his life, although he lingered in Scottish anecdotes as an outrageous 'backwoodsman' with a 'Blackwoodian' wit.[14]

After Galt died, his widow bundled up all his manuscripts into a trunk and shipped it to Canada, to be guarded by her emigrant sons there. Eventually the trunk arrived at the National Library of Canada. Letters, essays, short stories, biographies, dramas, sketches – all the prose of John Galt's experience is in Canada, ready for scholarly note-taking, analysis, and commentary. Fred Cogswell, in his graduate years, made a typescript of most of the Galt holdings now in the library of the University of Edinburgh. How Galt would laugh at such scholarly solemnity, just as he laughed at the intellectual fashions of his own time!

Scottish critics never knew quite how to approach and analyse his work. Indeed, the major Galt scholars have not been Scottish. Swedish professor Erik Frykman of Göteborg moved beyond his 1954 doctoral thesis, *John Galt and Eighteenth Century Scottish Philosophy*, into a thorough study, *John Galt's Scottish Stories, 1820–1823*. New Zealand professor Ian Gordon wrote *John Galt: The Life of a Writer* (1972), the definitive biography. French professor Henri Gibault published a book-length tribute, *John Galt: romancier écossais* (1979). Canadians contributed too: R.K. Gordon, then at the University of Alberta, did a pioneering study in 1920; Keith Costain, then at the University of Regina, Saskatchewan, contributed perceptive analyses to a number of learned journals; with the help of Dr Nick Whistler, I convened an international symposium at the University of Guelph in Ontario and collected essays by most of these scholars and others in *John Galt: Reappraisals* (1985). Only with the resurgence of nationalist spirit in Scotland did scholars there begin to convene conferences and to issue 'Scotlit' handbooks for schoolchildren being directed toward Galt's work.

His novels, on the other hand, were long enjoyed by common readers in Scotland. In the 1880s, the sentimental 'Kailyard' novels hovered over homely detail such as Galt had specified, and enjoyed a popular following as great as his had been. Galt would have enjoyed the fact that the Scottish creators of *The Stickit Minister* (1893), *Beside the Bonnie Brier Bush* (1894), and other such accounts were themselves Presbyterian ministers, latter-day brethren of the Reverend Micah Balwhidder, as sentimental as he and as imperceptive of real social and political problems.[15] In reaction against their sentiment, a 'counter-Kailyard' school emerged at the turn of the century, and Galt's sharper tones resonated again in George Douglas's *The House with the Green Shutters* (1901) and other dour exposés of the ironies of life in family and village. The genre that Galt had developed would continue, sometimes in parodic or parallel forms. Lewis Grassic Gibbon's novel *Sunset Song* (1932), first of his epic trilogy *A Scots Quair*, combined lyric with ironic tones in portraying the parish of 'Kinraddie'; Muriel Spark's *The Prime of Miss Jean Brodie* (1961) moved to the city of Edinburgh and featured a woman teacher rather than a minister, but Spark, like Galt, skewered the protagonist's self-delusions.

Before and after Galt left British North America, he had many readers and admirers in the colonies. In Nova Scotia, Thomas Chandler Haliburton, like Galt, had begun his writing career with statistical non-fiction: *A General Description of Nova Scotia* (1823) and *An Historical and Statistical Account of Nova-Scotia* (1829). He turned to fictionalized annals of his Maritime parish in a series of twenty-one sketches, collected and published in 1836 as *The Clockmaker; or, The Sayings and Doings of Sam Slick, of Slickville*. In 1821 Haliburton's mentor, Scottish-born Thomas McCulloch, had fruitlessly sent his comparable regional satiric sketches, *Letters of Mephibosheth Stepsure*, to Blackwood's, dreaming perhaps of taking his place in the Edinburgh circle later celebrated in the *Noctes Ambrosianae*; Haliburton, a generation later and Canadian-born, found a local publisher in Joseph Howe's *Novascotian* and a local group of friendly admirers. The Nova Scotia squire who acts as narrator in *The Clockmaker* duplicates Galt's trick of reporting without fully understanding, and Sam Slick, the devious Yankee clockmaker, is a fully developed portrait of the opportunistic American who spread his ideas of enterprise in *Bogle Corbet*. In the second *Clockmaker* series (1838), Haliburton added to the slick Yankee and the slower Nova Scotian squire a third character. This was the Reverend Mr Hopewell, a Loyalist minister, ninety-some years old. Like Micah Balwhiddder, Mr Hopewell provides a retrospective on a life of change, in this case changes in both the colony and the republic.

Much has been made of the influence on Haliburton of Dickens (since the Pickwick fad was just flaring when *The Clockmaker* was written), as well as of McCulloch. Other critics have emphasized the influence of early American humorists, including Washington Irving.[16] I myself hear echoes of *Annals of the Parish*. Perhaps the likeness to Galt is merely a comparable response to a comparable low-keyed world. Perhaps, on the other hand, it is a canny emulation of a successful contemporary, whose Scottish books had found a big sale in the new Scotia. Whatever the extent of Galt's influence, however, Haliburton would certainly not have called himself 'the Canadian Galt.'

Galt had many avowed imitators among contemporary writers of travel books. Caught in a wintry climate, soldiers and engineers, settlers and medical practitioners, and canal builders added his dry tone to the clarity and factuality of earlier explorers' reports. Most travellers claimed to write statistical accounts, in accordance with the Clydeside emphasis on fact.[17] Many Scottish travellers, however, also wrote because they loved words, loved manipulating sentences for comic or ironic effect, stringing out long sentences, snapping out short ones, as the Scottish books of rhetoric (and the example of John Galt) had taught them. Pushing through the swamps and rapids near Lachine and up the Rideau to Ottawa, for example, John Mactaggart, liveliest of all travel writers, in *Three Years in Canada* (published in 1829, the year of Galt's departure) wrote deferentially about 'Mr. Galt' – and mocked Tiger Dunlop, 'his beard not having been disturbed with the scythe for three calendar months.'[18] Mactaggart rummaged through his real experiences to patch together an account of canal builders, factual and funny:

On the bushy hemlock would we lie down; roast pork before the fire on wooden prongs, each man roasting for himself; while plenty of tea was thrown into a large kettle of boiling water, the tin mug [circulating] ...; while each with his bush-knife cut toasted pork on a sliver of bread, ever using the thumb-piece to protect the thumb from being burned; a *tot* or two round of weak grog

finished the feast, when some would fall asleep, – others to sleep
and snore; and after having lain an hour or so on one side, some
one would call *Spoon!* – the order to turn to the other – which was
often an agreeable order, if a spike of tree-root or such a sub-
stance stuck up beneath the ribs. (1:52–3)

It is a far cry from the heroic male world of Roderick Dhu.

To Samuel Strickland, another Galt admirer and employee,
we owe one of the many accounts of the founding of Guelph. In
Twenty-Seven Years in Canada West, Strickland wrote in glowing
terms of Galt, 'a true and affectionate friend.'[19] He had a sister
who had married a Scot, J.W. Dunbar Moodie. Susanna Moodie
came to Upper Canada (as Galt had done) with an established
reputation as a novelist. Hers were not satiric novels but sentimental ones. Upper Canada struck irony into her soul. Mrs
Moodie switched both her style and her publisher when she
came to report on Canada, probably in both cases under the
influence of her brother's friend and hero John Galt.[20] Her
experiences in Upper Canada began three years after Galt left,
and her working of those experiences into literary form waited
another twenty years, but *Roughing It in the Bush; or, Life in
Canada* (1852)[21] shows clearly that Galt's mode and motifs were
still very appropriate for Canadian use. Her style is as clear as
his, her structure as episodic.

Like him, she reports her life in the bush in a low register. As
in *Bogle Corbet*, she presents a dark view of the new country,
and her work smoulders with vitality, sour, disturbed, but
vigorous and involving. Like Galt, she wrote from a mix of
motives: to warn, to justify herself, to sell, and to impress. Like
him, Moodie eschews such novelistic stuff as flirtation, courtship, and intrigue; no great social movements unfold. As in
Bogle Corbet, some of the best characters (the still-hunter, for
instance) play no part in the central storyline. Many others of
Galt's cast of characters reappear: the slick, borrowing Yankee,
the shrill housewife, the dreamy solitary – 'the lone man' was
Bogle Corbet's term (128) – the Irish handmaid, the feckless
hired boy, who in both books sets a dangerous fire – 'siccan an

owre muckle a fire,' to quote Galt (126). But no minister: Mrs Moodie, an Englishwoman, did not come from a world where the presbyter played a role powerful enough to qualify for ironic treatment. Moodie adds 'didactic and analytical observations,' to quote Carl Ballstadt, her modern editor (xxv). The details she offers are coherent, cumulative, controlled. The account seems close to documentary, yet her sense of time passing turns her account into something personal and dynamic.

Susanna Moodie's annals of her Ontario parish stayed in Canadian memory and on Canadian bookshelves much longer than Galt's did. For one thing, her language bore no lingering trace of Lowland dialect. Her tone was ultimately affirmative and hopeful, unlike Galt's. Her narrator makes it out of the bush, to a new home in a town, with her china service intact and her marriage still strong.

The non-consequential sketch form that Susanna Moodie used, modelled at least in part on Galt, suited the desultory, disconnected life at the Canadian crossroads. Stephen Leacock used a comparable form. 'Mariposa'/Orillia has many of the qualities of Galt's 'Stockwell'/Guelph. Its ill-conceived festivities and its abortive efforts at grandeur call to mind the founding and the grandiose layout of Galt's 'metropolis ... fated with a high destiny.'[22] In *Sunshine Sketches of a Little Town* (1912) and *Arcadian Adventures with the Idle Rich* (1914), Leacock discriminated the same follies that had delighted Galt and treated them in the same kind of clever, sting-in-the-tail prose. Leacock's annals of his parish, like Galt's, bring quiet pleasure. The blood does not course; the heart does not leap; no one presses breathlessly on after plot developments or character surprises. This is prose in which the author's political science joins his delight in the absurdities of church, community, and business. Readers can relish their own follies, irradiated with the sunshine of Leacock's enjoyment.

That same tone, not sharp, but amusing in self-mockery, and full of Galtian wisdom and acceptance, marks the end of a time of reverence for Scottish legends and models and mores. John Kenneth Galbraith travelled back from his global sweep to a small Canadian town where he had grown up and reported his findings in *The Scotch*. Like Leacock, he brought his technical expertise as an economist into his analysis. He traced the effect of transportation from Scotland into rural southwestern Ontario. 'The transition from the spare, wet and treeless crofts of the Highlands and the Western Isles to the lush forests, deep soil and strong seasons of the land by the Lake could scarcely have been more dramatic' (57). Dramatic too the change in work ways: 'from an agricultural system in which they were guided by the experience of centuries to one where a very great deal depended on a man's capacity to figure things out for himself or imitate with discrimination those who could' (57). But stabilization had set in by the time that Galbraith was a boy. 'The formula "It was good enough for my auld man so it's good enough for me" combined a decent respect for one's ancestors with economy of thought' (58).

Galbraith details the life in his boyhood community, thrifty, dirty, levelling. 'If a man didn't make sense, the Scotch felt it was misplaced politeness to try to keep him from knowing it' (51). He characterizes the people of his region: hard-working, stiff-backed, money-oriented, family- and clan-centred, given to drink and to churchgoing, short on education, long on responsibility. A good region for the development of an ironist; a region with interests, customs, and attitudes very much like the Lowlands that Galt portrayed in his autobiography and fiction. Galbraith offers 'irony corrective' to the point of being 'corrosive': mockery of all the things – all the Scottish things – that he hoped to escape from when he left the farm and went to Guelph.

Galbraith was adding to comparable work in the form of full-length novels, regional fiction, none of it well received at home. Selwyn Dewdney, for instance, in London, 'doing a Galt' in *Wind without Rain* (1946), outraged the city. His story, incidentally, shows the persistence of Scottish names: Angus Macdonald faces off against James Campbell Bilbeau in an unsavoury struggle for school principalship. Dewdney's fiction becomes part of cultural history.[23] Morley Callaghan, using local Montreal detail in *The Loved and the Lost* (1951), added a comparable Scottish touch. The Canadians who outface racist prejudice in this Montreal novel are named Peggy Sanderson (Sandy's son?) and James McAlpine (faint echo of Roderick Vich Alpine of *The Lady of the Lake*?). Callaghan's suggestion of Scottish power in Montreal is the mark of realistic observation. As in the case of J.K. Galbraith, the local people felt he 'could have spared the reader some of the less agreeable scenery and ignored some of the less enchanting personalities' (*The Scotch*, viii).

Many besides Galbraith – and Galt – have considered it no breach of national pride to add some dark discords to the national anthem, though the local people, here and in Scotland too, will always want the sour song banned. In each country, galled communities responded acrimoniously to the 'truth-telling' reports. Galt's *Ayrshire Legatees* was not much relished in Ayrshire. Glasgow rejected certain later Galtian books (Alan Sharp's *A Green Tree in Gedde*, for instance), Edinburgh others (Muriel Spark's *The Prime of Miss Jean Brodie*, again for instance), depending on whether Glasgow or Edinburgh was being delineated. Most Canadians loved Margaret Laurence's *A Jest of God* (1966) for its Manitoba quality, but Manitoba schools banned it. Everybody relished her *Fire-Dwellers* (1969), except in Vancouver, where it was set. Peterborough led the battle to ban *The Diviners* (1974), which was partly set near that city. But allowing for local nerves, the general acceptance of the annals of local parishes waxed both in Scotland and in Canada.

The great Canadian place for seeing foibles most clearly is the prairie. People with no Scottish heritage had broken new literary ground there: Frederick Philip Grove with *Settlers of the Marsh* in 1925, Martha Ostenso with *Wild Geese*, also in 1925. Sinclair Ross's ancestry was Scottish. The family of his father, Peter Ross, had come from Shetland to Owen Sound, and his mother, Catherine Foster Fraser Ross, was born in Edinburgh. Like Galt, and like thousands in the days before university education was widely expected and available, Ross left high school at sixteen for a commercial apprenticeship, in his case at the Abbey, Saskatchewan, branch of the Union Bank, later the

Royal Bank of Canada. Four job transfers took him to Winnipeg; he had been combining bank work with writing since he was sixteen. Also like Galt, he left his homeland during war years. He spent 1942–6 in London as a sergeant at Ordnance Corps headquarters. Demobilized, he was transferred by the bank to Montreal, and from that 'exile' he continued to write short stories about the prairies. Many of his protagonists – Peter McAlpine, for instance, the farm boy in 'The Outlaw' (1950), who reappears in the Montreal novel *Whir of Gold* (1970) – bear Scottish names. The Scottish connection does not mean that Sinclair Ross had ever read or even heard of Galt's Lowland novels. It does mean that his ear was attuned to the same kind of talk, his experience was of the same kind of characters, and his irony had the same kind of tang.

After a series of short stories set mostly on isolated farms, Ross's first major novel described and deflated a prairie parish, adopting a dry tone like that of an American small-town annalist with a curiously similar name – Sinclair Lewis. The Canadian Sinclair's target, however, was not a Babbitt or a Willy Loman, but a minister, like Galt's self-deceiving Micah Balwhidder. In the old levelling spirit of Burns's 'Holy Willie's Prayer,' Ross caught a minister (Anglican this time) in the ironic spotlight. In *As for Me and My House* (1941), it is the minister's wife who (like Mr Balwhidder) passes along to the reader an incomplete perception of a prairie parish. Noncommunication between man and wife, a staple of Galt's irony in *Bogle Corbet* and other novels as well as in the *Annals*, darkens into the more complicated failure of Mrs Bentley either to see or to tell the truth about her husband.[24]

In Sinclair Ross's most Galtian work, *Sawbones Memorial* (1978), it is the doctor (traditionally the most respected figure in the parish, along with the minister) who focuses ironic attention. Each scrap of speech comes with a satiric undertone; every social gesture masks hidden relationships and attitudes; each specification of food, furniture, song, and streetscape slyly reveals Ross's view of the small prairie town, and of the Sawbones, Doc Hunter. He documents the 'fete,' held in celebration of Dr Hunter's none-too-willing retirement. Every one of the doctor's moves leads subtly to the realization that, in spite of the aging process discriminated in this novel and the apparent erosion of his control, his power over other individuals is still immense – immense and masked in matter-of-fact homeliness, like the skill of the author, who holds up his fictive doctor and his imagined prairie village, past and present, public and private, for our recognition.

The prairie village, in all its mores, customs, and interrelationships, is caught in the prism of a single night. Like a documentary tape, conversations at the party celebrating the Sawbones's retirement gradually reveal the life beneath the proper celebratory surface: meanness, silliness, narrowness, abortion, rape, infidelity, homosexuality, secret relationships, bullying. The air of sociable reminiscence, like Galt's, masks secret histories. Doc Hunter is himself the main channel for irony. He is aware of the community's inhibitions and secrets. His sense of waste is darker than the tone in Galt's novels, although *Bogle Corbet* has much of the same autumnal mood. Again, however, there is a sense of being at a crossroad of time: the past of drought and depression in a closed society, set against the present possibility of new life, with the promised coming of a new doctor and the presence of a sophisticated Englishwoman as wife of the town leader.

The nub of the novel is that old Doc, who has looked after the western community for many years, is being replaced by young Dr Nick, son of Big Anna, the Ukrainian cleaning woman. Gossips regard the young man askance. Not only is he a local boy; he is also a 'Hunky,' child of New Canadians. The irony of this story is that the young doctor, for all his exotic Slavic· heritage, is probably the unacknowledged son of the old doctor. Not a bad parable for the unacknowledged persistence of the old tradition within the new Canadian literature.

Like Galt, Ross has a keen eye for details of speech, manner, and social rituals. Pretensions perhaps seem most open to ironic treatment on the prairie, a place in new Canadian literature, to quote Laurie Ricou's memorable phrase, of 'vertical man, hori-

zontal world.' Silliness shines most clearly in the clear, empty
air of the west. Ross documents confinement and repression in
an austere land, fostered by puritanical religion and exacer-
bated by failure in communication, and he does so in what
Lorraine McMullen calls 'taut, economical, rhythmic prose.'[25]
This is not to claim a Galt echo. It is just recognition of a truth
(not promulgated by Burns and Scott) that irony is the best
mode for a lowland life; that specifying homely details of an
eroded, unpicturesque locale is a good way to endure them and
maybe even enjoy them.

At any rate, the reading taste for Galt's kind of 'statistical
account' of regional reality persisted until a critical mass of
fictions empowered storytellers to assume that Canadian settings and character types were now familiar. The dark forests –
and the unpicturesque villages – were no longer 'too silent to
be real.' Mapping and tabulating and photography and record-
keeping clearly were permitting the realization of Canadian
times and environments, and the incremental changes in both.

One still-active novelist completes my list of regional realists
working in Galt's mode of Lowland irony. Carol Shields's response to Galt's method is mediated through her admiration
for Susanna Moodie. Shields came to Canada from Illinois, via
a college in Indiana. She cut her Canadian teeth on Moodie: the
useful monograph, *Susanna Moodie: Voice and Vision* (1972)
emerged from Shields's MA work at the University of Ottawa.
In *Small Ceremonies* (1976) the twentieth-century author paid
direct tribute to the nineteenth-century one. In *The Stone Diaries*
(1993) the tribute becomes an acceptance of Moodie's method,
first-person memoir with intervals of poetry and meditations,
itself a method adapted by Moodie from John Galt.

The Stone Diaries gives a day-by-day account of a woman's
life, not in a single parish but in all the places through which
Daisy Flett flits: a quarry village in Manitoba; Winnipeg;
Bloomington, Indiana; Ottawa; and points between; and finally
Bradenton in Florida, where old, cold Canadians tend to go at
last. Intriguingly, the narrator slips from 'I' to 'she,' a device
suggesting the insecurity of identity in the supposed creator of

this memoir. For this book, like Galt's novels, is a pseudo-autobiography, so real it could fool an editor's mother.

Micah Balwhidder offers one key to Daisy. Like him, she is a warm but innocent participant and witness, impacted by all the changes of a lifetime but not able to square her self-analysis with the views of her held by the world (and the reader). Daisy recognizes a gap in her understanding of the events that shape her, although just occasionally she feels that 'the narrative maze opens and permits her to pass through' (190). Like Galt's books, the story is full of changes, both gradual and sudden. And like Galt, Shields is a hard author for the critical academy to take hold of. The huge sales of *The Stone Diaries* and the accolades conferred when it won the American Pulitzer Prize and was nominated for the British Booker Prize have been matched by critical puzzlement over its appeal. There is talk of 'chaos theory'; feminists stumble over the even-handed sympathy for men and women; nationalists ponder the significance of Daisy's return to the Dominion. No doubt right now the laptop equivalents of spotted coffins are filling up with notes on her works and their import.

People also reach for something in their reading that is deeper than facts and fun. Soothsaying rather than mere truth-saying, prose infused with passion as well as accuracy, style soaring from documentary into declamatory, affirmation and despair as well as scepticism and cool wit – Canadian readers in the twentieth century, like Scots in the Victorian period, wanted and needed these as part of their reading experience. In the time of nationalist emergence, people were ready to add to Galt's clear recording a richer, less rational fare. As part of the emergence of a new national literature, Canadian writers reached into a richer rhetoric, a more explosive passion. They responded to the lingering influence of another Scottish author, reproducing the pyrotechnic intensity of Thomas Carlyle.

Chapter Five

Carlyle, Mitchell, Laurence, and the Storms of Rhetoric

Thomas Carlyle, like John Galt, began his professional life as a writer of articles: encyclopedia entries, based on research and couched in careful, clear, colourless prose, as impersonal as a journalist could make it. Galt continued in a low key. Carlyle, when his times, the state of his country, and the devastation of his own ambitions came to ride him, dropped the cool prose of documentary. He put back his head and howled. A verbal lava erupted from his volcanic ambition and despair. He roared out an everlasting 'No!' against science and utilitarianism. He slumped into a desperately dreary centre of indifference (not calm, but the turgidity of depression). Then, beyond his vanishing point, his nadir of despair, Carlyle pulled his head and heart up and shouted out his everlasting 'Yea!': 'Forget self! Up, Up! Do the duty that lies nearest! Work!'

Carlyle had found his own work, writing – writing corrosive, image-laden, rhythmic incantatory prose, the kind of prose, that seemed to be the one thing needful for his times. In earlier times, Robert Burton in *The Anatomy of Melancholy* (1621), Sir Thomas Browne in *Hydriotaphia, or Urn Burial* (1658), and Laurence Sterne in *The Life and Opinions of Tristram Shandy* (1759–67) had wielded some of the same pyrotechnic skills. But it remained with the shaggy, bad-tempered, bilious, preposterous Scot to fracture the proprieties of Victorian English and recreate a language that could leap from the page, infuriate, arouse, and illuminate actuality.

Thomas Carlyle spent the major part of his life as a professional writer of non-fiction, not in Scotland but in London, England. But before he became a bearded Victorian sage in Chelsea, he had been an awkward boy in Ecclefechan, a hungry student in Edinburgh, a miserable teacher-secretary in Annan and Kirkcaldy, and a ferocious apprentice writer in Craigenputtock.[1] Few people other than Carlyle specialists read his London work today. If he retains a public, it is as the writer of 'Signs of the Times' (1829) and *Sartor Resartus* (1833–4), products of those lean years in Scotland.

And if he remains an influence on Canadian writers – and I believe his influence does linger, long after the habit of reading and revering him has gone – it is because of the aptness of his stormy rhetoric, his absolutism, intensity, existential penetration into depths of despair. He believed in a world of meanings, a world where truth can be found by fierce honesty. The symbolic method he developed for expressing his desire to disrupt traditional modes of living and writing would outlast the particular tradition he was born into.

Carlyle, born in 1795, almost ten years after Burns published the Kilmarnock edition of his poems, grew up in a community still very much like Burns's. Driven by poverty, toughened by an unpredictable climate, he was also scarified by Presbyterian conviction that this punishing life proved the dogma of man's sinfulness. In the little town of Ecclefechan, where Carlyle spent his childhood, the Presbyterian church of the Seceded Burghers preached a dark and frightening dogma. But unlike Burns, Carlyle left his strict, restricted, restricting village, and at fourteen, in 1809, he spun away to the University of Edinburgh. There, seized by the questioning spirit of modern science, he painfully wrestled with problems of faith and dropped his intention of studying theology and preparing for Presbyterian ministry.

For Carlyle, the road away from Ecclefechan was not easy. University scientists, working in the afterglow of late-eighteenth-century Enlightenment, offered no stirring alternative idealism to a stretching young man. Edinburgh innovators in medicine, engineering, biology, physics, and chemistry were working to derive useful and practical applications from the great Enlightenment burst of speculative free thought. For the undergraduate Carlyle, such mission-oriented science seemed petty, materialistic, soul-destructive, a let-down from the earlier ideals of the university.

He sank into depression, as many creative geniuses have done before and after him. Significantly, he worked out an oblique, defensive, and ironic way of expressing his despair. No doubt poverty, hunger, lovesickness, loneliness – and the darkness of winter-term Edinburgh – all contributed to a breakdown of Carlyle's nerve. From somewhere within his own psyche, however, in a strange epiphany of light and belief, he felt a sudden powerful up-welling of belief, a 'yea-saying' affirmation of life, self, nature, spirit, organicism. The 'Everlasting No' that pealed through his soul and the 'Everlasting Yea' that resounded in answer would be magnificently expressed, years later, in *Sartor Resartus*.

In the years between the epiphanic experience and the publication of that book, Carlyle wrestled in his mind as he reconsidered theology, science, business, war, death, duty, democracy – all the problematic issues newly clothed in nineteenth-century evolutionary, mechanistic, utilitarian form. As a young graduate, he briefly found satisfaction in mathematics. Then as a young teacher at Annan and Kirkcaldy he plunged into speculative philosophy based on ideas coming out of Germany. Yet German system-spinning seemed to lead into clouds rather than into clarity. At Annan, Carlyle received emotional as well as intellectual blows. His romantic dream of first love ran up against practical family considerations and a pretty girl's indifference.

When he dropped that dream and married a very different kind of woman, he moved to a new set of troubles. His marriage to icy-clever Jane Welsh intensified his stresses. Carlyle's marriage has long given grist to the gossip mills. This was not the hearty, healthy coupling of a Burns with a Highland Mary or a bonny Jean. Nor was it a marriage like Walter Scott's with his Charlotte, a happy follow-up to an earlier boyish frustration. Nor was it like John Galt's utilitarian marriage either: Galt married the daughter of his first editor – and barely mentioned her again throughout the hundreds of pages of his *Autobiography*. No, Carlyle and Jane were locked in a unique and significant nervous symbiosis.[2]

Striding the hills around Craigenputtock and struggling to put his tumbling thoughts on paper in a form that would suit *Fraser's Magazine*, he recognized the effrontery of his own literary ambitions, his desire to be a prophet, in an increasingly philistine day when prophecy and poetry were being pushed aside as impractical. Perhaps the harsh elements of the Craigenputtock landforms rekindled traditional conviction about the justified wrath of a punishing God. At any rate, Carlyle increasingly established in his work a protective, self-mocking stance. He was still in too small a community, too close to his own family and teachers, to openly avow his rebellion against orthodoxy. A society that mocked pride, a father who preached submission, a wife who added a sharp-tongued watch over delusions of grandeur, all constituted pressures on the writer to mask his most stretching thoughts, to find oblique ways to express the tissue of his new beliefs.

'Signs of the Times,' published in 1829, gave indications of a new style emerging. An old-fashioned kind of fiction would not hold his ideas. Around this time Carlyle dismissed the romantic novel popularized by Walter Scott as 'rose-pink sentimental': 'Literature *has* other aims than that of harmlessly amusing indolent languid men ... [T]here is little to be sought or found in the Waverley novels. Not profitable for doctrine, for reproof, for edification, for building up or elevating, in any shape! The sick heart will find no healing here, the darkly-struggling heart no guidance: the Heroic that is in all men no divine awakening voice.'[3] Yet if he wanted to catch a large audience, to heal and build and edify, reprove and guide his contemporaries (and he did want just that), he needed a form more passionate than essays, one which preserved some of the appeal of fiction – the appeal of an unfolding story that lures the reader into identifying with a protagonist and unravelling mysteries.

Instead of writing autobiography or a series of essays of the kind his American correspondent Ralph Waldo Emerson was already releasing, Carlyle concocted the imaginary story of a German philosopher (whom he ironically named Diogenes Teufelsdröckh – translatable as 'light-seeking devil's dung'). Teufelsdröckh's notes having been bundled into a series of paper bags, Carlyle adopts the voice of a bumbling editor who could only reveal the ideas in those bags in snatches and flashes. The background story of the philosopher's life, which in a conventional novel would constitute the principal story, would also tumble out, not in chronological or logical order, but in random flashbacks as the bags pop open.

Sartor Resartus[4] was a far cry from the standard fiction of Carlyle's day – the unruffled unrolling of a story by Dickens or Thackeray. Carlyle holds his disrupted narrative and unordered flashbacks together principally by symbolism. Of course, most novelists use symbols to enrich and deepen meanings. But Carlyle inverts the process. The symbols dominate rather than decorate the plot. Philosophical, social, and theological issues are presented muffled in metaphor, garbed in symbol. The hero's life story seems a fleeting distraction from his meditations on clothes, for example. 'Church clothes' stand for theology, garments woven by custom, once hiding wonders but now 'rent into shreds.' Diogenes Teufelsdröckh wrestles with the question of outward forms by references to clothes-making, clothes-rending, cloth-reweaving – vestments, from Adam's fig leaf to the whole of creation seen as the visible garment of spiritual force. Finally, beneath the vestitures of appearance that muffle, protect, and conceal a hidden body, he perceives that body as itself just 'clothes.'

The clothes-philosopher must himself don the clothing of style as he writes his notes. What sort of rhetoric (to ask a rhetorical question) would suit Carlyle's daring/cautious revelations? The answer was a spectacular style, Carlyle's fantastic phrase-making. Society becomes 'this sour mud-swamp of an existence'; the universe, 'one huge, dead, immeasurable Steam-engine, rolling on, in its dead indifference' (1:133); God, 'an absentee God, sitting idle, ever since the first Sabbath, at the outside of his Universe, and *seeing* it go' (1:130). Devastated by the nihilism of his times, troubled by his own ridiculous pride, Carlyle expresses his indignation by apocalyptic rhetoric.

He uses language heightened, enriched by all the orator's tricks; bombastic, staccato periods dropping to simple, almost naive phrasing; a turbulence of logic and rhapsody; sentence fragments and rolling periodic sentences. Typical of the style is a passage like this:

> 'Doubt had darkened into Unbelief,' says he; 'shade after shade goes grimly over your soul, till you have the fixed, starless, Tartarean black.' To such readers as have reflected, what can be called reflecting, on man's life, and happily discovered, in contradiction to much Profit-and-Loss Philosophy, speculative and practical, that Soul is *not* synonymous with Stomach; who understand, therefore, in our Friend's words, 'that, for man's wellbeing, Faith is properly the one thing needfull; how, with it, Martyrs, otherwise weak, can cheerfully endure the shame and the cross; and without it, Worldlings puke-up their sick existence, by suicide, in the midst of luxury': to such it will be clear that, for a pure moral nature, the loss of his religious Belief was the loss of everything (1:130).

Powerful vocabulary and startling phrases coil in repeated structures, and then lash out into the climactic simplicity of the final phrase, 'the loss of everything.' The style has the drive of the tides that push into Scotland's ragged coastline and then ebb leaving sand and gravel.

The hectic style of Carlyle is itself Scottish in origin. It comes from oral tradition – the exaggerations of ghost stories, drinking songs, and tall tales of local heroes told with appropriate heightening, and the quiet understatement of sadness and loss. It comes from old-style debating contests in classics-dominated schools; from the demagoguery of a democratic election system post-1832. Above all, it comes from visionary, apocalyptic sermons on hellfire and pearly gates, preached to counter hunger, the bareness of actuality, and the thinness of hope in this world. All of these were part of the linguistic traditions in Scotland.

In Scotland, too, there was richness of language in a community that had at least two languages at command, 'proper' English and colloquial Lowland Scots, with a third among the Highlanders, the lilting Gaelic. This linguistic richness and awareness guaranteed the continuance of ambiguous, mellifluous language.

The message rolling out in Carlyle's strange medium appeared in its time as a radical reaction against the solipsist self-indulgence of romanticism, the theological withdrawal into mysticism of the Oxford Movement, and the political clamouring for franchise of the era of the 1832 Reform Bill. The terrifying depression of many of his contemporaries not only in Scotland but also in England and America is articulated in 'The Everlasting No.' Furthermore, his enunciation of an 'Everlasting Yea' to answer that 'Everlasting No' seemed viable for his contemporaries at home and abroad. He became regarded in the United States and Canada as well as in England and Europe as a great 'sage,' a philosopher whose pounding style carried his ideas beyond his homeland. Emerson picked up and spiritualized many of Carlyle's themes; Thoreau put some of his commands into practice; Hawthorne adopted his symbolic methods. Biographers and autobiographers, including Newman, Ruskin, and Froude, followed Carlyle's *Sartor Resartus* in introducing intensities of anguish and affirmation – tides of feeling unlike anything traditionally unleashed in those genres.

Carlyle left the hard world of rural Scotland in 1834, the year he published *Sartor Resartus*. Briefly, he and Jane Welsh Carlyle considered emigrating to Canada, where he had a sister, a brother, and nieces and nephews; but the rest of his productive, disruptive, explosive life was played out in London. He would write many other works – massive histories like *History of The French Revolution* (1837), sweeping views of culture like *On Heroes, Hero-Worship, & the Heroic in History* (1841), rampaging meditations on contemporary events like *Past and Present* (1843), and heavy biographies like *History of Frederick II of Prussia, called Frederick the Great* (1858–65)[5] after he left Scotland. But *Sartor Resartus* had the greatest impact of all his work, both on his contemporaries and on readers and writers since. The force of his rhetoric opened the way for modern fables of identity.

Well into the twentieth century, Carlyle's work remained on the literary curriculum in Canada. In the 1930s and 1940s, Canadian schools still prescribed large doses of the raw and despairing Scot. His thought was close to Canadians' in its seriousness, its concentration on spiritual issues, its hunger for truths and imperatives. Its coruscating rhythms seemed to suit the rigours and harshness of the Canadian environment. Its theology, emerging from repressive Calvinist Presbyterianism through painful doubts into a new kind of absolutism, suited earnest Canada in the years between the First and Second World Wars.

As an undergraduate student, I was roused by Carlylean rhetoric, his iron chords. Here was something more relevant than the old ballads, more raw and rough than the regular rhythms of *The Lady of the Lake*. This seemed more like what language should do, shocking us into new ideas while reminding us of old ones. But world war loomed, and patriots saw a troubling correspondence between Carlyle's theories of 'heroes and hero-worship' and the Nazi dogmas of a master race. His concept of the strong man, the superman, was credited with influencing Nietzsche and, through Nietzsche, Hitler. By the time the war was over, Carlyle's heroics were discredited.

Yet even when the general reading public drifted away from him, his work remained a scholar's delight. The bituminous prose, the hectic rhetoric, the cartwheeling references to the signs of the times – all were grist for analysis, emendation, extrapolation. College courses on 'Victorian Prose of Thought' still involved dissecting the mannerisms, while deploring the messages, of the creator of *Heroes and Hero Worship* and 'Signs of the Times.' Surely this ironic turn of literary history would have infuriated and amused the blustering, subtle sage of the 1830s.

In the immediate post-war years, Henry Hall, dean of arts at Sir George Williams College in Montreal, was a disciple of Carlyle. As disciple, apostle, proselytizer, Dean Hall preached to the weekly assemblies of student veterans at the college the Carlylean 'Yea': 'Be no longer a Chaos, but a World, or even Worldkin. Produce! Produce! Were it but the pitifullest infinitesimal fraction of a Product, produce it, in God's name! 'Tis the utmost thou hast in thee: out with it, then. Up, up! Whatsoever thy hand findeth to do, do it with thy whole might. Work while it is called Today; for the Night cometh, wherein no man can work' (1:157). Strange dogma to preach to young men and women who had indeed done their duty, had strained for more than five years beyond their might, in France, Italy, Africa, Borneo, India. But Dean Hall's cheery Carlylean urgings sat well with these post-war people. The atmosphere of Sir George Williams in 1946 and 1947 was without anomie, without post-war stress.

I began my teaching career there in that time. To classes of two hundred students I lectured on Carlyle, along with Chaucer, Spenser, Milton, Browning, Tennyson, et al. The course ended, as my own undergraduate survey course had done, with Thomas Hardy and Joseph Conrad. My not-so-volcanic voice, sporadically helped by a public address system (it usually worked on Tuesdays), pumped out information and attitudes for these student veterans to commit to memory and regurgitate in exams. They read the three central chapters of *Sartor Resartus* ('The Everlasting No,' 'Centre of Indifference,' and 'The Everlasting Yea') with some pleasure. The roaring rhetoric seemed attractive in that fermenting time. They liked the idea of a raw wind from the north rejuvenating literature and life.

Dean Hall soon suggested to me, in an 'Up, up!' tone, that if I planned to stay in academic life, I should get a doctor's degree. When I returned to University of Toronto in pursuit of a PhD, Carlyle was not much in evidence there. Toronto had gurus, prophets, thunderers of its own. There was young Northrop Frye and young Marshall McLuhan, at Victoria College and St Michael's College respectively. Both had long taught and thought about Carlyle's work. Frye wove a Carlylean tissue of metaphor, proclaiming a gospel of imaginative correspondences between all orders of existence, offering to illuminate the mythic quality in every work of art, and luring students into a search for archetypes, grand universal permanences underlying the particular clothings of thought. McLuhan, as grotesque and provocative in his language as Carlyle had been in his, looked, as Carlyle had done, at the phenomena of the day and lifted them to prophetic significance. With such local sages, who needed to heed the bearded, burring sage of Victorian Chelsea?

In those post-war days, Canadian college students were also being carried beyond British literature to enthusiasm for other cultures. Melville's *Moby Dick* offered a rhetoric as sweeping and surprising as Carlyle's. James Joyce exploded ordinary syntax and included offbeat experiences as liberating as Carlyle's eruptions. But both Carlyle's medium and his message had been so thoroughly absorbed into the Canadian educational system that they lingered powerfully, even after his own writings were washed out of the required reading lists. There was a hard-rock pawkiness beneath his mystic soarings and a fearless earthiness in his details and metaphors that fitted Canadian experience better than Irish or American versions of vision. Canadian writers were still deeply affected by Carlyle's stylistic manner and his literary strategies and by his fierce concentration on absolutes.

A century after his death his methods resurfaced in tense and powerful Canadian writers such as Margaret Laurence and W.O. Mitchell. Fiery rhetoric and an absolutism like Carlyle's were impelling a thundering phase of Canadian nationalism in literature, following the cooler Galtian work of the regional realists. A new Canadian literature was flooding in, drawn in part from the memory of Scottish models, but with its own sweep and force. And at last some Canadian educators were taking notice. By the time I went back to my teaching job at Sir George Williams College, complete with a shining PhD, my specialized training in English Victorian literature seemed close to irrelevant. Sir George Williams was one of the first Canadian universities to proudly mount courses in Canadian literature.

Writers emerging in Canada at that time, whose works were being gradually added to college reading lists, included W.O. Mitchell, born in 1914, and Margaret Laurence, born in 1926. In spite of their difference in age, both shared the post-war sense of living 'between two worlds, one dead, and one powerless to be born.' In their strongest early work, both Mitchell and Laurence focused on the world of death. Mitchell's *Who Has Seen the Wind* (1947) used the perspective of a little boy; Laurence's *The Stone Angel* (1964) worked from the opposite end of the spectrum of life, adopting the point of view of a very old woman. But both shared the contemporary existential fascination with the 'Everlasting No.' In Laurence's *The Fire-Dwellers* (1969) and Mitchell's *The Vanishing Point* (1973) the point of perspective comes closer to the authors' immediate experience. The former features a woman in her thirties, the latter a man at about the same stage in life. Each moves toward a Carlylean epiphany, an 'Everlasting Yea' very much like his.

Let me trace the Carlylean elements that I find in these two books, my own perennial favourites among the fine range of work by the two authors, and the two novels that seem most interesting from a rhetorical point of view. First, however, let me note that both these authors voiced a renunciation of the controlling power of a Scottish heritage.

While Margaret Laurence was living in England in the 1960s, Alan McLean, her editor and friend, arranged for her to visit the country her family had so often spoken of as the old homeland.[6] Essays in *Heart of a Stranger* (published in 1976, but the relevant essays were written earlier, around 1966) report her finding that, contrary to the tenets of her upbringing, her real past was not connected, except distantly, with Scotland.[7] Thousands of miles away from home, she remembers (in 'A Place to Stand On') her Scottish pioneer forefathers, 'how authoritarian, how unbending, how afraid to show love, many of them, and how willing to show anger' (16). In 'Road from the Isles' she writes of revisiting the places from which her own ancestors

were cleared, betrayed by the chiefs to whom they gave unthinking loyalty. 'This, not the romantic swashbuckling figures
in Sir Walter Scott's novels, was the reality of the Highlanders'
(148). In Ross-shire she sees what she calls the 'mock Scots'
rituals put on for the tourists, 'slicked up, prettified' (155). The
details of Scottish life and scenery so effectively and ironically
observed help her to know where she belongs. She assigned
the same sort of trip, and the same sort of conclusion, to the
fictional Morag Gunn in *The Diviners* (1974). In '"There and Not
There": Aspects of Scotland in Laurence's Writing,' Colin
Nicholson draws attention to a decisive moment of repudiation
and identification in *The Diviners*[8] when Margaret Laurence,
having evoked Scottish romance, moves to an act of severance
and to a literary declaration of Canadian independence. That
sequence of possession/dispossession/discovery appears essential for self-recognition.

W.O. Mitchell's son, Dr Orm Mitchell, has recorded in comic
terms the story of his father's comparable 'struggle with his
Scots Presbyterian heritage.'[9] In a taped interview, W.O. Mitchell
recalled his grandmother Maggie McMurray – 'She looked a
great deal like a more finely drawn John Knox if he wore a
black velvet ribbon high around his neck' (115) – and for all her
influence on him, he hated his grandmother's oatmeal porridge and her theology (114). Partly because Mitchell, like
Margaret Laurence, was brought up in a largely Scottish community out west, raised in an Old Testament, prophetic Presbyterianism, he struck the Carlylean chord.[10] He drove himself
with the same self-immolating devotion to work and to truth
and created a comparable pyrotechnical prose. He pushed his
vision to the vanishing point, confronting absolute questions,
the 'Yea' and 'No' of belief and unbelief.

When W.O. Mitchell created a fictional hero who had to
radically re-tailor his beliefs and attitudes, he gave him Carlyle
as a first name, plus a surname, Sinclair, that would remind
Canadian readers of the prairie novelist Sinclair Ross. Mitchell's
Vanishing Point[11] carries his 'hero' beyond the prairies to the
foothills, where men must confront the Rocky Mountains. It

traces the spiritual travail of Carlyle Sinclair, using Carlylean rhetoric, metaphors, and fictional structures. The story of Mitchell's Carlyle Sinclair parallels that of Carlyle's Teufels-dröckh. He has gone through his own inferno: the death of his mother, a cold fostering by his Aunt Pearl, ill-treatment by a cruel teacher, loss of a dear friend, Mate, and the more devas-tating loss of his young wife, Grace, and their stillborn daugh-ter. He has reached a 'Centre of Indifference' as an alien teacher, in a Stoney Native reserve. Mitchell refers to the students as 'Stony Indians.'

Just as Thomas Carlyle used surface realities to form a sec-ondary level of metaphorical significance, Carlyle Sinclair pulls organic filaments out of real details to create a web of signifi-cance: plaster-statue Snow White and real 'red' girl Victoria; death of the oldest 'red man' in the tent of a white revivalist preacher. *The Vanishing Point* is set in a double geography of roads, bridges, and waterways in a modern city and its fringe. In Calgary the perspective lines converge in the conservatory where an old man named Ian Fyfe grows orchids, protected by glass from the snows, protected by Fyfe's swift action against the bee's natural fumbling efforts to cross-fertilize. In the city natural life is virtually dead. But outside the city, on the Stoney 'Paradise Reserve,' perspective lines converge on the 'shame' of the young and pregnant girl, Victoria. Ignorance, mutual misunderstanding, language problems, and economic depriva-tion threaten to prevent new life and love from being born.

Carlyle Sinclair wrestles with the problem of the 'Indians,' a part of humanity moved by those impulses and energies which western Europeans (and especially Scots Presbyterians) have been taught to control and condemn. Inside the city, Native peoples live as social outcasts, scavengers, misfits; yet they seem to hold some transcendental wisdom, some testament alternative to the Scottish-based orthodoxies. Gaining access to that alternative vision is as painful for the Canadian hero in fiction as was the period of doubt and searching for Carlyle's Teufelsdröckh. Carlyle Sinclair as teacher of Natives must be-come Carlyle, Native dancer.

The Native people are real – pathetically, comically, politically real. They are Carlyle Sinclair's students, his advisers, his antagonists, his burden, his hope. Their alternative to the Scottish work ethic is commonalty, generosity, improvidence. They are sadly and hilariously convincing as individuals and as a group. But they are symbols too. 'Native' stands for a part of Carlyle Sinclair's inner world. Natives reveal the part of himself he has subdued under the tutelage of Aunt Pearl, under the impact of Mate's death, under the blow of the loss of Grace. They represent urges he is ashamed of, simplicities he has lost, a language he cannot speak. The story of Carlyle Sinclair's dealing with the Native people teases us to consider every person's encounters with a hidden self, every adult's evasions of a part of the psyche. The Natives in *The Vanishing Point* 'work' both in the surface story and in the deeper level of symbolism.

To carry Carlyle Sinclair's vision of his own life with maximum impact to the reader, Thomas Carlyle's verbal constructs and mannerisms – the disrupted syntax, the vocabulary of words wrenched out of their ordinary uses, the sentence fragments piling up into tumbled heaps – reappear in W.O. Mitchell's novel.

So – wasn't all communication between all humans hopeless? Out of my skin and into yours I cannot get – however hard I try – however much I want to! All one could do was – wish it were possible – and know that illusion was the best that could be managed. The love illusion – possessing – being in each other – simply could not be brought off – love died instant death with each satiety ... What a weak bridge emotion was for people to walk across to each other – emotion swinging, unable to hold the heavy weight of communication. About as dependable as the goddam telephone line. Just illusion after all, for once the passage was made, the door was always closed. You stopped at the eyes, and you never left the home envelope of self anyway. (216)

The verbal static of Stacey MacAindra in Laurence's *The Fire-Dwellers*[12] has the same Carlylean pyrotechnic quality: 'Everything drifts. Everything is slowly swirling, philosophies tangled with the grocery lists, unreal-real anxieties like rose thorns waiting to tear the uncertain flesh, nonentities of thoughts floating like plankton' (34). 'Judgment. All the things I don't like to think I believe in. But at the severe moments, up they rise, the tomb birds, scaring the guts out of me with their vulture wings. Maybe it's as well to know they're there. Maybe knowing might help to keep them at least a little in their place. Or maybe not' (270).

Laurence's protagonist, Stacey Cameron MacAindra, with her double-Scotch maiden name and married name, burns in a female inferno. Ineffectual motherhood, suburban housekeeping, neurotic neighbours, too-available gin, all smoulder under the eye of the television screen with its reports of world terrorism intensified by the immediate focus on the atomic bomb. In *The Fire-Dwellers* Laurence uses fire as a constant symbol. The external, real fires in this novel are those in news headlines, stories of an atomic age, a holocaust. They are also those on escapist picnic beaches or in constraining kitchen cookery. But all are mediating symbols of spiritual and emotional modernity.

The 'fire-dweller' in Laurence's novel finds her ordinary world incandescent with meaning. Like Thomas Carlyle, she pulls 'organic filaments' out of everyday experience: a bird, a beach, or a bottle burn with an electric current, grabbing attention with a force as great as that of the unfolding story. '[T]he lunatic voices of the loons, witchbirds out there in the night lake, or voices of dead shamans, mourning the departed Indian gods ... the begone voices that cared nothing for lights or shelter or the known quality of home' (159). 'Stacey and Jen walk barefoot, picking up greywhite coarse clamshells, small purple shells paired and open like moth wings, greenly iridescent shells shaped like miniature coolie hats' (261).

For all its communication of a sense of deep significance in ordinary life, Laurence's story is richly humorous. For Mitchell too, the final epiphany in the Chicken Dance is comic rather than heroic. Life in Canada has drawn many Canadians into assuming a comparable mocking and self-mocking pose. The climate, the northern darkness of long nights, the soil impoverished by foolish practices of earlier generations; the cities small enough to be cold, big enough to be mean; democracy leading to mediocrity, technocracy replacing simpler machinery in dominance over humane values; the universal news of war and starvation reeling on – none of these troubles seem remediable. The old, dark theology looms; surely a punishing god must have decreed such a life. Canadians must deserve the cold, the rain, the mosquitoes, and the human gadflies. What if this mud swamp is the jest of an absentee god? What response to such a universe, a society, a god, except capitulation?

Beyond his vanishing point, Thomas Carlyle was able to formulate some rules for heroic action. A century later, his preachment of work, duty, and production had become an old, familiar, and unsatisfactory message. In western Canada in particular, the Protestant work ethic had proved ineffectual. To judge by fictional accounts, at least, it had brought few rewards, either personal, social, or economic.

W.O. Mitchell's hero has tried all too earnestly to follow Carlyle's edicts. He has worked; he has set his hand to the task nearest him; he has produced, and dragged the protesting Stoney Natives into productivity. But his work example and his work ethic have not changed Native ways or solved their problems. Carlyle's 'Yea' is about as useful as the oatmeal cookies with which later Scots Canadians fed Native children. Mitchell's story ends in what the Natives called 'grabbing-hold time': what Carlyle Sinclair's hand findeth to do is to grab hold of the Native girl, Victoria.

Nor will Carlyle's positive message serve Margaret Laurence's Stacey MacAindra. She has set her hand to the task nearest her. She has produced, if not a world, at least four 'worldkins' – two sons and two daughters. She has done her duty, as defined by patriarchy. She has worked for her husband, her father-in-law, her children, her neighbours. And she still dwells in the fires of anxiety and resentment. For her, happiness rather than blessedness comes, however; not from any heroic action, but from simple passage of time – time until her little daughter can articulate a few words in human speech.

Carlyle's 'Yea' sounds hollow to these modern Canadians. But in his 'Everlasting No' he had indeed articulated in borrowable terms the nadir of a common despair. This nadir is not the fear of death: Mitchell had faced that in *Who Has Seen the Wind*, Laurence in *The Stone Angel*. Rather, the 'Everlasting No' for the modern Canadian on the western prairie or in a Vancouver suburb, as for the early Victorian Scot on his unrewarding farm, is a sense of worthlessness, of powerlessness, of being the victim of a hostile world. For that continuing devastating nihilism, the Carlylean method seemed perfect.

Canadian novelists of the 1970s do in fiction what Carlyle did once in his own wild essay-diatribe form. They push readers toward the deepest questions of faith and despair, baring the everlasting 'No,' hinting at a possible 'Yea.' Their style does what Carlyle's did, disrupting the established patterns of prose discourse, flinging in firecracker metaphors, jumbling the distresses of current affairs into the clichés of romance.[13]

In *The Vanishing Point* and *The Fire-Dwellers*, Mitchell and Laurence voiced quintessential Canadian concerns of their day. I do not think that these books would catch a non-Canadian audience with the force they exerted here. They caught the times in themes that now date them. Mitchell's attitude to the Native people (Stony Indians, as he calls them), which seemed both sensitive and liberal in the 1970s, would now be unacceptable on several grounds. Laurence's nervous nodes – concern over napalm-burned forests, the draft dodgers from the United States, the peace marches, the ban-the-bomb signs, and the dream of a hippie life on the ocean shore – have been succeeded by new stimuli to terrors and new hopes.

These two novels are also distractingly gender-driven. Mitchell's concept of the Native girl, Victoria, is completely patriarchal, and the other women in his hero's life, the domineering aunt and the fragile wife, are conveniently dead, safely docketed in his memory as male-directed menace and solace. Conversely, the men in *The Fire-Dwellers* are all inadequate, unequal to Stacey in intensity and perception. Mac, the husband; the Reverend Matthew MacAindra, the father-in-law;

Buckle and Thor, the two phoney macho types; Luke, the impossible animalistic lover, together comprise the spectrum of
males, as reductively seen by a woman. All are apparently
acceptable characterizations for women readers, but for men
they seem shallow and unconvincing caricatures.

Margaret Laurence was in England when she wrote *The Fire-
Dwellers*, but her work is infused with the ideas rampant in
Canada at that time, as promulgated by the great contemporaries Marshall McLuhan and Northrop Frye. Stacey MacAindra
agonizingly recognizes herself as a citizen of what McLuhan
called 'the global village.' She also fits the paradigms set forth
in *The Mechanical Bride* and *Understanding Media*.[14] In her life,
the television is the medium. The 'ever-open eye' enters, punc-
tuates, and shapes her days. As for Northrop Frye, his vision of
archetypal patterns in literature seems to find a point-by-point
illustration here.[15] Laurence presents a full daemonic universe
of archetypes, from the ironic god Thor, through a human
range of unbending, stiff-necked generations of men, Matthew,
Mac, and Ian, right down to an animal kingdom where even
the bluebird is only a name on a street sign.

Both *The Fire-Dwellers* and *The Vanishing Point* are early products of a new Canadian self-assurance, representative of the
Centennial spirit. Both novels blaze with Carlylean energy. As
in Carlyle, the very intensity of their timeliness and prejudices
consumed them. For more lasting appeal, readers turn to
Mitchell's *Who Has Seen the Wind* and Laurence's *The Stone
Angel*.

A world very much like Carlyle's had been described not
only in Laurence and Mitchell but also in many earlier Canadian novelists, such as Nellie McClung and Charles Bruce.[16]
Elders in their books try to shape a society after the pattern of
Old Testament Israel; fathers combine pride with a hard-handed
discipline designed to induce humility in young people; schools
enforce narrow and rigid discipline. The Scottish names in all
these fictional villages are noticeably different from the names
in contemporary American novels – or English ones, of course.
A century and a quarter after Carlyle's social, familial, and

theological schooling, these novels imply, Canadian villages were being shaped by the same ethos that held Ecclefechan in 1800.

Carlyle broke heroically away from his village. Such a stand, once accepted as essential for fictional heroes, was downgraded in the novels of modern American and British stories. The anti-hero who concedes and accedes to convention was delineated, from Virginia Woolf's Mrs Dalloway to Kingsley Amis's Lucky Jim and from Sinclair Lewis's Babbitt to John Updike's Rabbit. Many modern Canadian writers, on the other hand, continued to focus on protagonists (male or female) who heroically set their faces against society. Many of these disruptive, questing, Carlylean Canadian heroes bear Scottish and/or Old Testament names. Many of them, like Stacey Cameron MacAindra, Vanessa MacLeod, and Morag Gunn, break dramatically from their own versions of Ecclefechan.

For any radically experimental writer, unorthodox fiction, symbolic metafiction, extravagant rhetoric, and above all self-mocking irony are the literary clothes that keep out the winter of desolation. Wrapping himself in his plaid, Carlyle could save a heroic, humorous remnant of identity and self-respect. Using comparable literary forms to confront despair, his later Canadian compeers could also be heroic in humour, heroic in honesty.

Everlasting Yea?

On both sides of the Atlantic, the 1970s brought intense activity and excitement, both political and literary. In song, story, essay, and polemic, Scottish writers moved into clear-sighted mapping in the Galt mode, and then beyond realism into a transcendent vision in the mode of Thomas Carlyle. Having articulated a Scottish 'here,' writers swung out in incantations, packed with local power words, home-grown metaphors, regional allusions. William McIlvanney's *Docherty* (1975), for instance, unleashed torrential localisms, astounding traditional critics. George Mackay Brown's *Greenvoe* (1972) reeled in history, mystery, and farce with extravagant rhetoric. Other writers, including Alan Sharp and Elspeth Davie, delighted readers with the sound of Scots used, not for comic effects or for discrimination of classes, but for the sheer pleasure of recording familiar and apt vernacular phrasing. By the mid-seventies it seemed that a new literary world was indeed about to emerge in Scotland, with Carlylean birth pangs.

The teaching of a national literature surfaced, matching and augmenting a growth in new writing. The work of Scottish writers, both contemporary and distanced by history, became a source of pride, amusement, and reassurance of presence for their compatriots. The School of Scottish Studies at Edinburgh, its turf hard won in 1951 from the English Department of the University of Edinburgh, and comparable groups at Aberdeen and Glasgow, Stirling and St Andrew's, moved to put more Scottish material on lower-school reading lists. Hitherto, academic articles on Scottish literature had appeared mostly in *Studies in Scottish Literature*, a journal published by Ross Roy, an expatriate Canadian in South Carolina. Now in 1974 the *Scottish Literary Journal* was established in Aberdeen by young academics there, David Hewitt and Ian Alexander, to offer critical back-up to teachers of Scottish literature, old and new.

It was a great time for centenaries and bicentenaries. The birth of Scott in 1771 was celebrated with international conferences and publications;[1] Galt's birth in 1779 was similarly recognized;[2] the centenary of the death of Carlyle in 1881 brought other volumes.[3]

Scottish critics and teachers alike delighted in reviving interest in the strong writers of the previous generation, whose work had been underestimated by the Englished literature departments: Hugh MacDiarmid, Edwin Muir, Lewis Grassic Gibbon, Catherine Carswell. Outside Scotland, however, the appeal of many of these twentieth-century Scots remained minimal. MacDiarmid and Gibbon were among the most powerful influences on subsequent Scottish writers, but it would be a fervent devotee outside Scotland who could course through their works without linguistic trouble. MacDiarmid gloried in beginning *A Drunk Man Looks at the Thistle* (1926) with lines like these:

> The elbuck fankles in the coorse o' time,
> The sheckle's no' sae souple, and the thrapple
> Grows deef and dour: nae langer up and doun
> Gleg as a squirrel speils the Adam's apple.[4]

Lewis Grassic Gibbon described Kinraddie in *Sunset Song* (1932) with a comparable overload of 'Scots-speak': 'Now Peesie's Knapp's biggings were not more than twenty years old, but gey ill-favoured for all that, for though the house faced on the road – and that was fair handy if it didn't scunner you that you couldn't so much as change your sark without some ill-fashioned brute gowking at you.'[5] 'Scunner' and 'sark' and 'gowking' may trail a faint memory of Burns's language for some readers, but Gibbon himself, worrying that the dialect words might cut down on his audience, provided footnotes.

Powerful, haunting, *Sunset Song* might have been expected to wield the kind of influence in Canada that once greeted Burns, Scott, and Carlyle. Instead, it remained virtually unnoticed. The days when influence spilled easily from a Burns or a Scott to a McLachlan or a Crawford were over. The newer Scottish voices were drowned out, in Canada, by powerful home-grown innovators.

Canadians, of course, shared with Scots the increasing desire to read, study, and present critical comments on their own literature. In those heady days, Canada seemed to be emerging as a bilingual, bicultural country. Led by Pierre Elliott Trudeau, biculturalism flourished. As part of a double heritage, Gabrielle Roy had long been revered; new names like Roch Carrier, Michel Tremblay, and Gilles Vigneault were now added to 'CanLit' reading lists (a parallel here to the way that contemporary Scottish educators had tried to widen appreciation of Gaelic poets and storytellers who created their work in that second Scottish tongue).

Helping to build up an infrastructure of teachers' support, young academics launched learned journals of CanLit criticism comparable to the *Scottish Literary Journal*. The *Journal of Canadian Fiction*, founded in Winnipeg by David Arnason and John Moss in 1972, is a case in point, and there were many others. For a brief time, readers, writers, publishers, and teachers were synchronized in forwarding national literature. A general public, moderately affluent, not yet totally addicted to television, bought both hardcover and paperback books from flourishing bookstores. A constellation of small publishers circled around the major publishers (in Canada these still included many with Scottish names: McClelland & Stewart, Macmillan, Douglas & McIntyre). Writers, both the old, well-established ones and the newcomers, supplied these institutions with displays of talent.

The old feeling of being at the outskirts of empire gave way to an assurance that local details were interesting. Canadian readers rediscovered writers, from Susanna Moodie to Stephen Leacock, who had chronicled those details, helping politicians to build the sense of national identity into a platform. Canadians had missed the opportunity to celebrate centenaries of the births of national icons such as Moodie, born in 1803, or Crawford, born in 1850, and could not yet memorialize deaths: McLachlan did not die until 1896, Leacock until 1944. National conferences were nevertheless convened, in particular the University of Ottawa 'Reappraisals' series, started in 1974.

Canadian English, so faintly differentiated on paper from American or British English, turned out to be an advantage. It was a fairly colourless medium through which highly differentiated Canadian materials could flow outward. Every town and village seemed to have its annalist, documenting regional idioms, accents, ceremonies, daily routines: Robertson Davies, Marian Engel, George Elliott, Jack Hodgins. Readers were tickled into saying 'I've been there! That's just what foothills people are like!' or 'Maritime winter roads – he's caught the sense of them exactly!' Canadians in the 1970s outside the bounds of the universities could glory in the availability of such books, not only nationally poignant but also universally meaningful.

It seemed as though the 'Yea!' for Canada – and for Scotland – would be everlasting.

Who could best raise a national voice? Galt and Carlyle had both left Scotland. Expatriates, they spent a good portion of life in London. Although Galt returned to his homeland to die, it was because his luck ran out. If his Canadian schemes had succeeded, he would probably have remained in Canada like his notable sons, rather than go back to Scotland. Nevertheless, though they were expatriates, Galt and Carlyle redirected the Scottish literature of their day into new and important paths. The phenomenon of expatriate Scots writing intensely Scottish works would continue, with Robert Louis Stevenson leading late-nineteenth-century Scottish novelists in new directions when he created *The Master of Ballantrae* while living in Saranac, New York, or *Weir of Hermiston* while in Samoa. The Canadian equivalent of this phenomenon would be Margaret Laurence writing her Canadian prairie novels while she lived in England or Mordecai Richler pinning Montreal to his Spanish board. Not a new phenomenon: Carole Gerson in *A Purer Taste* mentions Gilbert Parker, Charles G.D. Roberts, Bliss Carman, E.W. Thomson, Grant Allen, Lily Dougall, Robert Barr, and Sara Jeannette Duncan as dominating the Canadian literary scene from afar at the turn of the twentieth century.[6]

The reverse of this phenomenon in the emergence of nationalist literature appears in Austin Clarke and Audrey Thomas and many others, all one-time immigrants, who became recognized as leading Canadian novelists in the 1970s. The possibility of appropriation of national themes by an alien might lead to the false model 'of 'the outsider,' with its banal imagery of a fixed ontological gap between isolated artist and inauthentic society,'[7] according to Terry Eagleton, whose *Exiles and Emigrés* is a study of the 'heart land' and the 'found land' in writers such as James Joyce and Joseph Conrad. Eagleton concludes, however, that the phenomenon of peripatetic authors focuses literature, beneficially, on 'problems of value, consciousness, relationship and identity.'

Such questions of values and national identity were endlessly discussed in the 1970s. Young Margaret Atwood published two seminal books in 1972, *Surfacing*, a novel set in Toronto and in Quebec's cottage country, and *Survival*, a fiery thematic study of Canadian literature. In schoolrooms and college classes, teachers picked up the Atwood books and launched fierce arguments about her theses and her stories. In the late 1970s, discussion in schools and colleges about the Atwood theses was used to develop response to the Canadian books from which she had drawn her controversial and surprising theories. Teaching CanLit played an essential part in the surfacing of a national awareness of native culture.

Northrop Frye used to tell his graduate students (of whom I had been one) that it is impossible to teach literature; it is only possible to teach criticism. On the contrary, in the 1970s the teaching of Canadian literature, in the sense of talking to students about the writers, reading prose passages and poems to students, helping them push into the writers' ideas and notice the mannerisms of style, was a viable and important process. Another noted academic critic, George Whalley of Queen's University, postulated that there were in fact two kinds of students in any class on literature. He called them interns and patients. The interns are already dedicated to literature and hope to teach or write when they graduate. The other students, the patients, need expert help in developing mentally and emotionally, rather than training to join the profession. The books prescribed will help them in class, and they will carry the prescription and be helped by it all their lives.[8] Many academics in the 1970s believed that they could and should prescribe Canadian literature for the mental and emotional health of their students.

The results were exciting. For example, I taught *The Fire-Dwellers* in a course on Canadian women writers in a Women's Study program at the University of Guelph. My students were feminists, many of them 'mature students' who had at last sidestepped the responsibilities of home and children in order to do degree work. They identified with Stacey MacAindra's torments, although they condemned the emergence of her romantic interest in a self-satisfied bohemian lover down by the seashore. What they liked best about the book, and what surprised them most, was the unconventional style, the way Laurence wove news clips, memories, reveries, into the unfolding of Stacey's story. The barrage of words (which I saw as a Carlylean rhetoric) seemed to these students a fit, modern, and inevitable way to reproduce their own responses to life. My students, like Stacey, felt themselves to be 'between two worlds.' Laurence's style caught exactly their sense of disorientation and discomposure, and also the excitement and exhilaration of breaking old forms of language and life.

I once taught *The Vanishing Point* to an equally specialized but opposite group: young men in an English course required for Canadian students in agricultural science. Again the book was eminently appropriate. The hero, Carlyle Sinclair, as resident teacher on a Native reserve, reflected a 'between two worlds' state in land use. Conversion to machinery, adjustment from horsebreaking to cattle-tending, adaptation from dependence to production and providence – these were agricultural motifs readily visible as symbols of wider changes in agriculture. Carlyle Sinclair's obsession with Victoria, his desire and guilt and protectiveness, were also easy for the young men to identify with. Once again, and again rather to my surprise, the experimental form caught them. The freewheeling use of language excited them: it was close to their own experiences with disordered streams of consciousness.

I do not know whether members of either group ever picked up books so experimental in style for their later leisure reading. But I do believe that in both cases the classroom experience with this kind of book provided glimpses of essentially Canadian dilemmas, conveyed by deliberate mind-catching oddities of structure, metaphor, and language. Local details used metaphorically and local events transformed into fable could erase some of the walls not only of home and native land but also of self. Regional annalists might begin by clarifying local values and taboos; but if the writing was vivid enough, the book would leap local barriers and enter an international reservoir. The style of Mitchell and Laurence, heightened in a Carlylean way, permitted fictions to work for the 1970s students in the ways that Carlyle thought fiction should do: as 'doctrine ... reproof ... edification ... elevation ... guidance for the darkly-struggling heart ..., awakening of the Heroic.'

The study of Canadian literature was particularly popular in the new universities, founded in the 1960s. At Lethbridge, Regina, Sudbury, Guelph, Sherbrooke, Moncton, and Charlottetown, centres less cosmopolitan than the old university cities of Vancouver, Montreal, and Halifax, students responded very warmly to books about the world they knew. (In Scotland the same thing was happening. Scottish studies were strong in Strathclyde and Stirling and Dundee, stronger perhaps than in the older universities, where English departments were still likely to have an Englishman as head or chairman.)

The enthusiasm for Canadiana may have had some ultimately unfortunate results in the academic world. CanLit courses proliferated in most universities, becoming ever more specialized. Courses appeared first on Canadian fiction and then, as the scope grew narrower and narrower, zoomed in on Canadian women's fiction, then on Canadian women's fiction of the 1970s, then on the novels of a single Canadian writer – Margaret Laurence, for example. Furthermore, as the nationalist phase developed, we taught some strange, esoteric, elitist books simply because they were Canadian. In those halcyon days, books chosen by our English department curriculum committees were clever constructs, challenging to erudite critics and to ambitious graduate students, but not really confronting the interests of a mass audience and not truly engaging for the majority of our students. I am thinking of the admirable but difficult work of Dave Godfrey, Rudy Wiebe, or bp Nichol; of stylish books like Sheila Watson's *The Double Hook* (1959) or Leonard Cohen's *Beautiful Losers* (1966). Teachers read these books enthusiastically, ready to discuss structural niceties, Freudian subtexts, and verbal calisthenics. They were fun to teach.

They were not warm or enchanting for non-specialist readers. And they were too narrow for the curriculum committees in other departments and faculties. Professors in physical and biological science, commerce, social science, agriculture, engineering, architecture, and so on, gentlemen who had studied 'English 20: Chaucer to Hardy' in their own undergraduate days, checked up on something like *Beautiful Losers*, found themselves disenchanted and disinclined to include literature courses – not just Canadian courses, but any literature courses – on their list of compulsory subjects. In consequence, students in other faculties could graduate, not only without knowledge of Canadian literature, but without a shared awareness of all humanizing literary traditions.

Outside academe, there were other general consequences of the obsession with Canadian literature in the 1970s. Revered expatriate writers such as Leon Edel and A.J.M. Smith came home to tell Canadians that the new literary localism was provincial and that it ran against the cosmopolitan current of modernity. (In Scotland, opponents of devolution warned of 'Balkanization,' slippage into 'banana republic' status, if the new, avid nationalists had their way.)

In terms of cultural history, there was another consequence to fervid nationalism. The loosening of the bonds between the Scottish tradition and the new Canadian growth left an opening for other outside influences to flood in. In magazines, movies, radio, and television, an alternative flow was already powerful, the flow of cultural values northward from the United States.

Yet Scottish-Canadian links would persist. A strong Canadian nationalism was emerging, and there was some overt repudiation of strains in the Scottish heritage by major writers, but influence continued to flow from Scots whose choice of topic and rhetoric chimed with the new attention to local detail and with the passionate desire to experiment in strong modes of expression. There were still unshakable likenesses between the two countries in culture, politics; and geography. In both, two official cultures were augmented by growing cultural pluralism. Political attitudes were held in common in the two countries. Morals were linked with politics; respect for classical learning joined a casteless mercantilism. Fierce national ambition was masked in both by ironic self-deprecation. Independent individualism was countered in both by clannishness, and a missionary sense of responsibility for the poorer neighbours and nations was balanced by canny awareness of the strength of greater imperial powers and of their lack of interest in that wariness.

Both countries were set in a northern climate, but were increasingly subject to a southern economic control. And both countries still stretched in angular beauty from east to west, bordered by fringing islands where unique cultural colour was particularly strong. It is in those fringing islands that I find a metaphor for the next part of my study.

Part Three

Road to the Isles

Winter term, 1977. I am working at the Edinburgh Centre of Canadian Studies in George Square. Over my head as I work I hear the thumps and groans of Dennis Lee, beating out rhythms as he creates a new set of poems. He is here in Edinburgh for a year as Canadian exchange poet, much in demand for public readings.

Dennis Lee and I share occasional pub lunches and compare notes about the George Square ghosts: Sir Walter Scott, who was raised in the house next door to the Canadian Centre; Thomas Carlyle and Jane, who spent part of their turbulent early married years two doors down; and Arthur Conan Doyle, who lived at number 24. George Square in Edinburgh has welcomed many Canadians. In late Victorian times, for instance, Ralph Connor, Marshall Saunders, and Bliss Carman all came to Edinburgh to study; they walked this university square before going back to shape Canadian literature.

There's another Victorian ghost hanging around the University of Edinburgh: Robert Louis Stevenson, who once outraged the proprieties in his green velveteen jacket and loose silky shirts, garb as unconventional in his day as is Dennis Lee's brilliant cotton kitangi today.

Lee, like Stevenson, has an enormous popular following. Rather ruefully, he realizes that much of his popularity comes from the readings he has done across Canada, chanting his catchy children's poems. The voracity of a public ready to hear rather than read poetry troubles this print-oriented poet, first respected as a sophisticated intellectual. Dennis Lee never expected to find the kind of immortality that awaited Stevenson: enduring fame as a writer for little children.

Now, as elsewhere in the world, small Scottish children are responding to the chanting charm of *Alligator Pie*.

Studying influences, my colleague Mary Rubio and I travel around Scotland in 1982. We visit the places that were 'shrines' to L.M. Montgomery, the still-popular author of *Anne of Green Gables*. We are editing Montgomery's diaries and, following her honeymoon tour, we go to see Burns's grave, Loch Katrine in the Trossachs, and Abbotsford. We also particularly want to visit Kirriemuir, the village that J.M. Barrie sentimentalized as 'Thrums.' His work gave lifelong delight to L.M. Montgomery. She read and reread *The Little Minister* and eventually enjoyed it again as a movie.

People in Kirriemuir welcome us warmly. They don't want to talk about Barrie, however. They want to tell us how much they love *Anne of Green Gables*. They add that as children they didn't realize Montgomery was Canadian: 'Always thought Anne of Green Gables lived somewhere in the Scottish isles,' one elderly addict at Kirriemuir tells us.

Two weeks later, Mary Rubio and I see another instance of how deeply Montgomery's work could sink into the pores of readers far from Canada. We go on to Poland, this summer of 1982, at the invitation of Anne fans in Warsaw and to renew connections with Polish publishers of the Montgomery novels. Montgomery holds a mystical power for Poles: her work has been naturalized there since 1909.[1] During the war, soldiers were issued with copies of *Anne's House of Dreams*, so they could nourish their own dreams of peace, beauty, and domestic happiness. Now, forty years after Montgomery's death, we are fêted as designated co-editors of her journals. Everywhere doors open, restaurants produce meals after hours, museums offer solo tours, theatre audiences give us ovations when we are pulled on stage.

The Blue Castle is playing at a Polish theatre – a musical based on L.M. Montgomery's romantic novel about love and liberty in Canadian Muskoka. *The Blue Castle* is staged lavishly, in spite of the obvious poverty in Polish streets. And Montgomery's Muskoka life is conceived as being strongly Scottish. The character of Uncle Benjamin Stirling, in particular, has unleashed the Polish wardrobe mistress's most colourful dreams. Uncle Stirling is kilted in purple, red, and green; he wears a feathered bonnet at the family dinner table; and his hairy sporran, slung around his neck, rides high on his broad Polish chest.

Outside the theatre, Russian tanks still rumble through Polish streets, ensuring the end of an insurrection. At several street corners, flowers are massed in the form of a cross to mark the place where a patriot has died. We pass the flowery crosses on the way back from the theatre where Montgomery's escapist romance is feeding the Polish passion for freedom.

Violence – autumn storms of 1987 and the historic traces of ancient human violence – pounds the castle country around Aberdeen. Our grown-up daughters are pushing us through a holiday tour of Scotland. We have hit two weeks of stormy weather, and the wild, high winds don't make the ascent to ancient lookouts easy. Our daughters are castle freaks; we clamber through the ruins of Dunnottar, toil up to the tower at Crathes.

Finally we slip into the urbanity of Aberdeen Castle, the country house where Lord Aberdeen retired after his buffeting by the political and climatic violence of Canada in the 1890s. Beyond the formal Scottish gardens stands a 'Canadian shanty' built by the Aberdeens on their return from his work as governor general. It is a huge hall, with antlers, bear's heads, and crossed snowshoes high on the peeled log walls, bringing a whiff of the Canadian life the Aberdeens had experienced.

The present countess has arranged a theatrical evening for her overseas guests: a presentation of Edith Sitwell's *Façade*.

Pretty tinkling performance on the stage of the 'shanty'; horrible howling storm outside. The bear's head grins above our civilized heads.

The violence reminds my husband and me of another Scots governor general, the GG of our own early memories, John Buchan. Lord Tweedsmuir came to Canada trailing a tremendous literary reputation. His novels in the inter-war years thrilled us with their pitting of civility against desperate danger. In the 1930s each new Buchan book was guaranteed to shock and stimulate. In 'real life' we watched Lord Tweedsmuir gallantly working in Canada to keep the British-American alliance strong when the new war was brewing.

'Never heard of him,' our daughters say.

They are devotees, however, of the genres John Buchan helped to introduce: the mystery story with political overtones, the spy thriller, the tale of a fugitive pursued by violence. They recently found in Margaret Atwood's *Bodily Harm* the same pleasure of disturbance that once made us into Buchan fans. She is their oracle, their favourite deliverer of shocks. They are still reeling from the ferocity of *The Handmaid's Tale*. They watch for her new novels as eagerly as we once anticipated the latest Buchan.

My son and daughters were grown up by the time I began work connected with children's literature. I had co-founded *Canadian Children's Literature/La littérature canadienne pour la jeunesse* in 1975, but I waited until the end of my term as department chair before becoming actively involved. In 1980 L.M. Montgomery's son decided that I should co-edit, with Dr Mary Rubio, his mother's journals. Years earlier, when I did a little research on Montgomery's life and work, senior colleagues had warned me against endangering my career by entering such a marginalized field.

The word 'marginal' has always had special meaning in Canada and Scotland. Our countries were accustomed to being regarded as of marginal importance, not ranking, really, among the heavyweight nations. As to our literatures, the Dr Chews of the world had persisted in regarding them also as marginal in value. In the 1980s the term 'marginalization' stirred up new disturbance in geopolitics. In Scotland the rejection of political and economic marginalization had surfaced in the nationalist referendum of the 1970s; talk of devolution was becoming fiercer now. In Canada ferocious arguments about 'free trade' and NAFTA postulated the intensification of economic marginalization and the danger of losing the special tang of this country – itself a result (it can be argued) of our marginal position.

In the wider world, by the 1980s, 'marginalization' had become a call to arms of feminist critics, child-rights advocates, and minority spokespersons in every country. It was now considered wrong to push certain groups away from the sunny centre of life: the handicapped, the Native people, women, children, folk from the economically underdeveloped nations, and the psychologically disturbed (or challenged). The second emerging assumption about marginalization was that in all these groups certain values were to be found not present in the mainstream, but potentially valuable there.

In Scotland and Canada there had long been a countervailing mystique of margins. In both countries colourful life had flourished on the fringing isles, places of beauty and mystery at the geographical margins of the nations. The Hebrides, the Orkneys, and the Shetlands formed the tough selvedge of Scotland. There the threads of the great national plaid doubled back into a strong binding edge. There the dominant colours of Scotland seemed clearest. Theology and the arts flourished in the isles, although in forms scorned by enlightened urban pundits. Lullabies, ghost stories, comic skits, and ballads of long-ago loves and wars joined bagpipe and tongue music and traditional dance in the Scottish selvedges.

From all those rimming Scottish islands, many of Canada's early immigrants came, bringing strength in theology, politics, economics, and literature. But Canada has its own magic islands at the edges of the land mass: Newfoundland, Cape Breton, and Prince Edward Island on the east, Vancouver Island and the Queen Charlotte Islands on the west, the Thousand Islands on the south, Baffin Island, Ellesmere, and other Arctic islands on the north. All are places that harbour quintessential qualities of language, ethos, mores. The arts of the Canadian islands, like their Scottish counterparts, have had folkloric strength. From these margins come traditional Inuit carving, aboriginal totem poles, Newfoundland and Nova Scotia folk songs, and west-coast tall tales. In more recent times, Vancouver Island gossip has been neatly reshaped by storytellers such as Jack Hodgins; poems with a weird and ghostly twist came from Susan Musgrave when she was a west-coast dweller; Cape Breton fables have been retold with the force of incantation by Alistair MacLeod, and Newfoundland tall tales attached to young protagonists by Kevin Major.

The principle of the selvedge, the clear strength at the fringe of the fabric, also holds true in the literary realm in general. Tension and the brightest colours appear at the edges of respectable art, in the marginalized genres, mystery tales, children's fantasy, women's stories, comic sketches, thrillers, and sentimental romances. These are the kinds of writing once considered uncanonical, not quite worthy of academic study. Yet this is the selvedge of literature, the saving, tough, rereadable stuff that keeps the fabric from unravelling. Here essential readability survives. Thrillers and love stories offer respite from the banality and hostility in real life; children's literature reaffirms adventure and tenderness; books offering religious reassurance help hope and charity to survive. All offer the ministry of sentiment and laughter in a cold, patriarchal, unfunny adult world.

Belatedly, university departments recognized the power and the popular appeal in these genres. Why not give courses on those kinds of books known to have very wide appeal, best-sellers complementing courses on least-selling (but most academically admired) books? Once such a notion would have been summarily rejected. Now, in the mid-1980s, shrinking university support coincided with a rising interest in 'reader response' theory, in reader psychology, and in popular culture. Old favourites and new turned up on respectable courses, in women's studies, children's literature, or 'cultural studies,' which subsumed best-sellers such as sentimental love stories and mystery thrillers. Critics who had long worked in the mainland of canonized classics now took to the fringes.[2] Non-arts students began enrolling again, in courses recognizing the power that lies in the books at the edge of respected art.

On reflection, it appeared that many of these very popular books were written in genres in which, once again, Scottish writers had pioneered and had influenced Canadians. The standard reference, F.L. Mott's *Golden Multitudes: The Story of Best Sellers in the United States* (303–29), suggests the Scottish-Canadian sequence in the list of 'best-sellers': Robert Louis Stevenson's *Treasure Island* in 1884, J.M. Barrie's *The Little Minister* in 1891, *Dr. Jekyll and Mr. Hyde* in 1893, then Canadian Marshall Saunders's *Beautiful Joe* (1894), Ralph Connor's *Black Rock* (1898), Robert Service's *The Spell of the Yukon* (1907), L.M. Montgomery's *Anne of Green Gables* (1908). Popular Scottish writers had reflected national attitudes toward children, women, and violence. Most popular early Canadian writers had been infused with these Scottish traditions. Most of them had found an easy early path to publication in Canadian magazines and newspapers, partly because publishing in Canada was dominated for so long by Scots or Scottish Canadians.

Periodical publishing had early developed in the hands of Scots such as Hugh Scobie (1811–1853), born in Inverness-shire, who founded the *British Colonist* in 1838 and the *Canadian Almanac* in 1848; G. Mercer Adam (1839–1912), born in Loanhead, who founded the *Canada Bookseller* in 1865 and the *Canada Educational Monthly* in 1879; George Brown (1818–1880), born in Alloa, founder of the *Toronto Banner* (1843) and the *Globe* (1844). Prominent book publishers included Thomas Maclear (1815–1898), a representative of the Glasgow firm of Blackie and Son, who was a bookseller and publisher in Toronto, 1848–1887, and George Maclean Rose (1829–1898), born in Wick, who founded Hunter, Rose and Company in Quebec City in 1861.[3] The power to choose and publish stories remained with the great newspaper editors and proprietors in succeeding times: J.J. Stewart (1844–1907) of the Halifax papers the *Morning Herald* from 1878, the *Evening Mail* from 1879, and the renamed *Halifax Herald* from 1892; Hugh Graham, Baron Atholstan (1848–1938) of the *Montreal Evening Star*, renamed the *Montreal Daily Star* in 1869, and proprietor of the national *Family Herald and Weekly Star*; John Ross Robertson (1841–1918), owner of the *Toronto Daily Telegraph* (1866) and later the *Evening Telegram*; P.D. Ross (1858–1949), managing editor of the *Ottawa Journal* in 1886 – and a host of others with Scottish blood, in large centres and small.

All these individuals had kept publications of every stripe open to people with Scottish values, long after the number of Scots in the country began to diminish. The Scottish connection had remained strong also among teachers, ministers, politicians, and business leaders, all of whom helped to shape and maintain taste. The years of Confederation had opened with two Scottish-born prime ministers, John A. Macdonald and Alexander Mackenzie, and in ensuing years Scots of every stripe from radical to conservative had illustrated 'the Scottish proclivity for gaining the seats of the mighty.'[4] Of business leaders, 50 per cent of industrial leaders in the 1880s were Scottish in recent origin, according to the entry on Scots in *The Canadian Encyclopedia*; John Porter's *Vertical Mosaic* demonstrates the continuance of that disproportionate pre-eminence.[5] A 'fringe group' in terms of numbers, the Scots Canadians in education, business, and publishing kept the way open for writers ready to sound again the Scottish themes. People such as Montgomery, Ralph Connor, and Marshall Saunders would add a Canadian element to the Scottish formulas, but the connections with the tradition would remain strong.

It further appeared that although the impetus in these popular genres began in Scotland, the tide might well in later years flow in the other direction. Near the end of the nineteenth century, Canadian books would cross as easily, west to east, as Scottish ones once did, east to west. In many cases, the books travelling in the new direction by the boatload, as in the old one, would belong in those dear-to-the-heart genres once marginalized by academia: the romance, the thriller. Scottish children would relish *Anne of Green Gables*. Their seniors would weep and pray over Ralph Connor's *The Sky Pilot*.

A current had begun to run from the new country to the old one, in life as well as in literature. Soon it would be as common for Canadians to travel to Inverness or Aberdeen as it had once been for Scots to move to Nova Scotia or New Glasgow or New Dundee. Canadians would come to serve as visiting professors at the universities of St Andrews, Strathclyde, and Glasgow, just as their forebears had gone as humble students to study in those centres.

Canadian tourists would eventually travel to Scotland in their thousands. They would feel most strongly the pull of the Orkneys, the Shetlands, the Hebrides: Rum and Tiree, Skye and Barra and Lewis. Scottish singers had long celebrated the pull of the fringing islands, in 'The Road to the Isles':

> It's the far Coolins are callin' me away
> As step I wi' my cronach to the Isles ...
> If you're thinking in your inner heart braggart's in my step
> You've never smelled the honey o' the isles.'

Here I take the road to the literary isles. I celebrate the writers who have let us live as readers, enisled in the warmth, laughter, excitement, and reassurance of books, concurrently with so-called real life as daughter or son, student or stenographer, wife or husband or lover or parent. There is honey in the popular Scottish books that have given great pleasure to children, women, troubled people, and lonely ones, to embattled workers and repressed and victimized folk needing a safety valve. And strong trade winds of taste have run between these Scottish isles and the 'marginal,' uncanonical books by Canadian writers.

Chapter Six

Stevenson, Lee, and the Garden of Childhood

Robert Louis Stevenson created his sunny *A Child's Garden of Verse* when he was thirty-three years old and suffering from lung disease.[1] Shut into a small room, one arm strapped to his chest to prevent gesticulation, the room darkened so that he could not see the gorgeous flowers of the Côte d'Azur, he found a way out of adult trammels. He crossed the borders of imagination, back to a child's garden, back to childhood phrasing, innocence, and perceptions.

Stevenson kept his boyish zest for life gallantly alive in his books, even when illness pressed most harshly. A sickly child, a disease-ridden man, confined to bed with recurring lung problems, he defied the law of literary gravity to become the creator of wild accounts of travel, moving stories of comradeship, fascinating stories of dangerous double life. Gallant is the word for Robert Louis Stevenson. From his birth in 1850, he was feverish and cosseted in his Edinburgh home; but when he was transported into a merry circle of cousins at their grandparents' place, he emerged as inventor of games, centre of laughter and singing, leader of forays beyond the borders of timidity and propriety. He stunned his teachers with precocious skill in writing, stunned his family with refusal to follow the family professions of engineering and law, stunned Edinburgh society with his bohemian green velveteen and silken shirts and his flowing hairstyle and his nocturnal ramblings. The early dandified essays about his travels in 1876 and 1878[2] show the outrageous young man ready to work as hard on his writing as he did on his public persona.

Gallant young man, living in France in hope of a cure for tubercular weakness, he suddenly fell in love with an older woman, an American, separated from her husband, mother of two children,[3] and as suddenly followed her across the ocean to America, across the American continent to California, out of the Californian city to squatters' quarters in the silver-bearing hills. Who but Stevenson could turn these European and American expeditions into frivolous travel books?

Above all, gallant author: first at Braemar and then immured in a sickroom with tuberculosis, he set sail in imagination for *Treasure Island* (1883).[4] Here he found both the wish fulfilment of a sickly childhood and also the incarnation of childhood terrors: trapped in a barrel while a murderer lurks nearby. For young readers he also offered all the pleasures of free play: hide and seek, camping out, messing about with boats, and a chance to evade adult powers.

Stevenson's turn to writing for children was in tune with his times. In 1865, when he was fifteen, the English don Lewis Carroll had brought out his whimsical fantasy, *Alice's Adventures in Wonderland*. Scottish George Macdonald, publishing *At the Back of the North Wind* and *The Princess and the Goblin* in 1871 and 1872, had introduced moral seriousness into books for children. *Treasure Island* added something else: vigour, conflict, an exciting, exotic setting, an island where Long John Silver and the other pirates could give housebound young readers the pleasurable thrill of danger.

Inspired by the success of the little verses in Kate Greenaway's *Birthday Book* (1880), Stevenson worked up a set of short poems, to be published as *A Child's Garden of Verses* (1885). He had indeed created for little children a garden like the famous gardens of Scotland: not merely pretty but a mixture of wildness and order, spice and sweetness. In one poem in *A Child's Garden of Verses*, the child says, 'All the names I know from nurse' and then rattles off all the intriguing old-fashioned names: 'Bach-

elor's buttons, Lady's smock, / And the Lady Hollyhock ...'[5]
Like 'nurse,' Stevenson names, and in the process familiarizes
the child with, the small, nearby elements and also the majestic
greater presences, the wind, the sea, and the sun. 'Escape at
Bedtime,' he titled another of the poems in *A Child's Garden of
Verses*. From the troubles of maturity – illness, matrimony, insecurity – he led the escape to a bright night, a fresh wind, and
'thousands and millions of stars' (24).

Stevenson catches the voices of real children at play, at the
seaside, going reluctantly to bed in summer, playing at pirates
in the meadow (echo of *Treasure Island*). The Land of Nod, the
land of the sick child's counterpane, the Little Land of imagination where the child wanders in wonder among the jointed
grass, 'where the clover-tops are trees,' the land of picture-story
books – adults never leave these lands behind while they can
read the Stevenson verses to a child or to a remembering self.

The kind of child that Stevenson was himself – the kind he
conjured up as he wrote, in the throes of fever – is a Scottish
child, a bairn, not like Wordsworth's 'seer blest' but like Burns's
Babby that dances to his daddy. The poems in *A Child's Garden
of Verses* reflect an attitude toward children that is throughly
Scottish. The bairn is like a 'wee sleeket, cowran, tim'rous
beastie' to be regarded tenderly; like the cotter's children, enjoying a closeness enforced around the firesides in those long,
dark evenings. The child in Robert Louis Stevenson's garden is
also like the little catechist, being led to Calvinist assumptions
about the power of evil; like the Sunday school clansmen,
ready to 'fight the good fight,' with Presbyterian insistence on
the dignity and power of choice even of the smallest mortal.
Presbyterian theology had evolved, with its emphasis on evil
so absolute that the only counter was not just to be 'saved'
(implying some individual value) but to be 'elect' – chosen
before time by a merciful God's mere will and pleasure. Scott's
contemporary James Hogg had grimly fictionalized the possible extension of this harsh theology in *The Private Memoirs and
Confessions of a Justified Sinner* (1824). In Stevenson a Manichaean
doubleness comes often into lighter play. For a child, the legacy

of this absolutism begins with awareness of the 'Shadow.' (It will culminate for the adult in the legend of Dr Jekyll and Mr Hyde.)

Stevenson's garden of childhood is a Scottish one, a pleasant place, with wandering paths and glowing colours, but edged by a wall, a border, and by the knowledge that

> summer goes
> And winter comes with pinching toes,
> When in the garden bare and brown
> You must lay your barrow down. (90)

But Stevenson was also ready to carry children 'Over the borders,' committing, as he says in 'Keepsake Mill,' 'a sin without pardon.' He realized that older children were ready for a world beyond the garden wall. In *Kidnapped* he took adolescent readers to 'marvellous places, though handy to home!' (29). Exiled by illness to the soft south of France, he created in *Kidnapped* (1886)[6] the conviction of wild Scottish scenes, characters, and situations – the grey hills, the mists, the Jacobite angularity. He had discovered the margins of Scotland in a boyish tour of the lighthouses set on islands around the coastline. He used this memory in *Kidnapped*, following pawky David Balfour and that cock o' the north Alan Breck Stewart in an imagined adventure, destined to become a boys' classic.[7] *Kidnapped*, with its emphasis on chance, openness, and possibilities of change, underlines the irony of the author's own physical captivity.

Kidnapped presents young adult readers with a peculiarly Scottish version of the initiation myth. In the American classic *The Adventures of Huckleberry Finn* (1884), Huck the loner kidnaps an adult and cleverly manoeuvres him up the heart of the continent to freedom. In contrast, the Scottish youth David Balfour is kidnapped by a powerful adult, Captain Hoseason, taken in Hoseason's boat, the *Covenant*, round the margins of his country, and then led back to Edinburgh and a material inheritance. David Balfour, sombre, whiggish, Covenanting, conscientious, is led through a series of adventures by the 'glittering rascal' (as critic Edwin Eigner calls Alan Breck),[8] who defies propriety. The boy, who is aghast at his comrade's fighting, bragging, piping, and lying, nevertheless loves the active energy that erupts in all the antisocial ways. In the end, as is proper in a tale of maturing and initiation, the wild Alan Breck Stewart disappears, leaving douce David Balfour to come into his modest fortune. Writing *Kidnapped* for young readers freed Stevenson to release the daemonic element, the Mr Hyde, sublimated as a figure of heroic energy. Alan Breck Stewart, a trickster, outlawed for loyalty to a lost cause, like a 'little shadow' goes in and out with conventional David, on the ship, in the mountain caves and glens, on the high road where authority is murdered. For boys not yet ready for sobriety and responsibility, *Kidnapped* offers an irresistible, joyful reading experience.

Notably, there are no girls in this adventure story; this is a book for boys in the stage when 'romance' has no explicitly sexual undertones. *Kidnapped* offers an adolescent version of the *Waverley* story. Stevenson set *Kidnapped* in a time six years post-*Waverley* and chose a hero very much like Waverley both in his naïveté and in his bedazzlement by a Jacobite fanatic. Alan Breck reincarnates Fergus Mac-Ivor's Jacobite loyalty (though without his humourless fervour). Like Scott, Stevenson sets the pawky, sensible approach to idealism (David's way and Waverley's way) against a hell-for-leather, all-out fanaticism (Alan Breck's way and Fergus Mac-Ivor's way). Waverley's romantic interests in Flora and Rose have no strong parallel in David's younger heart. But the motif of travel, strong in *Waverley*, is stronger still in *Kidnapped*. Robert Louis Stevenson was a worthy (though very different) successor to Walter Scott.

In his last days, driven by ill health and wanderlust to the South Seas isle of Samoa, he overlaid the island ways with a lifestyle modelled on that of a Scottish laird, and went on to write *Catriona* (sequel to *Kidnapped*) and his darkest and also most Scottish novel, *Weir of Hermiston*, published, although uncompleted, in 1896, two years after he died.

This virtuoso author had opened new ways for a whole world of writers. Psychological thrillers, ghost stories, art nouveau lyrics, hide-run-and-be-followed stories, essays on the art of writing, dark novels of sin and judgment – all these genres show the effect of Stevenson's genius. Maestro of horror, mystery, escape, historical persiflage, and exotic landscape, he could also lead in other fields: rhymes for little children and quest stories for boys.

For pre-school children all over the world, he created a 'read to me' treasure in *A Child's Garden of Verses*. *Treasure Island* and *Kidnapped*, two memorable novels for children old enough to read for themselves, have now been working a century of magic, enticing young people to travel beyond the nursery-rhyme stage into the realm of imagination hidden in full-length books. Travel is a paradigm for the daily experience of growth, challenge, change, and restlessness in childhood. Stevenson's books for children offer exciting correlatives for the emotional and intellectual voyaging of young readers. All entice them into a garden of adventure and growth.

Just as Stevenson himself travelled from Scotland to America, to France, and to Samoa, his works bypassed national boundaries, first as an influence on writers for adult audiences. Conspicuously in Canada, his elegant travel essays impacted on what had always been a popular form of book. Reports of travel to Canada in the 1890s acquired a new glow, wit, and polish. Essayists also became lighter, more fanciful by 'playing the sedulous ape' to him. The 'At the Mermaid Inn' series of essays, in which Duncan Campbell Scott, Archibald Lampman, and Wilfred Campbell collaborated in 1892–3,[9] were very much in the Stevenson tone. Young poets – Bliss Carman, for instance – began to imitate not only the velvet jacket, the long hair, the big-brimmed hats, but also the short, singing verse forms, the bouncy, sensuous rhythms, the themes of wanderlust, quest, romance, and the joy in life and beauty.

Canadian short stories of the late-Victorian period tended to echo Stevenson's panache, his snap and polish and his jaunty fun with the language. They aimed for a touch lighter than Hawthorne's, brighter than Poe's. The legacy of Stevenson's self-assured control of brief narrative shows in such short stories of Duncan Campbell Scott as 'In the Year 1806,' 'Expiation,' and 'The Vain Shadow.'[10] The RLS line runs all the way to Alice Munro, whose comparable elegance, cadence, and intelligence are a formal cloak for vital, passionate stories.

Stevenson's adventure novels also enticed subsequent authors to recapture something of his thrills and terrors. Charles G.D. Roberts echoed Stevenson in several romances, notably *The Forge in the Forest* (1896). Critic W.J. Keith faults Roberts for his idolatry of Stevenson: for 'his apparent inability to realize that the art of the novel is not invariably linked to the creation of suspense.'[11] For younger readers, however, that suspense, RLS-style, would prove successful in sweeping interest onward.

Sixty years after Roberts, Farley Mowat followed Stevenson in this as in other aspects, in *Lost in the Barrens* (1956).[12] Mowat takes young readers travelling with two boys on a great circuit, not of Scotland, but of the Canadian north. The two young lads who make this perilous journey are differentiated, as David Balfour and Alan Breck Stewart were, in racial loyalties and wisdom, as well as in personality. Jamie Macnair, timidly venturing north from Toronto, and Awasin, son of Meewasin, headman of a Cree settlement five hundred miles north of Winnipeg, set out on a dangerous trip in search of caribou. They go up a chain of lakes and rivers, beyond the northern treeline, and tumble into deadly adventures, as exciting as those of David and Alan Breck. *Lost in the Barrens* is a boy's book, but it has values for all readers: vigour, clear character differentiation, and a breath-catching mixture of thrills and endurance. Farley Mowat is a great storyteller and in his own way as colourful a man of letters as was Stevenson: the kilt taking the place of the velveteen jacket as attention-getter.

More surprising are the connections with Stevenson in *The Root Cellar* (1981) by Janet Lunn. This time the two questors are girls. The *Kidnapped* northward swing is inverted: Rose and Susan travel southward from Ontario to Washington and back. This is a story of time travel to 1862–5; modern girls travel to the terrifying edges of the American Civil War, in a time not so very different from post-Jacobite days.

Janet Lunn acknowledges one debt to Stevenson directly. She begins this fantasy voyage with a quotation from *A Child's Garden of Verses*: 'I held the trunk with both my hands, / And looked abroad on foreign lands.'[13] The echoes of *Kidnapped* are probably coincidental. Yet Rose, disguised as a boy, calls herself 'David,' and the story of an adventure in a foreign country unfolds 'like some of them stories Susan's gran used to tell about ghosts and strange critters back where she come from in Scotland' (57). As in *Kidnapped*, the two friends are contrasted: one mystic and one practical, one adventurous and one shy, one confident and one inexperienced. They break away from peace and safety, meet physical abuse from desperate people, suffer hardship, and are falsely accused. Like David and Alan, they exchange talismans, lose faith briefly, and undergo a crisis of mistrust and dislike, but eventually are true to each other. Terror and humour mix in *The Root Cellar* in the same proportions as in *Kidnapped*. For Rose, as for David, there is no culminating 'romance' in the boy-and-girl sense, although both books are 'romantic' in their sense of wild possibilities and of the credible possibility of freedom from conventional social order. For a growing girl, the legend works in the same way as *Kidnapped* does, accepting doubleness, tipping the balance in favour of daring, movement, and love.

Lunn's style is terse, pithy, cleverly crafted. She offers a double challenge to the young reader: first to identify with a modern American girl temporarily living in a Canadian farmhouse and getting to know her Canadian cousins; then to go with her into the root cellar and emerge into fantasy. The time shifts back a hundred years as Rose goes over the border into the Civil War time in the United States.

The Root Cellar, like *Kidnapped* and like *Lost in the Barrens*, is *Bildungsroman* in the form of a travel tale. All three explore dualities in individuals and between friends; all use irrational conflict as an initiation into adult perfidy and cruelty. The critic Bruno Bettelheim postulates that violent and frightening fairy tales prepare little children for family and social antagonisms.[14] The same preparatory function applies to the violent and frightening books in which twelve-year-olds delight – books such as *Kidnapped*, *Lost in the Barrens*, and *The Root Cellar*. Part of the joy of reading fantasy or travel stories, particularly frightening fantasy or travel, is the unshakable knowledge that the book is just a book, and that the normality of home and everyday life lies just outside its covers. Young readers know that Long John Silver cannot really lay a hand on a shaking shoulder. They can make a wartime trip to the Civil War battlefields with Lunn without having to mop up the blood. Books offer adolescent readers the same immunity as little listeners found when they looked over the wall at 'foreign lands' or 'the Land of Nod' with Stevenson.

Nevertheless, following the Scottish writer, the Canadians imply the possibility of real-life growth in morals, decision-making, loyalty, and what John Buchan called 'the noble austerities of duty and courage.' Affirmations of endurance and honesty, inculcated by immersion in Stevenson's books, appear everywhere in Canadian literature for children. A peculiarly Scottish concept of childhood had come to Canada when families from the Highlands and Islands and Lowlands packed Ballantyne and Macdonald and Stevenson into their immigrant baggage. Subsequently, in spite of two hundred years of gradually multiculturalizing history, Scottish concepts still permeated the Canadian school system.

Not just Scottish influences in general but the influence of Robert Louis Stevenson in particular seems to have moulded Dennis Lee's very fine, very popular poetry for children. Lee moved into experiments with poetry for children at the age of thirty-five (Stevenson's age at the time that *A Child's Garden of Verses* was published). Like Stevenson in Edinburgh, Lee in Toronto was at the flourishing centre of an intellectual world. I assume that Northrop Frye's emphasis on a Blakean vision of childhood was one reason for the fine books for children written not only by Lee but also by James Reaney and Margaret Atwood. Lee, however, like Stevenson, was interested not only in childhood perceptions but also in tracing the geographical margins of his own country. Just as Stevenson in *Kidnapped* carried his readers around the rim of Scotland, Lee in 'Bundle-Buggy Boogie' chanted a litany of the Canadian fringes: 'Abitibi, Athabasca, Bona Vista, Malaspina; Bella Bella, Bella Coola, Batchawana, Baie Comeau!'[15] Like Stevenson, he moved to the margins in another sense when he turned from the accredited genres – personal essay, novel, lyric poem – to the undignified and undervalued form of children's verse.

The resulting lyrics, in *Garbage Delight, Alligator Pie, Nicholas Knock, Jelly Belly,* and other books of verse for children, show many similarities in tone and form to *A Child's Garden of Verses.* Of course, the motifs and themes and allusions reflect the meta-morphosis undergone as they crossed the Atlantic, and as ninety years of poetry and childhood ticked away. Just as an example, in Stevenson's 'The Swing' a sheltered child looks down over the wall of his green garden on 'Rivers and trees and cattle and all' (40). Dennis Lee creates a new song about a swinging child in the 1970s. He writes in the same rhythm: RLS's 'How do you like to go up in a swing?' becomes Lee's 'Who shall be king of the little kid's swing?' Lee's poem is as catchy, as unforgettable, as condensed, but it is pregnant with social suggestion of a very different life. Not a private swing, but one in the park; not a dear little nursie's boy, but a competitive kid who chants in public-park language:

Who is the king of the little kid's swing?
Jimmy's the king of the little kid's swing.
With a bump on your thumb
and a thump on your bum,
and tickle my tum in Toronto.[16]

Lee said of this poem, in a letter to me, 'I remember being conscious that Stevenson had written the classic swing poem and wondering if I could clear enough space to write a good one of my own.'[17] The impetus for Lee's children's poems, as he explains in *Alligator Pie* and again and again in interviews, was partly a desire to localize, to give Canadian kids a poetic ambience that felt like home.

Critics quote 'My Shadow' as foreshadowing Stevenson's interest in the doppelgänger or double, the Dr Jekyll theme. 'I have a little shadow that goes in and out with me,' the child in the *Garden of Verses* says, recognizing the strange doubleness of life (20). Lee reduces the accompanying double; his double is a zero, a nought, an egg: 'When Egg and I sit down to tea ...' (58). More notably, the rhythm of the 'Shadow' poem is echoed in Lee's 'I found a silver dollar but I had to pay the rent, / I found an alligator but his steering wheel was bent' (34). Like much of his poetry, this is nonsense, not discourse. Well, nonsense is one way of reducing anxiety. Rational confrontation – naming the shadow – is another. Lee took one path regarding mysteries, Stevenson the other.

A priggish child's cheerfulness is caught in Stevenson's 'Happy Thought': 'The world is so full of a number of things / I'm sure we should all be as happy as kings!' (27). Lee retorts, in the same rhythm: 'Tony Baloney is telling a lie: / Phony old Tony Baloney, goodbye!' (29). Double the sound play and deliberately none of the smug, goody-goody celebration.

Stevenson and Lee both focus on sleep and bedtime, flight, rain, lonely play, nature, animals, and manners (naughty or nice). So much for the content; but it is the poetic forms that strike the most interesting parallels. RLS sets up a rhythm and basic syntax in 'At the Sea-side':

> When I was down beside the sea,
> A wooden spade they gave to me...(5).

Lee echoes both:

> When Egg and I sit down to tea
> He never eats as much as me. (58).

RLS writes of night fears in 'Windy Nights':

By at the gallop he goes, and then
By he comes back at the gallop again. (10)

Lee uses the same tricks of repetition and rhythm in 'Billy Batter':

A dragon ran off with my dad,
My dad – ...
A monster ran off with my mum,
My mum – . (18)

This is a different kind of night fear, extending the fantasy to the edge of apocalypse.

How much of these correspondences was deliberate? I wrote to Dennis Lee, asking that question. He answered, 'As for taking Stevenson as a model deliberately when I started doing my own, I think I can safely say that I virtually didn't.' But at this point Lee added an intriguing comment: 'It's likely a deeper question, whether much of *Garden* sank into my pores and eventually had an influence on what I wrote.' Would that we all could respond to an influence with such verve and wit!

Was the influence benign, nurturing? Like Scottish parenting, yes and no. In a poem in *Nicholas Knock*, Dennis Lee prays to the Native spirit of Ookpik, in yet another off-key echo. The smug little imperialist who thinks happily of 'little children saying grace / in every Christian kind of place' (4) amuses Stevenson; Lee reacts with an anti-imperialist prayer to a new god, 'By your grace / Help us live in / our own space' (21). Maybe thanks to Ookpik, Dennis Lee creates something new, a Canadian children's poetry extravagant, ridiculous, transcending the local, a fantastic escape from limitations.

There are strange flowers in Lee's garden, native wild flowers with their strong savage names: devil's paintbrush, dog-toothed violet, jack-in-the-pulpit – and poison ivy. Today, children's books touch directly on topics formerly curtained off. Not just sexual topics but moral conundrums, questions of good and evil, once touched on, if at all, only obliquely, are now illustrated directly in grotesquerie and violence. *Jelly Belly* (1983), produced, I suspect, in response to the enormous popular demand for more Dennis Lee, releases shocks and troubles, ghosts and dinosaurs, 'over the border' in RLS's day.

Ruefully, Lee realized that his work in the marginalized world of little children's poetry was outselling and outstaying the other, more 'central' work. He eventually groaned to adult audiences,

> Alligator rhyme, alligator rhyme:
> Once you get the habit you're hardly worth a dime.
> First you turn to jelly, then you turn to crime,
> But you'll never get away from alligator rhyme![18]

Popular or not, children's literature – whether by Lee or by Stevenson – has been traditionally excluded from serious criticism, excluded from the list of courses required of honours students and from the graduate-course panoply. Most academic critics still bypass Lee's verse for children in assessing his work. The process of canonization – what Robert Lecker analyses as the 'forces of inclusion and exclusion'[19] – operates in judgments about genres as well as in judgments about particular works. In the 1983 edition of the *Oxford Companion to Canadian Literature*, for instance, Gary Geddes, allowed nearly two full columns on Lee, expatiated on *Savage Fields*, *Civil Elegies*, *The Gods*, and so on. Then he added, 'Lee has a talent for writing zany poems for children,' limply listing *Alligator Pie* and the other books.[20] Striking a comparable attitude, David Daiches, the finest critic of Stevenson's verses, having spoken of their clarity, says they are fine examples 'of their kind'[21] – and I hear patronage in that phrase. Many of the best critical works on Stevenson (Eigner, for example)[22] do not even include *A Child's Garden of Verses* in their index. Yet both poets brought gusto, tenderness, irony, gentleness, recognition of the independent life of the child, an unaffected use of the child's voice, and involvement with the child's concerns. As a consequence, both created work that has affected thousands of children and welcomed them to the garden of buoyant childhood reading.

Neither Dennis Lee nor any single Canadian writer has reached the continuing mass audience of Stevenson. Instead, Canadian writers en masse have achieved an astonishing reach. There is a surprisingly long shelf of writings for children by major Canadian authors such as Margaret Laurence (*Six Darn Cows*, 1979, and *The Olden-Days Coat*, 1979), Margaret Atwood (*Up in a Tree*, 1978, and others), Marian Engel (*Adventure at Moon Bay Towers*, 1974, and *My Name Is Not Odessa Yarker*, 1977), Mordecai Richler (*Jacob Two-Two Meets the Hooded Fang*, 1975, and other Jacob stories), and James Reaney (*Names and Nicknames*, 1978, and other plays for children). This phenomenon is unmatched by major writers in Britain and the United States.

Perhaps one reason for the unabashed entry into a downgraded field by these admired adult writers was the continuing pressure of Scottish attitudes on Canadian lives and memories. Even someone like Mordecai Richler, who bitterly resented the still-Scottish domination of the Montreal school system in the 1940s,[23] incorporated a good deal of *Treasure Island* into his *Jacob Two-Two Meets the Hooded Fang*. Perhaps this represents 'daemonization,' to use Harold Bloom's term: negative response or denial of influence. Perhaps there is something of the same negative response to Stevenson in Jean Little's obstinate offerings of 'bibliotherapy.' Her world is not a garden or a Treasure Island. The children in her books face their limitations, however painful. Little's books about damaged children, troubled ones, handicapped ones, offer a different kind of therapy from Stevenson's freewheeling adventure stories.[24]

When I first taught a course on children's literature in 1981, I found an astonishing pleasure in reading the books on the list. More astonishing was the response of the students, who told me, 'I have never really enjoyed my English courses; never enjoyed the supposedly marvellous books I had to read. But the books on this course are ...' (The concluding word might be 'challenging' or 'brilliant' or 'cool' or 'stimulating' or 'something else!')

Whether rereading an old favourite like *Treasure Island* or *Kidnapped*, or tackling *Alligator Pie* or *Jacob Two-Two Meets the Hooded Fang* or *The Root Cellar* for the first time, students reconnected with their own babyhood, childhood, or adolescence. The literary bonus was a chance to re-examine the essentials of style and to recognize the bare-bones power of children's books. Here setting, dialogue, and action unfold with the clarity and directness all too often lost in the sophisticated tangles of response and reflection that traditional literary courses had tied them into.

Canadian writers today help children enjoy reading at its best, absorbing them into the 'virtual reality' of intense, imaginative response. They also help adults rediscover the paths that Robert Louis Stevenson opened up: to treasure islands, to adventures with travelling comrades, to the garden of delight. In the case of the garden, being Canadian, it is a bush garden, with raw spots and a brief flowering season. And with a Hooded Fang and the occasional alligator.

Chapter Seven

Barrie, Montgomery, and the Mists of Sentiment

Gossip has always swirled around J.M. Barrie's life story. Biographies range from idolatrous to scurrilous psychoanalysis.[1] Never since Burns has there been such a fog of rumour, half-truth, and misrepresentation. Barrie himself fostered parts of the legend, emphasizing and exploiting the pathos of his story. Complex problems – a mother fixation, inhibited sexuality, inability to consummate his marriage, late obsession with small boys, and teasing relationships with married women – all pressured him to create misty evasions, fictions that sublimated his distress and made whimsical stuff out of the ugly aspects of poverty, puritanism, and impairment.

Barrie's *Peter Pan* turns childlike escape fantasy one notch beyond Treasure Island to Never Land. The boy in his play enjoys flight, fun, adventure, a circle of admiring friends, and a secure hidey-home. He taunts adults, defeats villains, lords it over a submissive girl and a guardian fairy. J.M. Barrie's own childhood was not like that. By the time he wrote *Peter Pan*, however, he had learned to veil angular actualities with a mist of sentiment.

His earlier novel, *The Little Minister*, had offered adult readers the same consolatory evasion of ugly reality. It was to become a major influence on later sentimental novelists, convinced, like Barrie, that the function of fiction should be to offer escape. 'Do you believe in fairies?' *Peter Pan* asked the theatre audience of 1904. *The Little Minister* asks readers, 'Do you believe in love at first sight, in softly sad situations that bring a gush of tears, in tender mother love and filial devotion, in happy endings?' A world of readers answers, 'Yes!'

James Matthew Barrie was a puny child, the late son of elderly parents, living in the eastern part of Scotland, north of Dundee. His father, a hand-loom weaver doomed by the death of the cottage industry, dragged his family for a short time from their Kirriemuir home to a struggling life in the town of Forfar.[2] Barrie's high-strung mother, Margaret Ogilvy Barrie, homesick for Kirriemuir and traumatized by the early death of three of her children, worked her way out of her depression by regaling the remaining children with her memories of the 'Auld Licht' Presbyterians, who followed the 'old light' of puritan joylessness. Her sharp little anecdotes about the Auld Lichts, eventually honed by her son into sellable sketches, would return to haunt her.

Out of homesickness while at school in Dumfries and later at university in Edinburgh, Barrie began writing. He turned out a series of melancholy but ruefully amusing comments about the Auld Lichts and sold them to the *Edinburgh Courant*. He emerged from college, not as the minister his mother had dreamed of, but as a journalist.

A London editor liked his arch little sketches. Soon an English audience was chuckling over the 'Thrums' folk in *Auld Licht Idylls* (1888). But Kirriemuir was aghast. Fancy telling the English about Scottish poverty and narrowness! Imagine making fun of the minister, Gavin Dishart, who 'tried to give an agreeable turn to the conversation by describing the extensions at the cemetery.'[3] Imagine inviting readers to laugh at Thrums honeymooners – 'On the Sabbath they had a gay day of it, three times at the Kirk' (77) – or to mock the poor housewife, hiding her poverty behind a façade of propriety and inhibition. Barrie presented his home-town people, grotesque in their loves and loyalties and rivalries, speaking a dialect tailored to amuse non-Scots by sounding quaint rather than rich. In England,

Auld Licht Idylls became a best-seller. But 'It's an ill bird that fouls his own nest,' said Kirriemuir.

The ill bird became distraught over his neighbours' distaste and his mother's distress. In *A Window in Thrums* (1889) Barrie made amends – embarrassing amends. He returned to Kirriemuir with a sentimental eye, wringing pathos from the story of a tender mother who waits for her wandering son through a hard but proud life, until her sad and pitiful death. In *A Window in Thrums*, the gentle mother watches for her erring Jamie, not knowing that he has been devoured by a 'leddy in London.'[4] (In the real case, it was not a lady but a devouring desire to succeed as a writer that had taken Barrie out of his eagle-eyed mother's ken.)

Again the fictional story was seen as 'merciless' by Kirriemuir. Barrie had anatomized old-fashioned Presbyterian conventions and assumptions, over-anxious family feelings, and the stiff-necked insecure Scottish community. Local shock! But the sentiment, the idolatrous treatment of mother love, and the touching specification of simple home life nevertheless turned out to suit the taste of a wider public.

Barrie soon found a niche a long way from Kirriemuir. Diminutive, whimsical, fabulously hard-working, he became a lively member of a circle of writers, actors, and artists in London. He developed a correspondence with Robert Louis Stevenson and a friendship with Arthur Conan Doyle, the aged George Meredith, and others.

In 1891 Barrie moved to a major literary success with his third novel, *The Little Minister*.[5] Returning to his Thrums setting, he produced a double romance. The comic but ultimately happy love of the young minister, Gavin Dishart, for the gypsy Babbie is framed by an older and sadder love story of Gavin's mother (named Margaret, like Barrie's own mother) and the old Thrums schoolmaster, Gavin Ogilvy (and Ogilvy was Mrs Barrie's maiden name). In this framing story, Margaret was tied by marriage to an illiterate, ill-spoken, working-class man; when he disappeared at sea, Margaret married Gavin Ogilvy and

gave birth to his son. The dreadful first husband returns; Ogilvy
leaves. Never can he reveal his still-undiminished love for
Margaret or claim her son as his. Thus Barrie assigns to his
young hero the secret patrimony of fairy tales, and mixes in
some odd play with his own mother's identity.

More fairy tale awaits in the young minister's romance. In
spite of his awkwardness, lack of sophistication, and narrowness of experience and ideas, Gavin is loved by the most charming of women. Newly installed in the Thrums manse under his
mother's watchful devotion, he secretly meets and falls in love
with a 'gypsy' woman, bohemian Babbie. She bewitches Gavin,
but she is in fact placed outside his social class, being the ward
of the local laird, Lord Rintoul. Babbie distracts the little minister from his ministry as well as from his mother and sets him
against his congregation. Gavin goes through theological and
political trials and a trial by flood in the glen wilderness, but
survives. The reward doled out to him in the fairy-tale ending
of the novel is a happy marriage to the ineffable Babbie, pretty
children, and an accepting mother, still watched over by the
self-immolating schoolmaster, Mr Ogilvy.

Fairy tales, according to Bruno Bettelheim, help children
dream their way into the problems that they will encounter in
the future: cruel queens, wicked wolves, confusions of identity.[6] A fairy-tale quality in adult fiction may help grown-up
readers slip away from such problems, post-encounter. Barrie
slipped into the imagined world of *The Little Minister* in the
stress of conflicting feelings about his mother, actress Mary
Ansell, his early beliefs, and his adult ambitions. So doing, he
created a fiction that could serve the fairy-tale needs of his
contemporaries, and of troubled readers ever since.

Mother worship was a Victorian addiction. Barrie's late-
Victorian audience wept readily when he waxed sentimental
over the mutual devotion between mother and son: 'Every
night Gavin was at his mother's bedside to wind her shawl
round her feet, and while he did it Margaret smiled' (14).
Margaret in turn 'tried, unknown to Gavin, to teach herself
writing and grammar, that she might be less unfit for a manse'

(16). Barrie had used his own sense of having failed to live up to his mother's expectations in creating this drama of devotion to an over-innocent mother. This misty, gentle, whimsical tone and the effective idealizing of the love between mother and son were also peculiarly appropriate for a Scottish writer. Sentiment over a mother's gentle love could soften a sense of guilt about the real struggle and sacrifice needed to put a 'lad o' pairts' into the way of advancement.

As for beautiful Babbie, dancing into Gavin's heart by guile and by pathos, she was also welcomed by a charmed audience. Readers loved Barrie's light and witty handling of the impact of the hazardous romance on the dour, respectable village. They chuckled at the sermons, thundered against women, at the moment the preacher is teased into falling in love with a lying, cheating, adorable woman. Babbie is also kind, generous, and a political activist. There was literary precedent for a Scottish heroine, sure of her own mind and ready to show frankly that she finds a man attractive, in Scott's Flora Mac-Ivor and to a lesser extent his Ellen, Lady of the Lake. Even Babbie's unlikely marriage to the little minister and her more unlikely acceptance by his parishioners and his mother were received with complacent smiles. The bewitching quality in young women was another Victorian cliché and, again, a specialty of Scottish folklore, from 'Tam Lin' to James Hogg's 'bonny Kilmeny,' whose 'beauty was fair to see.'[7] Robert Louis Stevenson wrote to Barrie that *The Little Minister* 'ought to have ended badly; we all know it did; and we are infinitely grateful to you for all the grace and good feeling with which you lied about it. You let yourself fall in love with, and fondle, and smile at your puppets. Once you had done that, your honour was committed – at the cost of truth to life you were bound to save them.'[8]

Stevenson, in his books for children, had presented a child's version of the dichotomy of good and evil: small child and shadow, innocent adolescent and same-sex traveller. Barrie's is an adult version of doubleness, presented in sexual terms. The male is douce, desiring to be good, self-examining, sermonizing. The female is wayward, beautiful, singing and dancing, a temptress, an aristocrat's ward who has been chosen to be Lord Rintoul's bride. Perhaps no happy melding is logically possible. Nevertheless, for audiences in Barrie's time and ours, the sexual dichotomy makes engaging reading.

He himself was always strained in his dealings with the women he met in London. In his Scottish youth, rigid Presbyterianism had combined with his near worship of a strong mother to inhibit pleasurable relations. Nevertheless, in London he managed to form a friendship in 1892 with Mary Ansell, a free-minded, energetic, young, bohemian actress; Barrie's attitude toward her was that of a childish playfellow.

The Little Minister became a turn-of-the-century best-seller worldwide because of the way it delicately suggested the tension between sex and inhibition. Since many contemporary readers shared the little minister's cliffhanging doubts about the relations between pure love, admissible passion, and unmentionable lust, they relished Barrie's fiction. Both the wit and the sentimentality in *The Little Minister* masked its author's real disturbance and confusion over sexual experiences. On the strength of its success, Barrie married Mary Ansell in 1894. The marriage was soon invaded by shattering news of the deaths of his mother and sister in 1895, within two days of each other. Soon the façade of a playful, friendly relationship eroded in the face of Barrie's inability to consummate his marriage.

In his next works, the two novels about a boy dubbed 'Sentimental Tommy' and an unabashedly sentimental biography of his mother, Barrie explored dark shadows. *Sentimental Tommy* (1896) presents a triangle again: Tommy and his possessive mother (both of them abused by his father) and Grizel, the forthright, friendly little girl who attracts and helps Tommy after his mother dies. In 1896 Barrie also published *Margaret Ogilvy*, a saccharine tribute to his dead mother. *Tommy and Grizel* (1900) introduces, through a very different mother, 'the Painted Lady,' mother of Grizel, the dark underside of village life that sentimental Tommy would like to evade: bastardy, suicide, prostitution, smuggling, drunkenness, poverty, and hopeless dejection.

Before the 'Tommy' books appeared, contemporary Scottish novelists bypassed these harsher realities in hope of duplicating Barrie's earlier success. Two Presbyterian ministers, S.R. Crockett and John Watson ('Ian Maclaren'), have already been cited as reviving John Galt's desire to present annals of a Scottish parish.[9] These late-Victorian novelists, however, set Galt's astringent irony aside and exploited Barrie's popularity by imitating the sweet sadness of *A Window in Thrums* and the whimsy of *The Little Minister*. Crockett's *The Stickit Minister* and Maclaren's *Beside the Bonnie Brier Bush* turned Barrie's pathos to bathos, but left untouched the titillating nerve of sexuality that he covertly stimulated. Presumably both the reverend novelists had seen the seamier side of life in their ministries, but their profession protected them and let them indulge in idealization. They hymned the humble yard where brier roses mixed fragile tender beauty with pungent kail, the homely soup-stock cabbage. Their contemporary J.H. Millar dubbed them 'The Kailyard School.'[10] Tough-minded W.E. Henley, friend of Stevenson and author of 'Invictus,' saw Kailyard novels as pale, nostalgic, gentle, static, and manipulating sympathy to draw readers into shallow moral judgments. Modern critics generally concur.[11] But readers misted the kailyard with sentimental tears and put Maclaren and Crockett along with Barrie on the best-seller lists, in Scotland and abroad.

Other contemporary Scots were producing stronger books, such as Neil Munro's *The Lost Pibroch* (1896) and *John Splendid* (1898). Yet a plethora of titles of weaker novels, such as *White Heather* (1885) and *In Far Lochaber* (1888), published before Barrie's success, by best-seller William Black, suggest how strong was the market for sentimental Scottishness. Even later writers, dissolving Barrie's sentiment, reveal his impact in the very strength of their aversion. As late as 1972, George Mackay Brown, in *Greenvoe*, remembers (and mocks) Barrie when he presents the little minister of an Orkney church as an alcoholic.

Barrie himself, however, moved away from Scottish parishes and from fiction into the brighter world of the London theatre. With his dramatization of *The Little Minister* in 1897, he had become a pet, a legendary little 'JMB,' whimsically present at rehearsals of his plays: *Quality Street, The Admirable Crichton, Dear Brutus,* and at least sixteen others, all excellent theatre still and published with charming stage directions.[12] His theatrical success climaxed in *Peter Pan* (1904). The story of Peter and Wendy was first told to five little boys, children of friends, whom Barrie idolized. On stage, it lifted him into the role of legend-maker. Like Defoe, Swift, and Lewis Carroll, he had created a character who assumed the dimensions of myth.

The gossamer prettiness of Peter Pan is the final antithesis of the Kailyard drab. Perhaps more important, *Peter Pan* stands in contrast to the optimistic apprenticeship novels so popular with early Victorians, all those Dickens stories of boys growing up into success and romantic courtship. For Barrie and other late Victorians, the preferred stories were about boys who did not grow up, like *Treasure Island* and *Huckleberry Finn,* 'boys' books' of male-to-male relationships, with no courtship and only impaired males as adult figures – Hook, Long John Silver, the escaped slave Negro Jim.

Something of Barrie's impairment is suggested in his strange attachment to Sylvia du Maurier (Mrs Llewelyn Davies), mother of the boys who were the inspiration for *Peter Pan,* and in his still-later dalliance with older actresses and political ladies such as Mrs Asquith. Feminized politics get whimsical treatment in *What Every Woman Knows* (1908), where Maggie (Margaret again), who manoeuvres her awkward husband into a cabinet position, is a young Scotswoman, less than beautiful but canny and ambitious.

Late in life, divorced from Mary Ansell, in an era that still regarded divorce with horror, Barrie wrote *Farewell Miss Julie Logan* (1932), a strange replay of some of the fairy-tale themes of *The Little Minister.* Again he fills the parish in the glen with angular, sternly conscientious, doggedly enduring people, poor and dour. Again the charm of a beautiful, dancing girl bewitches a young puritanical minister. The young man lives alone (no mother to twist his conscience); the green-gowned girl who haunts him is literally a ghost, caught in a time warp from an earlier century.

Tales of the macabre had long been a Scottish specialty. Burns's 'Tam o' Shanter' is just one witness to the fact that Scots in their misty glens or in the long, dark city nights had enjoyed whispers of the supernatural. Colin Manlove, in *An Anthology of Scottish Fantasy Literature*, attributes Scottish preoccupation with the supernatural to 'a desire ... to construct an "interruption" in this world, rather than, as in English fantasy, create a "secondary world."'[13] Through dreams and visions, he argues, Scots react against a condition of repression and explore and express a 'continuously mystic strain in the Scots' psyche, the sense of a deeper living world beyond or within this one' (10).

Among Barrie's Scottish contemporaries, Arthur Conan Doyle, in *The White Company* (1891), had infused historical romance with a spiritualist's sense of the thinness of the veil between the worlds seen and unseen. Barrie's 1920s play *Mary Rose*, like other para-rational tales in the fashion of the Celtic Twilight, had struck the airy, pretty note of things fey and inexplicable. *Farewell Miss Julie Logan* is a ghost story of a different kind. The aging novelist, indulging once more in a dream of ethereal loveliness, adds an inexplicable ending. He presents clues to prove that Miss Julie, in her long-ago grace and charm and beauty, did indeed visit her modern-day lover. Barrie had a string of novels to prove that such an incredible visitation by beauty could indeed happen, even to a troubled and repressed man. He had produced beauty, the gentle, wispy beauty of sentiment. Thanks to him, a veil had descended over fiction, like a Scotch mist, softening and refreshing the hills and lochs and the city streets.

Neurotic, perhaps, his obsessive sublimation of an ugly, unhappy life into a too-sweet beauty. When J.M. Barrie died in 1937, bereft of his wife, parents, and siblings, his friends, and a good part of his audience, his life had already become a favourite subject for biographers. Why should biographers so dissect a writer's life? Such prying has always been anathema to some; Browning parodied the petty probing: 'What porridge had John Keats?' The defence of a biographical approach is its illumination of the sources and appeals of the author's books, and also of the processes of the creative imagination. Barrie's work seems enriched when the linkage between it and his life is clarified. His process of transforming life into literature is complex; his mechanisms of repression and sublimation are subtle and delicate. The power of sentimental stories to move readers to tears perhaps results from the power of the pain that had to be sublimated and veiled.

Those facile tears – 'idle tears,' in Tennyson's phrase – in turn wash away some of the reader's bitterness, the stress and pain attached to real problems. Contemplating the interplay of life and book illuminates the way most readers move from experiencing to dreaming, from enduring to evading, and then back from reading to choosing, rejecting, enduring.

Robert Burns had sung of a rose – a red, red rose – as the eighteenth century ended and, coincidentally, Canadian literary history began. A different kind of rose came from Scotland to Canada near the end of the nineteenth century, not the red rose of passion but the white rose of sentiment. White rose bushes had once been planted by Scots in defiant memory of Bonnie Prince Charlie, for the white rose was his emblem. But the fiery rebellions of the eighteenth century had given way to milder acceptance of decorum and self-discipline, a sentimental prettifying of poverty and depression.

Lucy Maud Montgomery, who grew up in a Prince Edward Island community still overpoweringly influenced by Scottish values and still clinging to Scottish literary models, was deeply influenced by the sentimental Kailyard fashion dominant in her youth. In the next-to-last chapter of *Anne of Green Gables*, Anne plants a white rose on the grave of beloved, fatherly Matthew, 'a slip of the little white Scotch rose-bush his mother brought out from Scotland long ago; Matthew always liked those roses the best – they were so small and sweet on their thorny stems.'[14] The brier rose acts as a footnote to *Beside the Bonnie Brier Bush*, the Ian Maclaren novel immensely popular when Montgomery was a student at Dalhousie University in the 1890s. But as an adult novelist, she was more particularly indebted to J.M. Barrie. She read and reread *Auld Licht Idylls*,

The Little Minister, and *Sentimental Tommy.* In 1923 she wrote in
her journal: 'Barrie has to a superlative degree the power of
creating atmosphere and character, so that his books give us the
sensation of reading about people and places we have known
well, and consequently have all the charm of a newsy letter
from home. In a much smaller degree I have the same knack
myself and that is why my books are liked.'[15]

Before Montgomery wrote her novels, other Canadian romancers had admired Barrie and adopted many of his motifs
and a good deal of his style and tone. The taste for his blend
of sentiment and humour had been an instant import. 'Ralph
Connor' (Charles Gordon), after graduating in theology at
Knox College, Toronto, had gone to Edinburgh for graduate
studies in 1888, before coming home to enter the Presbyterian
ministry. After three years in a missionary post in western
Canada, he returned to Scotland on a fund-raising tour. This
was in the time when Barrie's Kailyard followers, Crockett
and Maclaren, were showing how uplifting (and profitable)
fiction could be wrung out of parish life.[16] Back home in
Canada again, Ralph Connor created his own sketches of a
wild western 'parish,' a place where Presbyterians must battle the temptations of a new world – drinking, fighting, womanizing. Collected as *Black Rock,* Connor's book became the
number one best-seller in the United States as well as Canada
in 1898. His second book, *The Sky Pilot* (1899), vividly depicts
intense rivalry between Auld Kirk and Free Kirk in Canada,
and adds harrowing demonstration of male rituals on liquor
'permit nights.' The story of 'Drunken Bruce,' whose redemption depends on a deathbed letter from his mother, is woven
into a plot compacting themes of emotional stress, idealized
love purified by suffering, wedded fidelity, impetuosity, faith,
prayer, and Christian salvation.

For his two next novels, Ralph Connor turned back from the
modern west to the eastern Ontario settlements of his childhood. Again there are signs of Barrie's influence. *The Man from
Glengarry* (1901) presents an idealized picture of the author's
mother and a somewhat less ideal portrait of his stiff minister-

father. The love between the backwoods youth, Ranald Macdonald from the Canadian Glengarry, and gay and frivolous Maimie seems like the uneven romance between Gavin and his Babbie. (Ralph Connor gives the story a fairy-tale conclusion, though the ending differs from Barrie's.) Like Barrie's Glen Quharity, Ralph Connor's Glengarry is peopled with 'auld licht' characters, touched in with the combination of pathos and humour. *The Man from Glengarry* sold 98,000 copies in its first edition in 1901. Its sequel, *Glengarry School Days* (1902), sold over five million copies over the next years.[17]

Following Ralph Connor's popular path, many writers such as R.E. Knowles, also a Presbyterian minister, kept the Canadian Kailyard writers on the path of respectability, satisfying sales, and a salutary sense of good influence through popular fiction. These authors faced an occupational hazard: lack of stylistic censorship. As privileged preachers, they were immune from editorial censorship of their indulgence of sentimentality. They also slipped easily into vapid moralizing and tended to be blind to ironies. Like Barrie, they were inclined to ignore and repress scenes of sexual passion.

Idealized portraits of Canadian Presbyterian ministers are strikingly different from the fictional vicars in English novels: domineering St John Rivers in *Jane Eyre*, for example; dusty Edward Casaubon in *Middlemarch*; slimy Obadiah Slope or uxorious Bishop Proudie or even the ascetic Francis Arabin in *Barchester Towers*. They are different also from American portraits of corrupt ministers, from Hawthorne's Arthur Dimmesdale to Harold Frederic's *The Damnation of Theron Ware* (1896) and Sinclair Lewis's *Elmer Gantry* (1927).

A minor reaction against Canadian sentimentalizing of the Presbyterian ministry set in. When Sara Jeannette Duncan created the officious Dr Drummond and the inept Reverend Hugh Finlay in her much-admired novel *The Imperialist* (1904), she was clearly working the old Kailyard vein in friendly mockery. Her heroine, bright as Barrie's Babbie, marries the Reverend Hugh and sets out with him for the west; but Duncan's whimsical tone implies that he will never perform the sentimental miracles of Connor's sky pilots.

A darker debunking of the sentimentalized vision of ministers appears in William Fraser's *The Lone Furrow* (1907). His
little minister must be rescued from the double menace of
Montreal and opium. In this powerful and sour counter-Kailyard
novel, the mean-spirited villagers are quite ready to replace the
minister when trouble brews. Physical poverty explains some
of the inhibitions and eccentricities on display in the novels
that followed Barrie's *Auld Licht Idylls* and his *Little Minister*.
Some Canadian versions imply poverty of spirit and ambition
as well.

The preponderance of successful novels about Presbyterian
congregations does not reflect the actual ratio of Protestant
churches in Canada at the turn of the twentieth century. It does,
however, reveal the continuing dominance of Scottish Canadians among the corps of editors and publishers who selected
and promulgated popular fiction for an ever-hungry audience.
The novels published by small firms such as Drysdale of Montreal, Bell and Cockburn of Toronto, and McKay of Hamilton
and, of course, by the major firm, McClelland, like their models
by Barrie, offer a necessary spoonful of sugar, a wholesome
relief from acidity. Paradoxically, these novels, performing a
secular ministry of sentiment and humour, were proffered,
often, by a minister's wife. *Duncan Polite: The Watchman of
Glenoro* (1905), by Mrs MacGregor ('Marian Keith'), is a typical
response to the fashion for Scottish clichés, presenting staunch
faith, old Covenanting zeal, Sabbath solemnity, and a minister
who can stand up against such village eccentrics as Wee Andra
and Splinterin' Andra.

Long before she was a minister's wife, Lucy Maud Montgomery was an ambitious, hard-working writer. Like J.M. Barrie,
she had endured a troubled childhood. She turned her troubles
into idyllic romances. Anne Shirley, the memorable hero of
Anne of Green Gables, recalls Barrie's Babbie in her lightness,
quick wit, unexpected shifts of mood, and ability to convert
antagonists into defenders. The Canadian village of Cavendish,
Prince Edward Island, where Montgomery grew up, becomes
'Avonlea,' treated with the same sprightly perception that Barrie
brought to Thrums.

Although she was a fourth-generation Canadian, Montgomery spent her childhood in a society still Scottish in all its affiliations, and in a family not unlike Barrie's in stiffness and narrowness. Her wit and high spirits, like Anne's and like Barrie's, overcame this early restriction. The influence of Scottish models was most obvious, however, in two other novels. *Kilmeny of the Orchard* is the first of these. Published obscurely in serial form before *Anne of Green Gables* brought fame to Montgomery, it was reissued as a novel in 1910, in the glow of popular response to *Anne*. Its title harks back to an old Scottish fairy tale, recast in a poem by James Hogg that was a standard in school readers in the Maritimes. Montgomery's Kilmeny has been laid under a spell, not by fairies, but by a stern, retributive God, punishing the sins of her mother and her grandfather by dooming her to silence. Unable to speak except through the medium of her violin, Kilmeny is nevertheless as charming and beautiful as any Babbie. Like Barrie's little minister, she is released from her closed, repressive, constricted world by a stranger coming from outside her society. In each case the outsider brings laughter and love and art.

The strange story of *Kilmeny of the Orchard* was not, and is not, a great favourite with the Anne fans. Under pressure from her publisher, Montgomery returned to a series of blithe sequels to the story of Anne of Avonlea and to two novels, *The Story Girl* (1911) and *The Golden Road* (1913), both of them filled with many traditional tales, retold by the 'Story Girl.' Herself imprisoned now in a troubled marriage (again like Barrie), Montgomery next spun a fantasy of romance and motherhood around the imaginary character of Anne in *Anne of the Island* (1914) and *Anne's House of Dreams* (1917). Then, after many years of struggling to cope with her husband's debilitating depressions and to hide them from his Presbyterian parishioners, she swung again into a different kind of story. Again, from Barrie she culled many of its qualities and motifs.

Like him when he created the romance of *The Little Minister*, Montgomery was in a dark, lonely, troubled phase. She was trapped in a community that discounted her gift as a storyteller and hopelessly aware that her passionate nature was unlikely to find companionship from her husband. Montgomery survived her problems by accessing a dream world of beauty and kindness. Structuring her escapist dreams into *The Blue Castle* (1926), she created the character of Valancy Stirling, who reads her way through a mean-spirited life. The first half of *The Blue Castle*, like *Auld Licht Idylls*, is a sharp-eyed report on a community like Thrums, dull, prim, narrowly conventional (as Galbraith would say, 'so – so Scotch').[18] In the opening movement of the novel, Montgomery reverses the gendered roles of *The Little Minister*. Valancy is the repressed, obedient, convention-dominated person, while Barney Snaith, like Barrie's Babbie, flaunts his freedom and disregards propriety.

The second half of *The Blue Castle* soars to a love story like that of Gavin, the little minister, and Babbie. Valancy finds a man who, like Gavin, has a secret patrimony. Barney Snaith, however, is not an impressionable little minister. He is abrasive, disturbing, antisocial, honest, and competent. His secret is that (like his creator) he writes about the beauty of nature. Valancy's union with this sophisticated, unconventional lover is like a long-drawn-out version of the unlikely happy ending of *The Little Minister*, that sentimental orgy that Robert Louis Stevenson (and thousands of subsequent readers) logically repudiated but emotionally wallowed in.

'What if?' Montgomery asked (like Barrie when he fantasized about Miss Julie Logan). 'What if all romantic dreams could come true? What if an unhappy and unfulfilled woman (who might be said to resemble Isabella Valancy Crawford) could find a perfect life in the simple rhythms of an island set in a misty lake of dreams? What if she could find a perfect alter ego, a secular preacher who could heal modern cynicism by the power of words?'

The reader may know such rapture is a dream and yet may be willing to believe in it, given the convincing and absurd reductiveness of the life from which the dream provides escape. To provide escape, the book must contain something of the repressive force that is beleaguering the reader in real life.

Montgomery was writing in the twilight of puritanical repression, especially family-based authoritarianism directed against uppity women. Valancy must fight against the propriety that hedged in Montgomery as wife of the Reverend Ewan Macdonald, the inherited Presbyterian propriety of her home in Prince Edward Island. Because of Barney, Valancy can become free, can dance and dress in green. Through him, she can find a wild island with a mysterious Native name. It is not an island she has been born to, like Ellen in Scott's *The Lady of the Lake*; nor is she living there under the protection of a loving father, like Ellen or Katie in 'Malcolm's Katie.' Indeed, even Barney is not the originator of Valancy's move to freedom. She changes dramatically in the book, to become not downtrodden but strong-minded like Babbie, though without any of her charms and wiles, the traditional weapons of a woman.

Besides purveying a sense of social surfaces, novels such as *The Blue Castle* or *The Little Minister* touch deep chords of myth. Pulling dreams or nightmares into narrative form, Barrie and Montgomery crystallize repressed feelings, desires, and angers, and bring refreshment. Tears come with pity, sympathy and identification with the characters in the books. Those sentimental tears crack the tight, ironic weariness of experience.

I 'grew up' on Barrie, his plays, his stories, his essays; graduation in my high school days had brought a presentation copy of *Courage*, a little book reproducing his installation speech as rector of the University of Edinburgh. I went back to *The Little Minister* when I began teaching a course on best-sellers. I went back to *Anne of Green Gables*, *Emily of New Moon*, and the other Montgomery novels – friends of my youth – at the same time, during the process of editing her journals. In those days, early in the 1980s, I was a member of several national boards, designate to innumerable local and regional committees. Daily I was doused in waves of conniving, politicking, upmanship and upwomanship, empire building, power struggles, snide remarks. What a blessing to be able to slip away to Avonlea or to Glen Tocharty in the evening! I could cope with the day's unkind pressures, and then pick up hope and gentleness and humour with the little minister and his doting mother and his enchanting Babbie, or with Anne and Emily, Kilmeny and Valancy. One of my colleagues was aghast. 'But Montgomery – her work is like *Peter Pan*! Sentimental twaddle!' Then he added ruefully, 'But I have a soft spot in my heart for J.M. Barrie.'

Many Canadians, and many Scots, have a very soft spot for all the sentimental novelists, whose whimsical, arch, fanciful fictions veil and soften trouble, bring on waves of laughter, reopen eyes to natural beauty, and restore faith in the power of language to transport us to a happy-ending world.

Chapter Eight

Buchan, MacLennan, and the Winds of Violence

Unlike J.M. Barrie, who was emotionally crippled by a neurotic mother and torn by a travesty of a marriage, John Buchan, by all early accounts (and many admiring accounts of his life were published in the years right after his death in 1940), enjoyed a successful companionable marriage and a marvellous public career. Yet it was Barrie who flew away in his books to a Never Land of romance, adoring mothers, and charming lovers. Contrariwise, Buchan's books present desperate struggles against murderous foes. John Buchan, victim of a serious accident in childhood and sufferer as an adult from the debilitating pain of a duodenal ulcer, made no fictional escapes, like those of the physically hampered Robert Louis Stevenson, to the garden of childhood or to light-hearted adventures. His books led into a wild and terrifying world of crime and danger.

Perhaps the contrast between the lives and works of these three popular Scottish writers is not as stark as first appears. Buchan, like Barrie and Stevenson, was torn between the austere Presbyterianism of his family and the sophistication of the circles he came to move in, later in life, in England. Like Stevenson and Barrie, he achieved a huge, devoted readership. Major differences remain, however. Buchan, born in 1875, matured in the twentieth century and played a role in the new complexities of national and international politics before and after the First World War.

His early biographers highlighted his successes, public and private. His sister Anna ('O. Douglas'), in *Unforgettable, Unforgotten* (1945), revels in her brother's Olympian progress. She does not linger over the near tragedy when, as a five-year-old, he tumbled from a carriage, and in consequence spent a year in bed and was scarred for life. Nor does she emphasize the boyhood years in a poor district in Glasgow where their father was minister. Instead, she celebrates his achievement at school in Edinburgh, his later progress away from Scotland at Oxford and in South Africa, and his romantic marriage to Susan Grosvenor, child of the family for whom Grosvenor Square and Grosvenor House in London were named, daughter of one of the brilliant Stuart-Wortley sisters, second cousin of the Duke of Westminster, great-grand-niece of the Duke of Wellington,

That high-born lady (who wrote very readable fiction herself), in *John Buchan, by His Wife and Friends* (1947), confirms the story of the Tweedside Presbyterian family, the soft Border speech, the code of 'moral austerity' and of quietly tackling difficulty. She writes with some asperity about Buchan's mother, but caps the story of her own courtship by Buchan with warm memories of their life together, when he was a happy father and a busy author of influential essays, biographies, and historical studies. The friends who add to her account include political leaders such as Lord Stanley Baldwin, historians A.L. Rowse and G.M. Trevelyan, and fellow writers such as Catherine Carswell.

Add to these feminine versions of Buchan the account of family life in three books by his sons, John Lord Tweedsmuir's *Always a Countryman* (1953) and The *'Wreath'd Trellis': John Buchan the Writer* (written in 1955 for the opening of the John Buchan Memorial Collection at Queen's University in Kingston, Ontario) and William Buchan's *John Buchan, a Memoir* (1982). Both sons stress that at their home at Elsfield, the country estate near Oxford purchased in 1919, all were 'absolutely happy.' The need to keep his sons in good schools, however, became one of the pressures that led their father to augment the prestigious histories with money-making 'thrillers.'

Memory Hold-the-Door (1940), John Buchan's autobiography, faces outward. He begins with stories of boyhood explorations in the Scottish countryside and the consequent sense of connection with Scotland's violent history. He includes portraits of his quiet, strong-minded mother, his gentle father, a Presbyterian minister, his brothers and sister, and the brilliant and brave young friends doomed to early death in the First World War. The autobiography touches on his public career as lawyer, diplomatic secretary in Africa, partner in publishers Thomas Nelson and Sons, politico in Peebles and Selkirk, pre-war envoy to the United States, intelligence officer during the First World War as director of information, member of Parliament for the Scottish universities (1927–35), and lord high commissioner to the General Assembly of the Church of Scotland (1933–4).

John Buchan (1965, 1985), a fine, authoritative, balanced biography by Janet Adam Smith, and her briefer version, *John Buchan and His World* (1979), carry the story through to the achievements of the later years: chancellor of the University of Edinburgh and governor general of Canada. He arrived with pomp, newly elevated to the nobility as Lord Tweedsmuir, in time to welcome the King and Queen for the first royal visit to what had once been a British colony. In 1939 he trekked northwards to the Peace River, the old Hudson's Bay posts, and the strange land beyond the timber line, the country that would inspire *Sick Heart River*. In the Second World War he helped to broker meetings between Churchill and Roosevelt in the interest of American support of the Allied cause.

In the interstices of all that public action, he wrote more than fifty books. The popular novels that he himself dismissed as insignificant – adventurous spy stories – still keep his name shining after all the public performances of this sagacious and balanced diplomat are forgotten.[1] Indeed, he created a twentieth-century genre, the violent, action-filled thriller. This courteous, civilized man doled out a lifetime of shocks to a world of readers voracious for violence.[2]

Buchan had put himself through college and university with writing of a very different kind, careful political reviews and personal essays, Stevenson-style, about fishing, reading, and the open road on a Scottish walking tour. Next, like Walter Scott, he pierced the wild places of his nation's history in an early novel, *John Burnet of Barns* (1898), dealing with the divided loyalty of a young Scot in the time of the seventeenth-century Covenanters. Then in 1900, the year that J.M. Barrie carried steamy sentimentality to its extreme in *Tommy and Grizel*, Buchan published the first of his modern action-packed adventure stories, *The Half-Hearted*, poising a fiery pen against the mists of sentiment.

Again, in 1910, setting himself against the whimsy of books like *Peter Pan*, Buchan presented *Prester John*, drawing a lad, like the boy in *Treasure Island*, into danger and violence, not in the Never Land, but in a world of real terrors. The world is Africa, which Buchan knew from his years in the reconstruction camps, post–Boer War. 'I let fiction alone until 1910,' he said, 'when, being appalled as a publisher by the dullness of most boys' books, I thought I would attempt one of my own.'[3]

Then from the heart of Africa back to heart-stopping adult adventure in Scotland with *The Thirty-Nine Steps* (1915). The novel was written early in the war. It imagined a heroic adventure that might have postponed the war's opening. Vicariously, Buchan had inserted himself into the action from which he was excluded by illness; vicariously, he involved himself in patriotic deeds. 'Into his books,' says his sister, 'he put all his longing for action and adventure that his health would not allow him to experience.'[4] He himself wrote in *Memory Hold-the-Door*, 'While pinned to my bed during the first months of war and compelled to keep my mind off too tragic realities, I gave myself to stories of adventure'(195). A modern critic, Paul Webb, adds, 'His war novels, *Greenmantle* (1916) and *Mr. Standfast* (1919), are partly wish-fulfilment: a way of fighting by proxy.'[5]

In *The Thirty-Nine Steps* each chapter revolves around the swift, successive shocks of unexpected events. In each, Buchan takes an ordinary, unexciting scene from a routine life like his own and adds a sudden, sinister twist. An unexpected caller comes to meet Richard Hannay in an unglamorous London boarding house, and murder comes to join him. Hannay takes a train from St Pancras to Scotland, changes trains, but leaves before he reaches his destination, fearing he is under sinister surveillance. An encounter with a literary stranger in an inn leads to flight in someone else's car. A political rally, addressed by an inept candidate, ends with the offer of an old bicycle, but the bicycle ride through a heathery glen culminates in danger: Hannay is spotted from the air by his pursuers. Entry into a Scottish country house leads to imprisonment. A casual glance reveals that a genial host can 'hood his eyes like a hawk' – a sign that here sits the malevolent mastermind of international intrigue! Dry-fly fishing is given a sudden melodramatic shot of violence with the announcement of another murder. Finally, at an English seaside cottage, thirty-nine steps lead down to a sinister rendezvous site for foreign emissaries and spies.

By the time the novel ends, the reader, like its hero, Hannay (and perhaps like Buchan), has been jolted out of boredom, dissatisfaction with sedentary ways, and the sense that nothing exciting ever happens. Like a secret code that can and must be broken, the novel offers access to hidden meanings and triggers unexpected passions, patriotic as well as personal.[6]

The Thirty-Nine Steps sold 25,000 copies in 1915 and 34,000 the following year.[7] And from that point on, a thriller a year. As the list of shockers piled up, from *Greenmantle* (1916) through *The Dancing Floor* (1926), *The House of the Four Winds* (1935), and *The Island of Sheep* (1936), to name only the ones that were Buchan's own favourites, certain constants appeared. In each book a group of men, comrades in arms, faces a clearly recognizable evil force, a force cold and destructive. Each character represents one facet of Buchan's self: Richard Hannay, brave and modest 'outsider'; Lord Leithen, lawyer and member of Parliament; Sandy Arbuthnot (later Lord Clanroyden), cool and intelligent; and Roylance, loyal and chivalrous. Each also seems to be drawn from memories of the brilliant circle of young men killed in the war, leaving Buchan, who had been a non-combatant, as the sole and perhaps shamed survivor.[8] He gives them a lost chance for furious action, throwing his fiction in the face of the fact of their stillness.

In each novel, Buchan confronts a hero with desperate challenge, threats to life and freedom, and conviction of national danger. Stealthy chase on the bypaths of a hill country, not necessarily Scotland, leads to open confrontation with villains. The hero glories in physical mayhem as he smashes his principal opponent. 'I found an ugly face close to me, fired at it, and saw it go blind,' says Hannay, in *The Island of Sheep* (64). To the well-bred group of heroes, Buchan later adds Dickson McCunn, citizen of bourgeois Glasgow, and the Gorbals Die-Hards, tough slum boys from another part of the city that he knew as a boy, son of the minister in an inner-city parish. The Glaswegians add a different shade to the violence in the novels.

It is hard to square those climactic moments in wild places with the portraits of John Buchan in the 1920s and 1930s at pastoral Elsfield. Edgar Allan Poe said that he invented the detective story in order to fend off madness. Given Poe's strange life, it is not surprising to imagine his desperate need to pull together his ratiocinative powers into fictions. But Buchan? What shocks did fate deal him? What need (to put it another way) to take on extra work and to add fiction to the unending, inevitable memos and drafts and papers that beset him as a public man?

Neither his autobiography nor the early biographies fully explain his lifelong escape into wild places of the imagination. In the years between the wars, Buchan continued to turn out thrillers, when one would have thought his life offered enough pleasant thrills: mountain climbing, social climbing, furthering the interests of other climbing young writers. Puzzles as to the secret source of his power and productiveness remained. In 1995 Andrew Lownie added a new speculation. Lownie's *John Buchan: The Presbyterian Cavalier* emphasizes Buchan's failures rather than his successes: 'bypassed' and 'out-manoeuvred' (296), 'an outsider all his life' as a Scot in the English Establishment, and a writer whose thrillers outsold his serious biographies. Lownie concludes, 'Many of these contradictions he suppressed in his own life and attempted to reconcile in his writing' (298). Secret personal disappointment may indeed explain why the winds of violence played so fiercely through Buchan's imagination. Yet frustration by failure to achieve goals set for oneself in youth is a common complaint, hardly sufficient explanation for that lifelong addiction to literary violence. I myself am tempted to speculate that marriage to an upper-class lady in caste-ridden England may have added repressions that needed violent release, a theory I will return to.

First, however, I will offer another explanation. Perhaps Buchan's Scottish heritage was responsible for his turn to violence. If the English ideal, as expressed by Matthew Arnold, was 'sweetness and light,' the Scots were more likely to exemplify 'sweetness – and fight!' 'Am I no a bonny fighter?' Alan Breck Stewart asked gentle David Balfour in *Kidnapped*. Certainly, there have been many bonny fighters in the panoply of Scottish heroes – historic figures like Bruce, Wallace, and the Black Douglas, fictional figures like Roderick Dhu and Fergus Mac-Ivor, and ferocious fellows in the borderland of fact and fiction, such as Rob Roy.[9]

Legions of less well known Scots had gone to every war in the world. Scottish regiments distinguished themselves, whether as part of imperializing British forces in the eighteenth and nineteenth centuries or as mercenaries in earlier centuries, driven by the structural violence of poverty into the overt violence of battle. At home, Scots fought in ragged, irregular troops as proscribed clansmen or as Covenanters, defying authority in the name of a harsh religion. In Scotland they fought not as regular, formal soldiery but as guerrillas who blended into their terrain, like colonials or Native scouts in the Revolutionary War. In Scott's day the glorification of rude, warlike strength, as opposed to smoother, prosperous commercial activity, expressed Scottish rejection of a prosperous overfed John Bull. The myth of the unbeatable, terrifying clansmen, the 'ladies from Hell' in modern Highland regiments, was based on a reality of Scottish violence. An individual Scot, even a manse-bred John Buchan, might harbour a fighting instinct in face of Oxford's sophistication. Winds of the north still blew in Buchan's memory, and the Scottish joy in a fierce fight lingered under the diplomatic façade.

So too did a different kind of tension. Buchan's Presbyterian upbringing had fixed in his soul the concept of original sin. Modern studies had transmuted that concept, in part, into a Freudian sense of wild places in the psyche, barely held under control by repression or sublimation. In *The Three Hostages* (1924) one of the minor characters talks to Richard Hannay about the relationship between the old theology and the new psychology. They have been discussing the new violence in detective stories written after the end of the war. Hannay comments, 'The poor old war seemed to be blamed for a good deal that I was taught in my childhood was due to original sin.' His friend counters:

> Oh, I'm not questioning your Calvinism. Original sin is always there, but the meaning of civilisation was that we had got it battened down under hatches, whereas now it's getting its head up. But it isn't only sin. It's a dislocation of the mechanism of human reasoning, a general loosening of screws ... Every doctor nowadays has got to be a mental pathologist ... [I]f you want detective stories that are not childish fantasy, you'll have to invent a new kind. Better try your hand, Dick ... Take all this chatter about psycho-analysis. There's nothing very new in the doctrine, but people are beginning to work it out into details ... [T]he fact of the subconscious self is as certain as the existence of lungs and arteries.[10]

Hannay's wife interjects, 'I don't believe that Dick has any subconscious self.' But Tom Greenslade contradicts her. 'Oh yes, he has. Only, people who have led his kind of life have their ordinary self so well managed and disciplined – their wits so much about them, as the phrase goes – that the subconscious rarely gets a show. But I bet if Dick took to thinking about his soul, which he never does, he would find some queer corners' (13). Out of his own queer corners, Buchan dredged his shelf-full of 'shockers.'

The production of literary shocks and thrills had been foreshadowed in Scottish fiction as far back as James Hogg's *The Private Memoirs and Confessions of a Justified Sinner*, most terrifying of all stories of the divided self, published in 1824, exactly a hundred years before *The Three Hostages*. Stevenson's *The Strange Case of Dr. Jekyll and Mr. Hyde* (1886) added to the literary legacy a strange absorbing story of dark topography, labyrinthine city, and a sinister sense of hidden byways and of secrets lurking under a respectable, civilized façade. In the late 1880s, Arthur Conan Doyle, another Scot, developed the formula of rational detective and slower-witted but energetic partner, still an accepted pattern. His Sherlock Holmes stories proved the force of thrillers, the fascination of fictional murder, disentanglement, and physical pursuit.[11] Buchan perfected the use of that force. Matters repressed in a controlled and elegant and successful life brought pleasure to readers living in a comparable tameness, and relishing a vicarious eruption of open enmity and secret contrivance of doom for opponents.

Buchan often referred to his popular stories as 'tusheries,' using one of the pet words of his literary hero, Robert Louis Stevenson. In 1927 he produced a different kind of 'shocker' in his historical novel *Witch Wood*. He had begun working that year on a scholarly biography of the Marquis of Montrose, expanding the briefer treatment he had published in 1913. In the midst of his historic research, he began to imagine what would happen if a proper young man, a Presbyterian minister in fact, were drawn from his orthodoxy into a passionate response to Montrose, and into deceit, disregard of responsibility, and the overthrow of discipline. In a sense, the story of *Witch Wood* had already been told with skill and grace by J.M. Barrie. Buchan creates a little minister who, like Barrie's Gavin Dishart, falls in love with a laughing, singing, dancing lady, who is out of his reach socially and who tempts him to throw Presbyterian propriety to the winds. The love story is played out against a dark background of witchcraft, a worship of darkness that has secretly obsessed the minister's parishioners. In Buchan's novel, unlike Barrie's, there is no happy ending, no marriage of minister and galvanizing woman. Here the dancing lady pays with her life for involving herself in the tragedy of the parish as it suffers from the ravages of the plague.

Women had played a minor role in most of Buchan's novels. They had been regarded romantically, sometimes taken along on the road to violence as accomplices or apprentice spies, but more often left safely at home while the men faced the shocks of encounters with evil spymasters, hidden enemies of goodness, loyalty, and manliness. In *Witch Wood*, however, a woman, surprisingly like Susan Grosvenor in background, appearance, and character, is a dominant, controlling character. The beautiful fictional lady comes to a shocking end, a dreadful sickness and death. This is the ultimate violence, and the motivation for producing this hypnotic, terrifying book is as puzzling as the force that led Barrie to produce *Farewell Miss Julie Logan*.

Buchan's final novel is virtually without women characters. *Sick Heart River* (1941) carries a final and different shock. Now the hero is not Hannay nor Roylance nor Clanroyden, all of them happily married, but Leithen, the lonely man. Leithen, hero of many earlier Buchan novels, brave Scot, stoic and intelligent, faces death, not at the hand of a foreign agent, but from the erosion of his own bodily strength. He comes to a remembered place that should restore body and soul – a place like 'Storm and Misty' in W.O. Mitchell's *The Vanishing Point*. With a French-Canadian companion and a Scots-Native guide, he endures a terrible journey northward, suffers betrayal and remorse. In the end he finds some spiritual redemption but no physical regeneration, no mercy in nature, where the cold north wind of mortality blows. After all the unfelt deaths dealt out by the good companions in earlier novels, Buchan in ultimate violence now turns the point of steel against his own heart, and his reader's. The novel pummels the reader with the slow, existential realization and experience of death. John Buchan had long suffered from a duodenal ulcer. He died, prematurely, of a stroke at sixty-five, with five books still unfinished and *Sick Heart River* just completed as a memento of that slow passage to silence.

The Second World War, in its first stages when Buchan died,

marked a watershed in literary uses of violence. Censorship, official and self-imposed, loosened dramatically. The increase of physical battering and bloody death in, say, a story by Alistair MacLean (1922–1987), compared to a Buchan novel, is exponential. MacLean, son of a Glasgow minister, parlayed fictional ferocity into best-sellerdom: his first book, *HMS Ulysses* (1955), sold 250,000 copies in the first six months. He rarely included women characters in his rampaging stories. Other post-Buchan Scottish thrillers, however, added a breathy dollop of sexiness and a luxury in settings, but counterbalanced these with raw brutality beyond Buchan's range.

That expansion of brutality is one post-war reaction to violence. The other is a dryness in style, the icy control of novels delineating ferocity beneath civilized surface. The cool, dry tone used in reporting inhuman destructiveness became pervasive after the Second World War. In the fictions of Scottish-born J.I.M. Stewart, writing as 'Michael Innes,' murder invades a super-civilized, Jamesian world, only to be quelled by an equally Jamesian detective. Stewart's life curiously paralleled Buchan's. He too grew up in an orderly, disciplined Scottish family. Like the traditional 'lad o' pairts,' he climbed to eminence as a university professor and settled into a peaceful English life. Like Buchan, he wrote scholarly tomes, but from an early stage in his life he also produced thrillers.[12] The old values of industry, self-denial, and ambition again built into explosive pressure under the surface of competence and success. Innes's *Lament for a Maker* (1938) is a curious Scottish pastiche in which a narrator like Barrie's old dominie watches a mad poetic laird in a lone tower, like Wolf's Crag in Scott's *The Bride of Lammermoor*. Blood on the snow brings urbane and elegant Inspector Appleby to cope cleverly with murder.

Writers other than Buchan continued to explore the 'stubborn anger that burns through Scottish history,' to quote Edwin Muir's 1935 *Scottish Journey*.[13] Writings by a later generation, such as Alasdair Gray's *Lanark* and *1982, Janine*, William McIlvanney's *Docherty*, and James Kelman's novels, though they ram home their vision of sexual and social violence in postmodern style, nevertheless serve the same function as the earlier 'shockers.' They give a cathartic outlet to the reader who is in impotent reaction against uncontrollable circumstances. In Kelman, verbal shocks add to recurring scenes of brutal battering, without the moral underpinning that Buchan held to.[14]

Canada had been an appropriate setting for tales of violence from the beginning, tales of Native ambush, tales of wild rides down foaming rivers, tales of Hudson's Bay trappers at war with their rivals in the North West Company. Most of the heroes of those far northern adventures had come from Scotland, and mostly from the Highlands and the Islands: McGillivrays, Macphersons, Camerons, Frasers, McGregors, fighting the wilderness, the savages, and each other for dominance in the far, lone land.

Wild rivalries of early days had been succeeded in Canadian history by the quieter but equally deadly battles of the financiers fighting each other as they built the country and its infrastructure, the railways, the steamship lines, the banks, the retail and tobacco empires – a second squadron of fighters: McGill, Strathcona, Simpson, Macdonald. Tamer days followed as the century officially celebrated imperial late-Victorian peace.

Paler stories replaced the early gothic accounts of wild confrontation by Richardson and Sellar. Sentiment doused sectarian battles in the Kailyard novels. The Scottish fighting spirit in Canada was dissipating. Came the dry stories of a new western wasteland, infused with the Old World Wasteland spirit of T.S. Eliot. Buchan's books, in contrast, brought a renewal of the joy of vicarious violence. In his own day, Canadians were among his greatest fans. Like their fellow readers around the English-speaking world, they waited in breath-stopping anxiety for the 'new Buchan.' Something happening in these thrillers – something to lift the reader out of the wasteland, into the heather on the hills. Here, for the dry lands, the dry times, was a literature of arousal.

When Buchan was in Canada as governor general, one of his aides-de-camp was young David Harry Walker. Scottish son of a military man, Walker left Buchan's service to go to war. He returned to Scotland to rejoin the Black Watch regiment, in which he had served since 1931. His war experiences included battle as an officer in the Black Watch, followed by five escape-oriented years in German prisons (1940–5). After the war and after a time in India as comptroller to the viceroy, he returned to settle permanently in Canada. There, in the post-war years, he produced some strong and popular stories set in Scotland, Germany, and India, combining piquant use of Scots themes and scenes with the traumas of war and imprisonment and the equal devastation of rebellion against authority. Like Buchan, Walker turned out shockers. He titled his 1984 autobiography *Lean, Wind, Lean*. In his novels as in his life, however, the lean winds of influence are out-roared by the winds of violence. Yet like Buchan's, his novels assumed the virtues of honour, duty, courage. *The Storm and the Silence* appeared in 1949 and *Geordie* in 1950, together establishing Walker as a successful producer of both suspenseful novels and comic local-colour ones. When *Harry Black* was published in 1956, it revealed a novelist ready to probe Freudian disturbances in family and love relationships.

Walker shifted to Canadian settings in another series of highly readable thrillers, including *Mallabec* (1965) and *Black Dougal* (1973). *Black Dougal* is my personal favourite, my most rereadable Walker book. The Montreal setting helps: I can relate to lunch at the Ritz Carlton. The unexpected helicopters descending from the sky over the south shore of the St Lawrence, guns blazing, in a James Bond style of retribution against the bad guys – after weeks of work on the Montgomery diaries, how glorious to move into this shock of virile action, where violence descends in the person of a powerful Scot!

The most generally popular of Walker's Canadian productions, however, was *Where the High Winds Blow* (1960). Like Buchan's Leithen, Walker's hero returns to the Arctic region in search of its curative, restorative power. Like Leithen, the new hero experiences absolutes of loneliness and despair. But the winds of the north that finally seemed to Buchan to blow with the chill of death are for Walker invigorating. This novel of a northern Canadian testing, however, received little critical attention either from literary critics or from cultural historians intent on tracing that myth in their academic studies.

I interviewed David Walker in 1975, when I was preparing a paper on best-sellers for a conference. I found that he felt his exclusion from the academic canon sharply and was resentful of the bypassing by Canadian critics. He cited his enormous sales as a base from which he could well scoff at academic neglect, but he was justly proud of his own craftsmanship and irritated at how cursory and perfunctory the Canadian reviews of his novels seemed.

David Walker deserved better. Into his late novel, *Ash* (1976), he built danger, hiding, escape, all the stuff of Buchan's action thrillers: flight through the underbrush (Canadian bog cedars rather than Scottish heather this time), the road to the north, where solitary courage is pitted against hazardous nature and relentless human pursuit. He added a wry love story involving Ash and his brother's wife. *Ash* further suggests the stress of a writer, producing a book in spite of the distresses of aging, family animosity and betrayal, adultery, and alcoholism. Perhaps this story cuts too close to the bone, and perhaps that cutting quality disturbed academics, even while it satisfied common readers looking for the fillip of disturbance.

The story of the reception of Walker's novels takes us back to the question of marginalization. Walker was bypassed not only because his fiction, enormously popular, sat squarely in the genre of shocker or thriller, but also because he fitted into no national norm. In Scotland, folks had chuckled over *Geordie* and thrilled to *The Storm and the Silence*, but as years passed (and Scottish nationalistic criticism waxed), few Scottish critics took any interest in the subsequent works, set often in Canada and featuring always transatlantic manoeuvres and intrigues. Canadian critics found this New Brunswick author overly attached to the scenes of his youth, too likely to include Scottish scenes and myths, even in books featuring Canadian characters.

Conversely, both the academic critics and the general readers have relished the shocks administered in Hugh MacLennan's novels. MacLennan (1907–1990), most philosophical of Canadian post-war novelists, wrote about articulate, conscientious, puzzled people, men and women very much like Buchan's circle of friends. His urbane novels nevertheless moved towards climaxes of physical brutality.

MacLennan, like John Buchan, was a courteous, civilized man. Like Buchan, he grew up in a Presbyterian home and held a comparable fond attachment to his sister. As a child, he was taken to England while his father completed specialist medical studies; the sojourn ended with a memorable visit to Edinburgh. MacLennan, too, progressed mightily: to Dalhousie University, on a Rhodes Scholarship to Oxford, and then on to Princeton. Like Buchan, he married an alien woman, a woman not from his own ethnic group or country but an American artist, whom he revered and perhaps regarded as in some ways a social superior, more sophisticated and aesthetic than himself. The distance between MacLennan's parents' marriage and his own represented something that could not be easily assimilated into the Scottish tradition he was born to. With Dorothy Duncan he returned to Canada to teach in Montreal.[15]

MacLennan's first book, *Barometer Rising* (1941), is literally explosive. It pounds with the terrors of the Halifax explosion of 1917, a horrific event experienced by MacLennan when he was ten years old. Indeed, this book has a double explosion, for a gun burst had hurled the hero, Neil Macrae, two years earlier, out of his overseas imprisonment. In *Barometer Rising*, time is condensed to a single week, setting restricted to Halifax, but the plot expands Buchan's typical actions: deadly pursuit, secret rendezvous, sudden reversal, twist of chance, macabre moment. Neil Macrae, aided by Angus Murray, searches for Alec MacKenzie, who holds his secret talisman. The names signal that MacLennan, like Findley in *The Wars*, assumes that a Canadian hero should have a Scottish name.

MacLennan emphasizes the Scottish tradition not only in his native Nova Scotia but also in Montreal, where he taught for many years at school and university. In his best-known work,

Two Solitudes (1945), Huntly McQueen represents English-speaking Montreal. 'Two solitudes' has become a commonplace for characterizing the politically explosive relations between French- and English-speaking Canadians. Users of the commonplace forget that MacLennan prefaced his book with a quotation from Rainer Maria Rilke emphasizing that two solitudes can 'protect, and touch, and greet each other.' In spite of this emphasis on conciliation, he opens the story proper with an unforgettable metaphor of violence. The very elements, ocean and land, seem to be at enmity: 'a sword had been plunged through the rock from the Atlantic to the Great Lakes and savagely wrenched out again' (1).

Even in Grenville, the imaginary town in Ontario where *The Precipice* (1948) opens, the Scottish names continue: Bruce Fraser will eventually love Lucy Cameron, one of three daughters of John Knox Cameron. This book, however, is set largely in the United States and centres around an American businessman named (neutrally) Lassiter. It is a study of modern, American-style marriage between sophisticated people. MacLennan introduces an allusion to Buchan to suggest the difference between the new kind of book he is attempting and old-fashioned works. Prim Jane Cameron says John Buchan 'proved that a man can be a great writer today without even mentioning sex' (36). She finds justification for her inherited puritan prejudices in Buchan's 'stately and inexorable progress from a Scottish manse to the House of Lords and the Governor-General's mansion in Ottawa' (35–6).

By the time that he wrote *The Precipice*, MacLennan had reached something of Buchan's status as a novelist of whom his nation was proud. Each new novel was welcomed by book clubs and by a very wide Canadian readership, and received major attention in popular newspapers as well as in academic journals. His essays and reviews gave his authorial voice extra currency. Meantime, his wife, Dorothy Duncan, was also building a strong reputation as a writer of non-fiction; she had received a Governor General's Award in 1944 for *Partner in Three Worlds*.

In *Each Man's Son* (1951) MacLennan returned to his native region. He set this story in Cape Breton, where, he postulates, the Highlanders brought not only pipes and clan feuds but also an ancient curse, the Calvinist absolute division between the saved and the damned in life and afterlife. Calvin's harsh doctrine had been intensified in Scotland by Knox. This puritanism is a steel spring, compressed, too tense; shattering the self and others in its explosive release. (This theological interpretation appears in 'An Author's Note,' added at the suggestion of MacLennan's editor.)[16]

MacLennan pictures Archie MacNeil, a used-up prizefighter, violent in the ring, violent in the barroom, returning from the United States to Cape Breton, to find both wife and son drawn away from him. The baffled Cape Breton Highlander creates dreadful havoc, committing bloody murder before the eyes of his wife and little son. His reaction is brutal, horrifying, a dreadful initiation for little Alan, his son – each man's son.

The story is dark, and so is the regional setting: natural world of fog, wind, rain, tides; social world of endurance, poverty, repression;[17] and personal world of wreckage and castaways. The curse of Highland ferocity, explosive when repressed, appears both in Archie and in the doctor who covets Archie's son. Dr Ainslie's Highland temperament is chillingly controlled, but it takes its toll on him and his easygoing, easily affectionate American wife. Demonic energy, fear, and desire fester in many of the Scots Canadians in MacLennan's novels, as perhaps they did in MacLennan himself. By the time that *Each Man's Son* was published, his wife had suffered the first of a series of embolisms, threatening paralysis. Apprehension had added an edge of darkness to MacLennan's work.

In his next novel, *The Watch That Ends the Night* (1959), a sad, rational man named George Stewart watches as his gifted wife dies (as Dorothy Duncan had done in 1957). The novel, however, erupts with savage power when a third character, Dr Jerome Martell, uncovers memories of his childhood in New Brunswick, in a savage world of floggings, loneliness, and fights, culminating in a dreadful scene where the child listens to sounds that accompany the brutal death of his mother, a ferocious woman who rains blows on her attacker: 'crack – crack – crack – of hard fists driven expertly home ... a yelp ... a gasp of pain, then a crunching shock more terrible than a fist blow. Then silence' (181). This wild scene reprises the climax of *Each Man's Son*, where another boy witnesses an equally violent killing.

Bloody accidents begin and end the most devastating of MacLennan's books, *The Return of the Sphinx* (1967). Alan (MacNeil) Ainslie, now an older man, grieves at the memory of the horrible death of his wife, Constance, in 'a completely senseless street accident' (16). In his alienation from his son Daniel, Alan Ainslie thinks, 'That truck that broke Constance's skull broke the life of our whole family' (232). The son's life as a Québécois separatist agitator culminates when his car hits a police barricade – 'a wrenching crash, the steering post struck his chest, there was a crack on his forehead' – and police discover the bomb he is carrying (290).

MacLennan's final novel, *Voices in Time* (1980), came from a late period of his life, when he was happy in a second marriage and in the admiration of fans and disciples. It swings beyond the present into a vision of terrible destruction (and not-very-convincing regeneration).

Critics both before his death in 1990 and since then have pondered the mystery of MacLennan's incessant movement into darkness.[18] Some cite the influence of his classical studies and his absorption of an Oedipal myth. Others note the later acceptance of Freudianism. In *Under Eastern Eyes*, Janice Kulyk Keefer dismisses him as a 'Middlebrow *Agonistes*' writing for 'educated Sunday readers' (214). The major biography of MacLennan, by Elspeth Cameron, avoids such reductiveness and also avoids the admiring awe that characterizes the early Buchan biographies. Cameron explicates the pressures of making a living and paying for medical bills, often leading to the need to bow to requests of editors and publishers contrary to his own vision. T.D. MacLulich confirms the dark focus on father figures and reiterates Cameron's point about the influ-

ence of Gordon Rattray Taylor's *Sex in History* (1953). MacLulich
also postulates that MacLennan felt neurotically a 'patrist/
matrist' shift characteristic of his times.[19] I see the violence in
MacLennan as also marking his Scottish heritage.

Soon after the death of his wife in 1957, he had gone to
Scotland, returning for the first time since he had travelled
there, first as a boy and later as a college student. In *Scotchman's
Return and Other Essays* (1960)[20] he details the beguiling and
dangerous beauty of the Highlands, the sheep-stopped roads,
the emptiness, and the sense that 'everyone who ever mattered
is dead and gone' (5). He speaks of his own Scottishness as 'a
kind of doom from which I am too Scotch even to think of
praying for deliverance' (1). Yet returning to Canada, flying
over Cape Breton, MacLennan looks down and sees as a tiny
speck the house where his mother and sister lie asleep; now he
can think of Canada as home. He asks, 'Is it true that it is only
now, after so many years of not knowing who we were or
wanted to be, that we Canadians of Scotch descent are truly at
home in the northern half of North America?'(12).

In the title essay MacLennan catalogues what he sees as
Scottish qualities: 'the perplexity and doggedness of the race ...,
its loneliness, tenderness and affection, its deceptive vitality, its
quick flashes of violence, its dog-whistle sensitivity to sounds
to which Anglo-Saxons are stone-deaf, its incapacity to tell its
heart to foreigners save in terms foreigners do not comprehend, its resigned indifference to whether they comprehend or
not' (2). The melancholy tone is reinforced in the titles of other
essays in this volume: 'Sunset and Evening Star,' 'October and
Smoke.' Yet he can strike a darker, sardonic note and in 'The
Future of the Novel as an Art Form' can say wryly, 'I am Scotch
and by nature inclined to anticipate doom' (158).

MacLennan was particularly conscious of his Scottish Calvinist legacy, the 'compressed spring' which he referred to in
Each Man's Son. The spring was compressed in Canada as in
Scotland by poverty, by ambition, by a religion that enforced
self-examination and encouraged a sense of guilt, by a patrist
society cutting harshly into tender and companionable feel-

ings. The spring was tightened over the years by the need to move with the times into new attitudes to the relations between men and women. MacLennan's stance, in his life and his novels, does not represent a case of being influenced by Buchan, but of being influenced by the impact of the same changes on a comparable inherited value system. Like Buchan, he directed his disturbances into his fiction.

Meditative, ironic, MacLennan would not have been pleased to be analysed as a purveyor of shocks and violent thrills. He revelled in the critical consideration accorded to his works as philosophical penetrations into the human dilemma. Readers, however, not only in Canada and Scotland but wherever a veneer of complacency covers malaise, relished MacLennan's offer of fictional release less for the philosophy and more for the unexpected, sudden wildness, the eruption of violence, mindless, barbaric, in terrifying juxtaposition to the civil surface of society. His books came, like Jerome Martell, from wild places – of which there are many, psychological as well as geographic, in Canada as well as in Scotland. These stories bring a pleasurable shudder to readers living in not-so-wild places. With the shudder comes a fair dose of fear if the reader happens to be a woman.

Braggart's in My Step

When conventional critics speak of books like *The Little Minister* or *Anne of Green Gables* in the same way as statistical geographers might consider 'insignificant' places like Saltspring Island or Eigg, readers can outface their scorn. They know from experience that power inheres in the literature of the fringe, as in places geographically marginal. The books read most intensely, reread most frequently, are frivolous romances, whodunnits, science fiction, dark studies of schizophrenia, vampire tales, swashbuckling 'through the heather' stories, children's books, South Seas adventures, and dandified costume histories of pageantry and disguise. Such books are the fringing isles of life, the loci where the pace of events can be controlled, harsh places misted over, natural forms held in small perspective, troubles grasped and weeded out.

The power of the formulaic book rises in part from the life story of the writer, who pumps perilous and complex stuff into a shady, shaky vehicle. Robert Louis Stevenson turned his physical weaknesses into an escapist return to childhood happiness or vicariously sailed into far places, dangerous moments, wild trips through the Highlands and Islands. Barrie evaded his troubles by misting them over into sentimental romance. L.M. Montgomery channelled her traumatic life into blithe stories. From secret sources, Buchan and MacLennan unleashed violence. In each case, the strength of the story rises from the strength of the author's frustration in life, combined with the professional's craft in wrestling frustration onto paper.

An inordinate number of Canadians who have been recognized as major writers have chosen to produce thrillers, children's books, and romances. When a Margaret Atwood packs her annual stint of writing into a murder mystery, she concocts the haunting *Alias Grace*. When a Margaret Laurence decides to write a children's book for the Christmas market, the magic result is *The Olden Days Coat*, one of the most poignant time-jump fantasies imaginable. Mordecai Richler produces his Jacob Two-Two stories, and children everywhere accept with delight. Dennis Lee works in Stevenson's garden, in accordance with educational practice of building from known to unknown. Farley Mowat, disturbed by the pallor of books for children after the Second World War, imitates Stevenson in snap and polish in order to restore to young readers the joy of suspense, challenge, and surprise. Excellent Canadian writers have shown what formulaic work, work at the fringe of the established canon, can be at its best and most unexpected. When a great writer works in a minor genre, the effect can be astonishing. Vision and sensitivity and structural skill, when condensed into a formulaic container, may well carry the despised genre to surprising heights.

Let's face it: Canadian writers, like Scottish ones, have been good at producing best-sellers because they were anxious to make money and willing to practise the art of readability. From Scott's day on, the connection between literary success and a comfortable income had pressed on consciousness – particularly the consciousness of Scots, whose awareness of money has always been both a cartoon feature and an actuality. Canadians, perhaps especially Canadian women, have felt the same hunger for a money-making activity, combined with an awareness that storytelling might well be that activity. Again the Scottish examples motivated Canadians, from Moodie to Montgomery, to write something that would sell. If we detect some Peter Pannery in L.M. Montgomery, we can note in her journals how often she read Barrie and how anxious she was to write a best-seller of her own. Concerned to live by her pen, Montgomery would gladly use any material that came her way, whether from literature or from life. She would probably not be horrified to learn that a successor in turn lifted plot motifs and phrases from her work, as Colleen McCullough is suspected of doing. She would recognize a valued motivation, to please and to sell.

In the less-intellectual genres, the marginal, the uncanonical, there has never been an anxiety of influence, but rather an intention of grabbing on to an appealing model. Canadian writers in popular genres, formerly considered uncanonical, have continued to rework motifs picked up from Scottish models, proved effective in terms of reach and appropriate because of shared psychological, theological, and practical pressures. So Canadian romancers dealt with love in sentimental, evasive pastels drawn from Barrie. Shockers kept up the pull of plot, teasing readers as to 'what happens next,' muffling the drift in false clues, and untangling with sharp suddenness, all in Buchan's manner. All, at least in part, in hope of achieving a market share.

That motive may be at the outer edge of literary inspiration. Once again, however, the edge turned into a tough strengthening of the flow of creativity. In 'Scotch' communities the products had to be good to warrant readers' spending the hard-won pounds or dollars. The books written to sell had to give the purchasers what they needed – reassurance, comfort, escape – or, to put it another way, catharsis, symbolic release, and sublimation; relief and empowerment, defences, expectations, fantasies, and transformations that are essential to well-being. Paradoxically, best-sellers usually also had to give access to an immaterial world in which getting and spending pressed less strongly than in real life.

Let me weave one more thread into the metaphor of the fringe. Canadian and Scottish writers have proved that books themselves – any books, the canonical ones and the marginalized, though they may seem to be at the outside edge of real life – do in fact hold more colour and strength than that so-called real life at the crossroads of 'getting and spending,' of business and housekeeping, career and sports. In an hour at the grocery store, a person lives through sixty minutes. In an hour with a book, one lives through years of tension or a lifetime of happiness and sorrow.

There was a time when I worried that I was shirking my responsibilities when I snatched time from preparing lectures or sorting diapers to read a new best-seller or reread an old favourite. Eventually I learned that I could combine my joy with my duties: I rocked babies and read books, stirred stews and read books, chaired tedious meetings with a book in my lap. Now I know that my real life was as much in the books as in the babies. The reading habit proved to be not an addiction but a nourishment, not an evasion but a deepening of experience. Reading is the selvedge of life that binds colours in more clearly and creates a firm fabric that will not unravel, as the passing preoccupations of the day tend to do.

Nowadays, of course, it is easy to clamber into technological alternatives to book reading. Into the tape deck in the car goes a recorded version of *Alligator Pie*. The children sit side by side in front of the computer playing an interactive game based on *Treasure Island*, helping Jim Hawkins decide whether to confront Long John Silver openly or to hide in a barrel. 'Would you like me to read to you?' (a question well received when they were babies). 'Thanks, Gran, but not just now.' For now they are hypnotized by the computer game. Tiny figures beep and leap and glide, are zapped, puff off, dissolve, flip back onto the screen. The accompanying sound is an ear-eroding little tinkle of bing-bing-beep-bing, no recognizable melody but random computer-generated repeats of an innocuous sound combination. The small boys crouch, intent, in front of the computer screen.

Into the VCR the older children slip a video titled *Hook*. *Peter Pan, or The Boy Who Wouldn't Grow Up* has grown up indeed in terms of reach, from pantomime to Broadway extravaganza to film and on to this million-dollar caricature (or travesty), *Hook*. Tinker Bell flits across the screen, a sexy charmer. For adults, the video port also welcomes *The Little Minister*, recreated in a classic old-time movie featuring a young Katharine Hepburn as Babbie. Another choice is *Anne of Green Gables*, in reruns of old films or in the 1982 television series and its Avonlea sequels.[1]

Audio-visual versions are indeed at the 'cutting edge.' They cut away and into the sense of self. They impose their pace, their vocal tone, their visual specification, which distorts the individual's own timing and imaging. They blur the resonances in the text, stop the ear from catching, pausing over, surging after, or stopping to reconsider. When I read *The Thirty-Nine Steps*, I can turn back a page or so, to recall a cadence, an allusion, hardly noticed at the first run through but perhaps a clue to what will happen later in the story. Reading *Kidnapped*, I can push a private pause button and catch breath between blows, or speed up to get the final horrors over with. Reading *Farewell Miss Julie Logan*, I can creep into a ghostly world and linger there, closing the book uncompleted, unwilling to end the spell. Wrapped in the warm plaid of my book, I can outface the World Wide Web that now lurks on my personal computer as a substitute for books.

Perhaps as we move, via the World Wide Web, into the global village, national oddities will disappear, and we will no longer bristle when another nation mocks our own peculiar accent. Indeed, Frank Davey assumes, in his study of works such as *The Wars* and *The Diviners*, that the post-national state has already arrived.[2] When Margaret Atwood (clearly not to be thought of as a Scottish-Canadian writer, although maybe there is something Buchanesque about *Bodily Harm*, that dark tale of intrigue and flight and explosive politics) comes to Scotland, she speaks in an international tone. When she is interviewed on television, her flat Canadian voice delights listeners as she battles questions with her own weapons of understatement and irreverence. Atwood's books are everywhere in Scotland, in the libraries, in the bookstores, in the bags that students take to school. In books with such appeal, questions of nationalism and of influence are almost irrelevant.

In earlier days, real-life travellers in Canada imported the clothes and the culture of Scotland: plaid on their backs and Burns in their pockets. They rode behind a steam engine invented by James Watt in Galt's Greenock or walked a road paved in imitation of McAdam of Ayr. Nowadays, Canadians travel on an international net of airlines and airwaves. They wear multicultural dress. As for reading, most Canadian bookshelves do contain MacLennan and Montgomery and Findley, but these native products must jostle for space against Salman Rushdie, A.S. Byatt, and Toni Morrison.

Yet even in the global village, readers still need the comfort of books written in a familiar idiom, presenting a locally appropriate stance toward nature, society, family, body, and mind. Canadians need Canadian books; Scots need Scottish ones. In spite of universal, instantaneous communication by fax and e-mail, we are still insular. We still feel closest to people who share our language and some of our climatic and political experience. Here is one function of best-sellers. Books for children, thrillers, and sentimental novels, Canadian and Scottish, preserve precious national qualities. They remind our own people of the significance of our polar extremes and stark antitheses, of our strange fringing islands as well as of our warm and reassuring centralities.

Best-sellers have a second function. They reach out across national lines to a worldwide readership. Indeed, popular Canadian books and Scottish ones have established our two nations as a continuing part of mythic geography.[3] They have helped a world of readers to take exciting journeys from sea to sea: North Sea to cold Atlantic in one case, Atlantic to warmer Pacific in the other. The journeys have encompassed a trip to the Highlands and the Lowlands, the Hebrides and the Orkneys; to the Laurentian Shield, the Prairies, and the Rockies and to Bella Bella and Newfoundland. Borderlands have been important in both journeys: the shires just north of the English border; the pastoral and populated strip just north of the American border. There have been crossroads: a chance to leave Scotland and make for London and the prosperous home counties;

a choice of staying in Montreal or going to New York and Florida, Chicago and Texas, Seattle and California. There have been high winds and resounding music: bagpipes and fiddles and the traffic noises of Aberdeen and Calgary. Gardens, carefully tended, have attracted the traveller away from adult pragmatism. Mists in the glens became a fog blurring Glasgow angularities; mists softening the autumn colours drifted into Halifax and Vancouver as drizzle and into Toronto as smog. Violence erupted in these two countries that have tasted their blood in brawls and raids and strikes. Above all, there have been voices, gossiping and declaiming as the people in two countries talk their way to a sense of personal identity.

Part Four

Open the Door!

This 1991 conference at the University of Edinburgh probably marks my last visit to Scotland. My crossings reach back a long way, to a first tour when I was a schoolgirl, through many research trips and appearances at conferences, on Scott, on Galt, on Canadian 'unity and disunity.' Now we are here to discuss Scottish-Canadian connections.[1] We are housed in student residences, near the handsome home John Buchan inhabited when he headed the Edinburgh publishing company of Thomas Nelson and Sons.

We begin each day with breakfast in the student cafeteria at the University of Edinburgh. The porridge is thick and the accents are thicker. The words and the lilt both charm and baffle me, a third-generation Canadian. When the students turn politely to me, the seventy-year-old stranger in their midst, they swing into a homogenized English. There is a hovering burr, but otherwise they sound as bland as the BBC. We find common ground in discussing American television shows.

Then they relax. They talk to each other. Drama, humour, taunts, affectionate raillery. Anecdotes, gossip, mockery. The accents grow stronger, the atmosphere richer. Like all students everywhere, they are moving into self-awareness, a sense of identity, and also into a sense of relatedness, of community.

They are talking, telling, voicing themselves, their age, and their country.

I feel homesick.

We are back home in Ontario, at the Highland games at Maxville, Ontario, in August 1994. Our small, red-haired grandson has had a Canadian flag painted on his face. The points of the scarlet maple leaf ride high on his Slavic cheekbones, inherited from his other grandfather, who is Czech. We are here to watch his young cousins compete in the Highland dancing contests.

A field full of plaid, kilts flipping and swirling. The little girls are on stage now. They whirl and fling, performing the ancient dances, once the preserve of male warriors. They do the 'Sword Dance' and 'Shaking the Trews' (ritualizing the old defiance of English proscription of the tartans). They swelter in wool and velvet under the hot Canadian sun.

Booths festooned in bunting sell tiny books of Burns's poems, along with mini-dirks and sprays of dried heather. And then the pipers – a hundred pipers and a' and a' – swing ponderous down the field with banners flying. The drummers flaunt leopard skins; the leaders toss the heavy batons into the air, twirling and catching to point up the tempo. Everyone beats time, with pleasure, to the tunes of old glory.

Every piece they play reminds us of a story. 'The Skye Boat Song,' 'The Campbells Are Coming,' 'Up wi' the Bonnets of Bonnie Dundee,' 'Hey, Johnny Pope, Are Ye Marchin' Yet?' The Canadian grass turns dusty beneath the domineering feet.

Now that I am retired, I have time to notice new things – new ways of dancing old dances, new ways of talking, new ways of thinking about literature and nationalism. I find, with surprise, that the critical methods I picked up over the years as part of my teaching equipment remain with me, ready to throw new light on my favourite old books.

For one thing, I have developed something of a feminist perspective. Many of my mentors and friends, I now realize, were feminists before the term came into common usage. Mossie

May Kirkwood, my favourite professor at the University of Toronto in the 1940s; Wynne Francis, keeping a critical eye on groups of poets in Montreal in the 1950s; Mary Quayle Innis (who did not like to be known as 'Mrs Harold Innis'), editor of *The Clear Spirit*, a Centennial celebration of Canadian women by Canadian women writers published in 1966; Clara Thomas, beginning her long list of critical revelations with her publication on Anna Jameson in 1967; Francess Halpenny, taking over the general editorship of the *Dictionary of Canadian Biography* in 1969 – this is just the start of a list, and the names on it are all Canadian.

International feminism had been sweeping over me too, with major markers coming at roughly ten-year intervals. Simone de Beauvoir published *The Second Sex* in English translation in 1953; Betty Friedan's *The Feminine Mystique* appeared in 1963; Kate Millett's *Sexual Politics* followed in 1970.[2] In 1976 came a book that began the particular linkage between feminism and literature for me: *Words and Women*, by Casey Miller and Kate Swift.

The sweep of avowedly feminist literary criticism has continued. Now I can take a new look at all the familiar, long-loved books with eyes dilated by modern feminist criticism. Most of the books that raised my literary consciousness were by Americans: Patricia Meyer Spacks, Elaine Showalter, Sandra Gilbert and Susan Gubar, Carolyn Heilbrun, Annis Pratt, Annette Kolodny, Rachel Blau DuPlessis, and Jane Tompkins.[3] How pleasant to feel the old anti-Americanism diminish! In the 1970s, to be Canadian was to be anti-American; in the 1980s, women reached across the border to shake hands in shared revelations.

Reading *Anne of Green Gables*, for instance, from a feminist perspective brought out elements unperceived by little girls. After studying Gabriella Åhmansson's *A Life and Its Mirrors*, I could go back to the familiar story with new awareness of the ways in which that old classic had empowered women through its subtexts of self-worth, resistance, and persistence.[4]

But the feminist approach was not the only one that opened for me during my time of teaching. Narratology, the theoretic analysis of storytelling, also emerged as reputable and challenging over the last fifty years. As a teacher of fiction, I picked up annual doses of new narrative theory every spring when I attended the meetings of the Canadian learned societies. (The Canadian 'Learneds' are larger and more complex than inter-disciplinary gatherings in Scotland, kindlier and more enriching than the corresponding gargantuan meetings in the United States.) Each year I updated critical approaches. 'What's that name?' I would whisper to a neighbour in a session on Isabella Valancy Crawford, maybe, or on Sinclair Ross. 'Merleau-Ponty,' she would answer (or 'Bachelard' or 'Kristeva'). '*Very* important in current criticism.' I would return to teaching, my lectures newly enriched. Foreign names bedewed my lectures: Lacan, Derrida, Foucault, Jakobsen.[5] For my students I deconstructed stories, recognizing the implied meanings that had been slipped in by allusive metaphors and by suggestions of binary oppositions. In lectures on fiction I unravelled the hermeneutic, proairetic, and connotative codes. I noted metafictions and subtexts.

Now, my involvement in teaching is over. Yet I find myself rereading my old leisure-time books in a decoding mood, noting implications that slipped by me in earlier days, when my eyes were sharper in one sense, less sharp in another. With bifocal vision now, I look at stories as a newborn feminist and narratologist. In my revisionary readings, I recognize again some important Scottish qualities: Scottish pressures on the life of women, especially of women writers; Scottish assumptions about fictions and ways of discourse. I see again some parallels between the Scottish tradition and Canadian developments.

John Knox, the founder of Presbyterianism in Scotland, preached furiously against woman – Eve, seductress, teller of falsehoods. Women enjoy the other half of that Scottish anecdote: an old Scotswoman in Knox's church picked up her stool and hurled it at one of his successors in rebellion against his chauvinism.

Placed at the outskirts of power by the patriarchy of church and state, few nineteenth-century Scottish women took to stool-throwing. Instead, they unleashed the power of words. Most had had schooling opportunities not always open to their English contemporaries; training in rhetoric and composition no doubt made their verbal thrusts more telling. Scottish women learned to use their tongues to redirect male dominance. In home-making, child-rearing, teaching, and health-care jobs, women used stories, from ballads to local gossip, to add laughter, compassion, and surprise to the national sobriety and practicality. Scottish women who were professional writers offered stories featuring sharp-tongued, strong-willed, and often frustrated women, Spark's articulate Miss Brodie being a prime example. Women poets duplicated the cleverness as well as the passion and frustration.[6] Male writers in Scotland had put together their own portraits of strong-minded womanhood, from Scott's Flora Mac-Ivor and Galt's Lady Leddy to Barrie's Babbie, all of them talking their way through the world. Modern literary historians now turn sharp attention to stories, formal and informal, oral and written, by women writers, the forgotten and the well remembered, the conformists and the viragos. *A History of Scottish Women's Writing*, edited by Douglas Gifford and Dorothy McMillan, is a first and important gathering of analysis and celebration.[7]

Substitute Canada for Scotland in these generalizations. Here too a good educational system combined with official restrictions to produce generations of women clever enough to convert storytelling to their own subversive ends. Women like Mrs Moodie and her sisters, from the outskirts of Canadian political and economic power, raised voices that would establish and modify the identity of the nation. *Re(Dis)covering Our Foremothers*, edited by Lorraine McMullen, opened the door to a study of nineteenth-century Canadian women writers; *Silenced Sextet* moved in for a closer look at women writers whose achievements had been overlooked and underestimated.[8]

The women's stories were often casual, in a shaping talk apparently directionless, without the structuring of formal discourse. Such desultory talk had long seemed insignificant to deep thinkers, intellectuals. But as serious attention turned to women's history, women's ways of telling and listening began to catch critical attention. The new theorists of storytelling moved beyond Barthes, Heidegger, and Kierkegaard, who distinguished important, intellectual discourse from trivial 'idle talk.' Swinging the focus to gossip, vocalization, and focalization came another group of critics. They examined the connections between formal narrative and other forms of discourse, including gossip, traditionally linked to the women's world.[9]

Patricia Meyer Spacks, whose work on gossip underpins new interpretations of American and English writers,[10] places gossip and printed texts side by side and considers the way each consolidates and uses social power to affect status and opinion in a community (20). Spacks's subtext is that traditional association of gossip with women led to critical downplaying of 'the values of gossipy attentiveness to the minute, the personal, the human' (263) and suppressed recognition of the value of women's subversive 'speculations and inventions.' Feminist criticism has revalorized gossip.

Each community – and each nation – can recognize its own distinctness by listening to the gossip that women share, and reading the novels and short stories they write. It follows that it is important for Scots and Canadians to take another look at women's discourse. A study of the writings of Scottish and Canadian women illustrates the colonial/post-colonial, patriarchal/feminist, high/low literature oppositions and relates them to national peculiarities, Scottish and Canadian.[11] Women's storytelling now appears as one of the determinants both of people and of 'peoples,' that is, nations.

For, in spite of the international sense of sisterhood and the general sense of entering a global village in an age of electronic web-weaving, national sentiments persist. Spacks warns that nationalism can be 'an exclusionary alliance,' and collective talk can be a 'restrictive and reductive force' (260). Nevertheless, national discourse (both in literature and in gossip) helps to define relationships of individuals and a bordered country. Not geography and not economic pressures, but human talk sets the borders of a nation. Public discourse and private chat, or both of these, pulled into narrative and made into fiction, maintain national identity.

Storytelling of this identity-establishing sort has long been a specialty in Scotland. Narrative patterns reflect Scottish traditions of sermonizing and analysing sermons, and the long tradition of 'taking the Book' and rolling out the biblical cadences and committing the Bible stories to memory. Emphasis on story also comes from being a misty, sight-challenged, aural nation, and a double-language nation at that.[12] In Scotland, storytelling rises in part from the geography of isolating glens and survives in the stratified groupings of cities. Scottish storytelling is traditionally droll, with a mournful edge, passing on the folk tales and the gossip and the scandal and the needed practical information to listening families and neighbours. Many Scottish stories are ambiguous and open-ended. My Scottish friends used to joke about 'Caledonian anti-syzygy,' the Scottish refusal to come to a clear yoking of ideas into a single conclusion. Yet that is a recognizable feature of many Scottish fictions. It is also one of the features recognized as 'postmodern.'[13]

Canada, too, had to be a storytelling nation if social customs and connections were to be preserved in the face of geographical distances, physical barriers, regional separations. Some of the stories that early Canadians told and listened to were imported, and the native new ones tended to fall into imported patterns. New vistas opened as the Canadian air filled with a cumulation of voices, naming, re-naming, re-membering, re-counting. Increasingly, Canadian stories also featured the qualities recognized as postmodern: the fragmentation, the ambiguous endings, the play with voice, and the validation of experience once masked for propriety's sake. Linda Hutcheon, internationally respected as an analyst and apostle of postmodernism, clarifies the links between postmodernism in fiction and the contemporary state of Canada.[14]

Postmodernism in literature, in spite of the overlap between its features and those that feminists claim as having been strong, historically, in women's writing, is certainly not limited to female writers today. Postmodern writers, both male and female, transcend the traditional modes of storytellers. Male writers have absorbed narrative theory about codes and metafictions, and have observed the feminist resurrection of gossipy voice, ambiguity, and fragmentation. They sit comfortably holding that stool which the old woman once flung at chauvinism. How pleasant to feel the feminist fury subsiding, as we see male writers bow to the pressure of postmodernism and build into their work devices tentatively and perhaps unconsciously developed by earlier women writers! Modern practitioners, both men and women, put in play the newly available potentials of fiction. At the same time, in Scotland and in Canada at least, they add vistas of memory, subsuming the oldest layer of story-telling.

Here, finally, I open a door, first to view the work of women writers of past generations, Scottish and Canadian. These women told stories about women's concerns, interests, achievements, and frustrations. They told stories about falling in love and getting married, and also told stories that have nothing to do with those romantic courtship conventions. (Although, if the world is to be populated, those love stories must go on beaconing, beckoning.) They reported what people said in public and in private and how they said it, and they suggested the ways in which what people said differed from what they thought. They wove the small details of domestic life and personal relations into the bigger fabric of national interests and time-tied concerns.

Beyond that door another opens, revealing the writers, men and women, who build on the strengths of those early fictions, adding postmodern consciousness and techniques to traditional elements, Scottish and Canadian. These admired writers still make up new stories that, among all their other functions, reflect and create emerging and changing nationality.

Chapter Nine

Sinclair, Saunders, and the Outskirts of Story

Sinclair is not a name with the resonance of Burns or Scott or Carlyle. There are no Sinclair societies, no Sinclair newsletters, no annual toasts to 'the Immortal Memory' of Sinclair. But Sinclair's novels rivalled Scott's in their enormous and continuing sales; Sinclair's work was as dear as Burns's poems to thousands of nineteenth-century children; Sinclair was for a time a figure as well known for eccentricity and for comments on contentious issues as Carlyle.

Literary historians bypassed the Sinclair phenomenon when they retold the story of literature in Scotland. They postulated that a long hiatus yawned between 1832, when Scott died, and 1882, when young Robert Louis Stevenson emerged as a new 'wizard of the north.' In fact, however, literary historians saw a hiatus only because the most successful mid-century writers, and most of their readers, were women. The so-called hiatus was filled to overflowing with lively, readable books, satisfying the needs of women readers.

The life of women in democratic but Presbyterian Scotland was paradoxical. Barred from positions of power in kirk and state, yet educated beyond the level of English girls, they learned the stratagems of indirection. They converted their ambition into a fierce pushing of sons and brothers into desirable positions, and they wrapped quick talk and laughter around the hard life of a rarely affluent society. They governed by gossip.

They used story in lieu of sermonizing. Middle-class women used their new leisure in reading the work of women with interests like their own. Outstanding among the mid-century novelists who satisfied this Scottish audience was Catherine Sinclair.

Born in 1800, she was a bright child, daughter of a prominent political figure. The Right Honourable Sir John Sinclair had collated the *Statistical Account of Scotland* (1790–9), a very different kind of writing from the stories that his daughter would eventually produce. Her childhood was protected by his wealth and enlivened by her happy, boisterous brothers. The brothers, naturally, went on to college. Catherine, naturally, stayed home. But the 'women's sphere' of visits and shopping and household supervision was breached in her case. From the time she was fourteen, she added to her feminine pursuits a job as secretary to her political father. He died in 1835, and she was then more free to develop her own talents and to work on her long series of novels.

She had inherited enough political savvy to dedicate *Modern Accomplishments; or, The March of Intellect* (1836) to the young Princess Victoria, heir apparent to the British throne. But just as Sinclair had been barred from playing a strong role in politics because she was a woman, she was barred also as a storyteller from using what the poet Yeats called 'the supreme themes of love and war.' She could not, respectably, write of amorous adventures; nor could she recreate battles and bloodshed. Scotland had always treasured its storytellers, but the honoured epic bards had always been male. Catherine Sinclair turned to the kind of gossipy stories that women tell each other.

In the preface to *Modern Accomplishments*, she promised to 'draw from life' a picture of misguided educational practices leading to affectation. The show of outward prosperity fills the lives of the characters she creates: two sisters in winter residence in Edinburgh, principally because each has a young daughter of sixteen who must be 'married off.' One of the sisters is a vain socialite, the other a bluestocking, pretentious about her learning. There is a third, unmarried sister, over-conscious about her religious practices and as concerned about sanctimonious formalities as the others are about social proprieties. 'Modern accomplishments,' in other words, do not amount to much except a sterile formalism in education and religion.

Modern Accomplishments presents a woman's world of manoeuvres and manners, dress, furnishings, and the social rituals of visiting, tea parties, and churchgoing, exposing follies not with mordant irony but with quiet amusement. There is a Jane Austen touch here, but Sinclair is closer to unromantic Galt in her specification of dialect, diet, domestic arrangements, and clothing and her disdain for the hypochondriacs and the religious fanatics of her day. Two similar books, *Modern Society* (1837) and *Hill and Valley* (1838), followed *Modern Accomplishments*.

Her next accomplishment was a modern one indeed. In *Holiday House* (1839) she created the first and still-admirable non-didactic English-language book for children past the point of delighting in fairy tales, according to standard reference books.[1] Catherine Sinclair, once the fourth daughter in a large, lively family bent on hiding its feckless doings from a rather stern father, recreated pre-adolescent realities in Harry and Laura Graham, noisy and naughty, warm-hearted and mischievous, full of fun and notably without pious sentimentality. These children are not protected and supervised like Alice or Christopher Robin. They reflect the openness of an upper-class Scottish childhood.[2]

Sinclair returned to fiction for adults with *Modern Flirtations* (1841). She realized that adult women did not live in a 'holiday house.' Their work had changed with a changing economy and technology. The need to spin and card and weave at home was over, but 'fancy-work' must still weave the badge of success and status into household linen and apparel. Agricultural changes brought food products more varied and easier to prepare, but cookery must increasingly show affluence and style. Flirtations must centre on men who could settle women's social status. Other novels of the period, such as *Jane Eyre* and *Wuthering Heights*, featured male heroes (Heathcliff and Mr

Rochester) likely to please male readers as well as female ones because of their wild, macho qualities. Strong-minded Catherine Sinclair created no such portraits of domineering males.

Her life had settled into non-flirtatious spinsterhood. She became obsessed with religious controversies. Small wonder: in 1843 Scotland was torn by the 'Great Disruption,' a schism within Presbyterianism that threatened to be as divisive as the controversies of the Reformation or of the Covenanters. The Great Disruption absorbed all the reasoning, polemical powers of a preaching nation. Catherine Sinclair's next books concentrated on the need to remember and battle an old common foe. 'Popery' or 'Romanism' threatens the enslavement of young Scotswomen in *Jane Bouverie, and How She Became an Old Maid* (1846), *The Business of Life* (1848), and *Beatrice; or, The Unknown Relatives* (1852).

Mixing theology with stories of courtship proved a very saleable strategy. *Beatrice* reached sales of 100,000 in a few weeks; in England it outsold its 1852 competitor *Uncle Tom's Cabin*. Sinclair did not find sympathetic literary colleagues to hail her success or foster her talent, however. Although as a young woman she had been a welcome guest at Scott's Abbotsford, she was never part of the male circle of authors, editors, publishers, and reviewers who made Edinburgh a great literary centre. She lingered at the outskirts of storytelling.

Yet in spite of critical neglect, a world of great readers relished her novels. She had perfected the Scottish turn for lively chat, gossiping about minor eccentricities, local feuds, and social commonplaces. Each of her thirty-seven novels blended, in unthreatening form, the mirroring function of Galt and the preaching, teaching function of Carlyle. She added her own sense that the mirroring should be directed toward the life often hidden indoors among women, and the preaching focused on curable foibles rather than on existential doubts.

As she reached the far edge of middle age, Catherine Sinclair emerged as one of Edinburgh's eccentrics, a 'notable old soul' moving through the city's streets, square and solid, a juggernaut going where proper ladies never ventured – to the crowded markets of the lower town, to the tenements in old houses, a shocking contrast to the elegance of the New Town, the world of her fiction. Sinclair gave money from her considerable royalties to set up 'cooking depots' (forerunners of the soup kitchens of later depression periods). She outfitted a volunteer corps of peacekeepers and provided uniforms for a band of musicians. One lingering trace of her campaign to alleviate animal suffering appears still at some Edinburgh corners, where watering troughs for long-gone horses still carry plaques naming Catherine Sinclair as donor.

Her name is not listed in the excellent full index of Francis Hart's *The Scottish Novel* (1978). That index does list Margaret Oliphant (1828–1897). Oliphant was a fit successor to Sinclair in popularity and productivity, but a different kind of critical 'silencing' of women writers appears in her case. Her first novel, *Passages in the Life of Mrs. Margaret Maitland of Sunnyside*, was published in 1849 when she was only twenty-one years old. She pulled into her domestic sieve that all-important event of the period, the Disruption of the Presbyterian church. Margaret Maitland is an elderly spinster whose advice helps a young minister to cope with religious conflicts, while she also helps and advises him in his courting of her pupil, an heiress named Grace. Scottish critics generally refer to *Margaret Maitland* as the best fictional treatment of the 1843 schism.[3] But *Johnny Gibb of Gushetneuk* (1871), another Great Disruption novel, by the male Aberdonian author William Alexander, though stilted in tone and uncomfortably thick in dialect, has been graced with a modern reprinting, while *Margaret Maitland* has slipped into the 'out of print indefinitely' category.

Mrs Oliphant, like Carlyle, left Scotland for England (though with less drama: she went with her family to Liverpool). She eventually supported a silly husband and a drunken brother by 'scribbling' one, two, and sometimes three novels a year between 1849 and 1884, amounting to at least fifty-two novels.[4] Her best-known works, the 'Carlingford' series, are set in a vaguely English village. But books such as *Merkland: A Story of Scottish Life* (1851), *Harry Muir* (1853), and *Katie Stewart* (1853) proved the lasting sales potential of a Scottish setting.

Oliphant, in leaving Scotland, had gone to a country where

there were more markets for her work. She joined the nine-teenth-century parade of ex-Scots, including Byron, Ruskin, Carlyle, and Gladstone. England was also for Oliphant a place that accorded women critical recognition as well as monetary rewards. George Eliot, Charlotte Brontë, Mrs Gaskell, and their sister authors received the same welcome in reviews and in bookstores as Dickens, Thackeray, and Trollope.

Other 'scribbling women' continued to work in Scotland. (The phrase is Nathaniel Hawthorne's. A kindly man, loving husband, and good friend to individual women authors, Hawthorne still resented and mocked the female novelists – who cut into his own potential audience.) Robina Hardy, Catherine Crowe, Harriet Jay, Henrietta Keddie ('Sarah Tytler'), Mrs Howitt, Mrs S.C. Hall, and Dinah Mulock Craik published often in the proliferating family journals such as the *British Weekly*. London-based magazines, however, put pressure on Scottish writers to keep their local allusions whimsical, a political pressure on Scottish women that added to the general Victorian pressure to repress unpleasantness in their stories.

One late-Victorian Scotswomen who 'stayed home,' Annie S. Swan (1859–1943), enjoyed a career both popular and profitable. But she lived away from the centre of the literary scene in Edinburgh and Glasgow.[5] Scottish intellectuals subjected women writers like her to scorn, for their sentimentalism and simplicity. Annie Swan retorted that the writers of contemporary 'high' literature 'have, with a strange insistence and mysterious, dynamic force, clothed their meaning in imagery the simple-minded find it difficult to grasp.'[6] For their 'simple-minded' audience, these women dealt less with romantic love and more with the friendships between women, who entertain, enjoy, and amuse one another. From 1878 almost to the time of her death, Annie Swan produced novel after readable novel, over two hundred all told. She worked at the same loom as Sinclair, deftly weaving quiet stories about the lives of Scottish girls and women.

Threaded through these orthodox stories, however, subversive subtexts glint. Everyone knows about the sub-plots in Shake-

speare: the secondary stories in which clowns subtly under-
mine the grand drama of the courts. Nowadays, critics, especially feminist critics, talk not of sub-plot but of subtext. Mockery
of the notion that every maiden will find a hero and live happily ever after is built in (say subtext watchers) by metaphors
and allusions. Through such obliquity, emphasis is placed, not
on bonding and submission, but on flight and resistance. With
or without a 'happy ending,' such an enriched story can appeal
to repressed urges and fears and desires of the readers. The title
of a seminal study, *The Madwoman in the Attic*, by Sandra M.
Gilbert and Susan Gubar, is a witty allusion to *Jane Eyre* as a
sample of such oblique embedding of subtexts.[7] Annie Swan
could match Brontë in quiet subversion.

The gentle stories by nineteenth-century Scottish ladies make
easy reading. I first encountered the novels of Catherine Sinclair
and her successors during a bout of 'serious' research at the
National Library of Scotland. In off-hours I slipped easily into
their light stories for amusement – and found revelations of wit
and finesse.

Some of the latecomers among Scottish women writers were
less submissive. There was still no equivalent of the Bloomsbury
Group to harbour them. Virginia Woolf might demand a room
of her own. Her Scottish contemporaries, Catherine Carswell,
Violet Jacob, the Findlater sisters, and Willa Muir, found little
privacy. Few doors opened to them other than those in their
own households. Novels such as Carswell's *Open the Door!*
(1920) and Willa Muir's *Imagined Corners* (1931) underline the
degree of repression that was accepted as normal. More serious
in their concept of the function of fiction, they never achieved
wide popularity.

For a while they were also excluded from serious critical
consideration. Recent feminist criticism has increased their
respectability and widened their audience. In particular, the
neglect of Willa Muir's *Imagined Corners* has roused feminist
ire. The work of her husband, the poet-critic-translator Edwin
Muir, was showered with academic attention, gracefully tem-
pered with little notes to the effect that his wife played a large

part in 'his' productions.[8] Isobel Murray has recently suggested that Willa Muir's novel opened the door to many of the ideas that turned Lewis Grassic Gibbon's *A Scots Quair* into a national icon. Willa Muir's work, published when Gibbon was beginning his trilogy, helped the now-revered novelist construct his female character, Chris Guthrie.[9]

Indeed, the focus on a woman's life by Gibbon shows the popular conception of womanhood. Chris is largely defined by her series of marriages. By some critics, she has also been seen as a symbol of Scotland, 'Chris Caledonia.' Again, her marriages – first to a wild Highlander, next to a Presbyterian minister tied up in intellectual confusions, and finally to a worker who leaves and goes to Newfoundland – may represent a sequence of epochs in the life of Scotland. Certainly, they delineate three of the Scottish elements that contributed to the downgrading of womanhood.

Gibbon's portrait of a woman garnered a great sheaf of critical commentary. Catherine Carswell's *Open the Door!* appears nowadays on reading lists for courses in women's studies, but there were virtually no analyses of it in Scottish literary journals before the 1990s – seventy years of neglect.[10] Regardless of their intricacy of structure and the subtlety of psychological analysis, *Open the Door!* and *Imagined Corners* are still at the outskirts of the literary canon, although they now appear in the new reprint finery afforded by feminist presses.

Even in the bland and pleasant stories of their gentle contemporary, O. Douglas, subversive subtexts lurk. In non-literary life, Douglas, Tweedside author of the 1920s, was Anna Buchan (1877–1948), stay-at-home sister of the overachieving John Buchan. Her *Penny Plain* (1920), *Pink Sugar* (1924), and other novels, like Catherine Sinclair's books, ostensibly tell stories about young people finding happiness in love. But each also puts the gender stamp of value on quiet decency and unobtrusive self-sacrifice. Each O. Douglas book presents a picture of a quiet girl left behind by a more fortunate brother. In *Penny Plain* a little act of kindness brings Jean, the quiet girl, a Cinderella bounty of wealth and a chance to help her brother, away at college, and a second brother, preparing to go to college too. No longer a 'beggar maid,' Jean can accept a lordly suitor without loss of pride. Happiness is crowned by a trip away from rainy Scotland to see *As You Like It* performed in sunny Stratford – a metaphoric climax to an unlikely romance. (On the night before her fairy-tale wedding, Jean's younger brother, Jock, mocks *Romeo and Juliet*, '[a] silly love-play, but there's a fine scene at the end where they all get killed' [302].) Having married her lord, Jean gives him her version of the 'King Cophetua' fairy tale: 'I've no doubt it was all right for him, but it can't have been much fun for the beggar maid ... But ... Money only matters when you haven't got any' (312). This beggar maid's book ends not with lovemaking but with friendly talk.

Pink Sugar has a sadder ending. This is in part the story of another little minister, marrying a pretty girl from far away (like the author's brother John Buchan marrying Susan Grosvenor). But there is a sister, left behind by romance. She speaks with deadly honesty to the charming lady who has fostered the romance. 'You thought, because I was dumpy and had a red face and uninteresting hair that I must want brightening ... What do you know about keeping a house? Have you ever got up on winter mornings and lit fires and washed front doorsteps? Do you know what it is to wash dishes and scrape pots until your hands smell of dish-cloths, and you can't keep decently tidy, and life is one long preparing of meals and clearing them away?' (252). 'And now I'm losing Rob ...,' she continues. 'I think he has made a foolish choice. I know nothing against the girl, but she's young, and she's English, and not likely to know much about housekeeping, and as for managing a kirk –!' (253). This is 'writing beyond the ending,' the romantic happy ending.[11] Later, when her own thin dream of romance ends, Rebecca weeps 'a few hot difficult tears' (310). *Lachrimae rerum* – not the tragic tears for death in battle but a woman's small tears, falling in bitter self-pity, or rather, held back from falling because of pride and propriety. In the last moment of the O. Douglas book, however, again 'beyond the ending,' Rebecca makes a pudding, 'not a plain rice pudding ... but a bread pudding with jam on the top' (312). It is a homely and wholesome Scottish equivalent for pink sugar.

Penny Plain and *Pink Sugar* take their titles from the candies that gave Scottish children a dose of sweetness to keep energy high in the cold days. A character in *Pink Sugar* cries, 'I do *hate* people who sneer at sentiment. What is sentiment after all? It's only a word for all that is decent and kind and loving in these warped little lives of ours' (167). 'Quite so,' says her male interlocutor drily, and she is silenced – momentarily, at least.

Like many other women, O. Douglas adopted a nom de plume that disguised the fact of her being a woman. It did not save her from critical condescension. The best that reviewers could say was that her style was something like her brother's.[12] Like so many others, she was the victim of a peculiarly Scottish patriarchy. It was a patriarchy tender and protective, but un-yielding and imperturbable, perpetuating the position of a lover who sees his girl as a 'bonnie wee thing,' of a son unthinkingly grateful to his mother for sacrificing so much for him (though not for his sister), of churchmen encouraging mission bands and money-raising auxiliaries but barring the pulpit to women. O. Douglas was barred from many fields that welcomed her brother. But she was not timid in depicting the real longings of women of all ages for the sweetness of love, home, security, independence, and understanding friends. She worked well in her narrow plot and achieved a devoted readership.

Canadian women worked hard in their gardens, in the bush, in the villages, and in the suburbs. They grew roses as well as cabbages. Housework and child-rearing were hard too, but from the beginning women in Canada found time to read: stories in the religious journals – the Roman Catholic *Pilot*, the Presbyterian *Witness* – and in the farm papers – the *Family Herald and Weekly Star*, the *Farmer's Advocate*, the *Prairie Farmer*. Most of the journals came to the man of the house, but the story sections found their way into women's hands. They were passed around after church or at tea parties or temperance rallies.

Many of the reputable books and magazines designed for women came from the United States – *Godey's Lady's Book, Youth's Companion* – but a few were Canadian. Books by Catherine Sinclair, Annie Swan, and O. Douglas also came in steady succession to Canadian readers.

They suited an ever-growing audience of women readers, supplementing rather than competing with home-grown products. In Canada too, there had been a growth in women's education and in leisure for reading, imported or native. Between Haliburton's *The Clockmaker* in 1836 and Leacock's *Sunshine Sketches of a Little Town* in 1912, both world best-selling authors, there had occurred in Canada also (again, according to literary historians and critics, most of them male) a hiatus in local fiction. Here again, however, as in Scotland, women writers in fact filled the gap.

Their work followed the same sequence as Scottish writers: from gentle, amusing stories in the 1860s to brilliant complexity in the early twentieth century. *Silenced Sextet* documents the presence of at least six polished professionals among the 'regiment of scribbling women.'[13] Many more names could be added to the six: Lily Dougall, Agnes Machar, Jean McIlwraith, Isabel Ecclestone Macpherson MacKay – the 'pulled-out-of-the-air' list rings with Scottish echoes. The ever-hungry popular press, represented in Canada most strongly by the *Literary Garland* in early days and later by the *Canadian Illustrated News*, the *Canadian Magazine*, and others, gave them an opening, an incentive, and a model for writing. Some sent their work to American publishers. *Sybil Campbell; or, The Queen of the Isle* (1861) by May Agnes Fleming came out first from Beadle and Adams of New York. The title suggests that even an Irish Canadian like Fleming was well aware of the selling power of Scottish names and themes.

Writers such as Margaret Murray Robertson and Margaret Marshall Saunders, just to name two with strong Scottish affiliations, dominated publishing in production and sales. Like their Scottish models, they reflected little of contemporary turmoil. Their work contained no Darwinian speculations about nature, no loss of belief in a benign, reasonable, God-created universe, no sense of hidden vice, no resentment of class or gender exploitation, no urban malaise or labour troubles. They did not soar to heights of any kind of passion, whether religious, sexual, or aesthetic.

Margaret Murray Robertson (1823–1897),[14] in *Shenac's Work at Home: A Story of Canadian Life* (1866), dramatically underlined the differences for women between Scotland and Canada, the old world and the new one. *Shenac*, like Sinclair's *Holiday House*, was written for young readers. But the youth portrayed on the Canadian backwoods farm is not frolicsome or flirtatious; it is sombre, dominated by harsh necessities of productiveness. Shenac MacIvor's work is hard seasonal farm labour, necessitated by the death of her father. She forces her shy self to bargain with the neighbour farmer for help with the harvest, then for a market for the wool she spins and the lengths of cloth she weaves to make sturdy clothing, blankets, and rugs. Her entrepreneurial spirit links with quiet piety as she moves toward maturity.

By tracing Shenac's humble love for the local Presbyterian minister, Robertson draws the readers of the book into the religious turmoil of Canadian Presbyterian revivalism of 1864. The forming of the Free Church in Canada in that year created upheaval similar to the Scottish Disruption of 1843. In this focus, though not in grace and lightness, *Shenac's Work at Home* is comparable to Oliphant's *Margaret Maitland*. The attitude of the young Canadian minister to the hard-working farm girl is, however, very different from that of Oliphant's hero to his cultured, sensitive, and socially adept Scottish love, so aptly named Grace. Shenac is sent away to Montreal for schooling that will make her fit to marry a minister. The author explains, 'In Shenac's country, happily, it is not considered a strange thing that a young girl should wish to pursue her education even after she is twenty' (407). Certainly, the result appears satisfactory: 'In the manse, and in the parish, Shenac has never, in her husband's estimation, failed to fill well her allotted place' (409). She lives in an old Calvinism, the Presbyterianism of the

Covenanters, the faith that her contemporaries embraced when they walked out of the old kirk into a church even more rigid. How could she resist the benign patriarchy of her husband without the impiety of resentment against her stern, patriarchal God?

The pious quality of *Shenac's Work at Home* is reflected in its publication first by the American Sunday-School Union of Philadelphia and then its republication by the British Religious Tract Society in 1868. Its wider appeal, however, is evidenced in the fact that the major publishing house of Nelson in London and Edinburgh reissued the novel in 1889, with reprints in 1892, 1901, and 1904. In Canadian terms, it was a best-seller.

Margaret Robertson had been born in Scotland before her family emigrated. Some of her novels – *The Bairns* (1870), *The Inglises* (1872), and *David Fleming's Forgiveness* (1879), for instance – are divided between Scottish and Canadian settings. Others, such as *The Orphans of Glen Elder* (1868) and *The Twa Miss Dawsons* (1880), are set in Scotland, aiming more directly at the audience that Sinclair and others had established. None of Robertson's books is more Scottish than *Shenac's Work at Home*, though it is set entirely in the Canadian Glengarry. Women characters appeared in her stories in plain, decent dress, without idolatrous gilding or vainglorious elaboration. Literally, the dress might still contain a touch of plaid, since the taste for tartan, long ago spread by Scott, still lingered. But the cut of the dress was Canadian.

Robertson was an ingenious professional, good at finding topics and markets. Nevertheless, in Lovell's directory of addresses for Montreal, where she lived for many years with her brother, who is listed as 'Lawyer,' she simply appears among 'others of the household.' Her nephew, the Reverend Charles Gordon, writing as 'Ralph Connor,' wrote stories of the same sort about the Canadian Glengarry backwoods. His books were taken much more seriously by critics. The Ralph Connor stories quickly attracted the attention of (male) literary historians and held that attention for a century. Margaret Robertson, on the other hand, though she made a good living out of her writing, was still at the outskirts of her profession, kept there by traditional academic inattention. *In Re(Dis)covering Our Foremothers*, papers from a symposium on nineteenth-century women writers edited by Lorraine McMullen, Carole Gerson presents important and startling statistics on 'Anthologies and the Canon of Early Canadian Women Writers' (55–66). She quotes a scathing comment: 'What is commonly called literary history is actually a record of choices' (65). Most choices are made by anthologists oblivious of women's claims. (Gerson does not even list Margaret Robertson among the excluded, so thoroughly has she been forgotten.) In part, this is just a variant of what was happening to women, especially to women writers, everywhere. In part, however, it showed some peculiarities traceable to the still-strong Scottish strain, legacy of a peculiar Presbyterian patriarchy.

Sara Jeannette Duncan (1861–1922) is among the elite few women writers remembered, respected, anthologized. Her work has been thoroughly praised and analysed by a wide range of critics – a tribute much greater than any of her contemporary Scotswomen has been accorded.[15] No amount of study can diminish the freshness, the charm, and the relevance of *The Imperialist* (1904). Few of the male Canadian writers who were her contemporaries in the early twentieth century could rival her on even one of those counts.

Among its other claims to attention, *The Imperialist* should be a required text for feminists. Advena is a fine study of a young woman's ability, yearning, self-awareness, and self-delusion. As she moves westward, she is ready to change the pattern of her life, to justify her strange name – a 'new woman' indeed. In Canada, attitudes to gender roles were changing more quickly than in Scotland. From her reading, Duncan knew enough about the Scottish heritage to delineate the imported norm and to discriminate the Canadian deviance. Just as Canadian politicians were taking the lead in discussing trade constraints with the 'mother country' in the political sections of *The Imperialist*, so Advena's openness is set against the double closures of the two Presbyterian ministers: Dr Drummond, practical and manipulative, and Hugh Finlay, unworldly and quixotic, with a hypersensitive conception of honour.

The Imperialist is a major locus for tracing the persistence of Scottish traditions in Canadian life, both domestic and theological. It should also be required reading for anyone interested in post-colonialism and the process by which a country moves toward a lessening of imperial ties. Duncan wrote the book in part as an optimistic report on the erosion of old imperialisms. The imperious male power in marriage and in the church was giving way to a new 'common wealth' approach in international relations.

Sara Jeannette Duncan left Canada. She married an Englishman and moved to India. She wrote a splendid series of novels set in imperial power circles there. The colonial life of even a simple memsahib left her free to write as she pleased – and she pleased to write with a Jamesian elegance and sophistication impossible to achieve in Scots-Canadian 'Elgin,' Ontario.

Ontario had produced a small hero for another Canadian woman, roughly contemporary with Duncan. Margaret Marshall Saunders (1861–1947)[16] made her name and her fortune telling the story of a dog named, with irony, 'Beautiful Joe.' From her own day to the present, Saunders's reputation as a writer of animal stories for children has blurred the real value of her achievements as a novelist.

Margaret Marshall Saunders grew up in the Maritimes. Born in Milton, Nova Scotia, she moved with her family to Halifax in 1867. She was sent to finishing school, not to 'the Boston States,' as was common for girls in Nova Scotia, but to Edinburgh.[17] There one of her great dreams was to meet George Macdonald, author of *At the Back of the North Wind* (1871), the tender story concerned in part with a poor boy's attachment to a horse. She was disappointed; Macdonald's Edinburgh visit was cancelled. But the Scottish model helped to shape Saunders's first efforts at writing. She began work on animal stories, a genre as old as Aesop but newly attractive in the post-Darwinian period. The new strength perhaps began with Macdonald and moved through Anna Sewall's *Black Beauty* (1877); after Saunders's

Beautiful Joe (1894),[18] it finally circled back to Edinburgh with Eleanor Atkinson's *Greyfriars Bobby* (1912).

Saunders was of a generation that still felt the need of a non-female pen name. 'Maggie' to her family and to the Scottish friends she made during a year at school in Edinburgh, she chose to send out manuscripts under the sterner name of Marshall. Eventually that name would be famous worldwide as that of the author of excellent animal stories. Her first full-length animal story, *Beautiful Joe*, written on the spur of a publisher's challenge, became a best-seller. She was also, however, the author of adult stories, wrongly forgotten.

In *Beautiful Joe*, Saunders speaks in a male voice. Unusual: many men have claimed to express the psyche of women, from *Clarissa* and *Pamela* to *Madame Bovary* and *Portrait of a Lady*, but women rarely reverse the process. Saunders writes as an unattractive, mutilated male animal, the dog named 'Beautiful Joe.' As such, her persona is free to wander, observe, and involve himself in many unsightly and dangerous situations – freer in movement than a female would be in 1894.

Saunders's adult stories focused on young women who moved with equal, and equally unusual, freedom. *Rose à Charlitte* (1898),[19] an Acadian story, features two women, underlining the difference between freedom and restraint. The first, Rose (known, like 'Malcolm's Katie,' as an attribute of a man, Charlitte de Forêt), harbours the traditional women's loves, for her family and her child. But Bidiane, the girl dominating the second half of the book, steps out into the political sphere, rallying women to fight for the rights of the underprivileged Acadians of Nova Scotia. Bidiane is a new kind of heroine.[20] The story of Bidiane and Rose is again told from the viewpoint of a male narrator, Bostonian Vesper Nimmo.

Bidiane is followed in Saunders's later novels, first by Berty Graveley in *The Story of the Graveleys* (1903). Berty espouses the kind of causes that Saunders had herself worked for in Halifax – control of child labour, temperance, community action, parks and playgrounds. Women in the book support her, but the men do not. Berty says sadly, 'You men don't suffer ... You men all have votes.' Next, in *The Girl from Vermont: The Story of a Vacation School Teacher* (1910), Patty Green fights for the rights of abused children, all the way to court, where she makes an impassioned political speech. She also argues as a pacifist and as a feminist against the patriarchal judicial system. Here is a sharp difference from *The Imperialist*. Sara Jeannette Duncan presents her Advena as venturing into new areas of thought but leaving politics to her brother. Lorne and his cronies discuss imperialism in the dining room, while Advena and the young minister discuss Browning in the library. And the mother works in the kitchen, preparing an oyster casserole for the old minister, Dr Drummond.

Saunders set her enterprising young women in American settings, on the advice of an American publisher, in hope of reaching a larger audience. She herself, though she lived for a while in Bangor, Maine, and in California, returned to Canada and continued to support herself and her sister by her work. She wrote an endless popular stream of animal stories – *Golden Dicky: The Story of a Canary and His Friends*, *Pussy Black-Face*, *'Boy': The Wandering Dog*, and so on – always tucking some subversive politics into the children's stories.

For one of the last of her books, Marshall Saunders chose a half-Scottish name: *Bonnie Prince Fetlar* (1920). The prince is a Shetland pony. An American boy named Dallas Duff, visitor at a cottage in Muskoka, rides him to an adventurous climax. But the real centre of the story is Cassowary (her real name is 'Jeanne Mance,' after the saintly nurse-teacher in historic Montreal). Cassowary is an unsaintly rebel – disobeying rules and taunting one of the boys that he is adopted. It turns out that she is the one that was adopted. Cassowary is no effervescent orphan like Anne of Green Gables.[21] She is turbulent and mean, a dark shadow in a happy holiday house. Saunders introduces poetry into the story, not 'The Lady of Shalott' but the rough camp songs that even a proper girl could sing at campfires in cottage country:

I'm Captain Jinx of the Horse Marines;
I feed my horse on pork and beans;
I kiss the ladies in their teens –
For that's the way in the army!

Saunders had published so many animal books that no one
paid any attention to this one. As a young 'lady in her teens'
in Montreal West, however, I found *Bonnie Prince Fetlar* both
exciting and disturbing. Cassowary opened too many doors of
frustration and rebellion.

Saunders lived long enough to be known, like Catherine
Sinclair, as an eccentric old body. She built a house, not at the
outskirts of the city, but on a ravine in the heart of downtown
Toronto. It was a strange building, with open porches at the
bottom of the ravine to give a winter home to the squirrels and
raccoons and foxes that proper Torontonians avoided. Win-
dows on the middle floor were open so that birds could fly in,
flutter up an inside shaft, and fly out again at the top level.
Saunders played an active part in the Canadian Authors Association. L.M. Montgomery, who met her there, found her odd
but enjoyed reading *Golden Dicky* to her own son, Chester.

Like other Canadian women serving the huge reading public
of the early part of the twentieth century, Margaret Marshall
Saunders followed the Scottish moralists in building didactic
messages into her energetic, realistic novels. Her stories of the
clash between self-fulfilment and duty were in part at least a
legacy from Scottish models. Like the Scottish women writers,
she sensibly avoided dealing with battle scenes and moments
of high ritual. Notably, she drew on a wide range of relationships other than those of courtship. Perhaps this was a result of
the fact that, like Catherine Sinclair, she remained a spinster.
Perhaps it simply reflects her recognition of the interests of her
readers. She knew that (whatever men may assume to the
contrary) women do not spend most of their time thinking
about men.

But her novels were swept aside by reviewers, who preferred
the stronger stuff of contemporary males such as Frederick

Philip Grove and Morley Callaghan. These two authors, like many other male writers of less appeal, are accorded full-chapter treatment in the *Literary History of Canada*. Saunders gets sixteen consecutive lines in the chapter on fiction, including a bare reference to her earliest adult novel, *My Spanish Sailor*, and a kindly glance at *Rose à Charlitte* (1:334–5); four lines and sporadic name references in the chapter on nature writers (1:382, 396–7, 399). Elsewhere her name appears only in long lists of also-ran writers.

In Canada, women like Margaret Robertson, Marshall Saunders, and 'Marian Keith' had absorbed from their readings of Scottish imports the idea that writing stories about women's work and home life was a proper and profitable employment for a lady. The unbroken succession of successful women writers in Canada showed the cumulative effect of confidence. A prime example of a modern writer's acknowledgment of the empowerment she felt when reading the work of an earlier woman writer is Alice Munro's 'Afterword' to L.M. Montgomery's *Emily of New Moon*. 'What's central to the story,' Munro says, '... is the development of a child – and a girl child at that – into a writer.' She continues, 'We're there as Emily gets on with this business, pounces on words in uncertainty and delight, takes charge and works them over and fits them dazzlingly in place.'[22]

When Munro says 'We're there,' she means 'I was there,' as a girl born to be a writer but still unsure if such work was possible. She is writing of empowerment, the empowerment of one writer by another's assurance, the empowerment of one Canadian writer by an earlier Canadian woman writer's relevance and effectiveness. The work of reassurance goes back from Munro through Montgomery to Isabella Valancy Crawford, perhaps, and from there back through Susanna Moodie to Scott and Galt, and to Catherine Sinclair, the forgotten successor to Scott and Galt.

In Scotland the success of Catherine Sinclair and Margaret Oliphant encouraged Scotswomen to think of writing as a career and to expect to find publishers for lively, low-key, unromantic stories. One did not have to be a great intellectual like George Eliot or a neurotic genius like Emily Brontë to set out on a writing career. Remembering Sinclair and Oliphant and *their* predecessors, including Susan Ferrier and Elizabeth Hamilton, many Scottish women writers could and did produce well-wrought, engaging novels, from Annie Swan to other underestimated but successful writers such as Helen MacInnes, Mary Stewart, D.E. Stevenson, Dorothy Dunnett, and Josephine Tey. The names of Scottish women writers who have received more critical attention swell the list: Violet Jacob, Catherine Carswell, Willa Muir, Muriel Spark, Naomi Mitchison, a long catalogue of women encouraged in their ambition to write by the success of their forerunners.[23]

Nevertheless, about all the forerunners, the now-forgotten women writers who opened the door to modern success, it is appropriate to quote the questions – and the comments – which end *Silenced Sextet*:

> Are these novels indeed the work of writers who knuckled under in tough circumstances and dissipated their talents? Or are they the work of writers clever enough to embed still-powerful messages in formulaic stories and stereotypical characters? Did these works disappear because they lacked depth, or were they unfairly bypassed by a biased academy? Must we assume that they are inferior to the works that have been judged valuable by recent critics ...? Have we here a case of non-survival of the fittest? ... As a group they ... offer us a broad and richly detailed view of the literary activity and exchange of their times, the models and taste of their country and its regions, the channels of dissemination of entertainment and ideas, and the modes and pressures of critical reception. Besides performing these solemn and honourable tasks, [they] can still be counted on to provide all the ingredients of a good read – laughter, suspense, pathos, stimulating ideas, and vicarious thrills. We hope they can be taken seriously by future literary historians – but not so seriously as to undercut their primary function – to capture and captivate yet further generations of readers. (207, 208)

Chapter Ten

Duncan, Munro, and the Vistas of Memory

Scottish fiction turned a corner away from compliance and sentiment soon after the end of the Second World War. Muriel Spark (b. 1918) published her first novel in 1957; her best-known work, *The Prime of Miss Jean Brodie* (1961) has a tart tone far from O. Douglas's gentle subversions. Spark exposed the life of a woman liberated in career choice and in sexuality, though not free from pressures social, professional, or psycho-logical. One of the elements that characterizes and changes Miss Brodie's Edinburgh world is gossip, of the malicious sort: the gossip of her colleagues in the staff room and the gossip of the little girls who defeat the dream of her prime. Miss Brodie epitomized the frustration of post-war women, at home in Scotland and abroad in comparable societies (including Canada), where liberation into careers and work outside the home did not bring freedom from gender stereotyping and limitation. Spark's sympathy is dipped in a sophisticated acidity, directed at the protagonist as well as at the unrealizing world. There are several touches in her novel that smack of the postmodern. She builds in a portrait of an artist, a painter, with some of the qualities that Spark or any artist must have – self-absorption, obsessive immersion in art. Second, she makes suggestive use of old songs, songs of Scottish history, assigned to a rather laughable, or at least a victimized, character. *The Prime of Miss Jean Brodie* is her only truly Scottish novel, although some critics have found it worth arguing the opposite.[1] Muriel Spark moved away to London when she was eighteen. For all the works of her long career she has been well rewarded with sophisticated reviewers' attention, not least in Scotland.[2]

George Mackay Brown stayed – stayed to fully explore the Scottish narrative tradition and the labyrinths of Scottish personality. In *Greenvoe* (1972) he uses narrative devices like Margaret Laurence's: camera eye, memory bank, rhetorical rant mixed with homely detail. 'Carlylean' is a fit tag for Brown, as for Laurence. His inferno is not just the Carlylean fire of personal doubt and disbelief, however. The village of Glenvoe and the whole Orkney isle of 'Hellya' are consumed not only by human weakness and by natural disaster but by the machines of a mindless technological 'progress.' Brown draws on memories of the Highland Clearances, but he sees displacement as still to come.

Violence seethes beneath the surface of the Orkney village. Here, as in *Witch Wood*, is a little minister; but this one is addicted not to a beautiful woman but to alcohol. His mother tortures herself with Calvinist terrorism, a daily interior inquisition into her guilt and shame. That is just one thread in an absorbing, poetic book.[3] As in *The Prime of Miss Jean Brodie*, the figure of an artist is built into *Greenvoe* – a writer, The Skarf – who adds a self-reflexive note to the novel, with his sonorous readings of ancient Orkney sagas. The storyteller connects village life with ancient history and myth, opening a long vista into the past. There is another 'writer' in *Greenvoe* too, however, a stranger who makes destructive, reductive notes (mostly wrong) on everyone in the village. In the whirl of farcical personalities, Brown himself, the true creator, almost disappears. Shifting perspective, incongruous juxtapositions, and apparent randomness of order add to the sense of sudden violence in the story. Chaos adds to the richness of reading experience, according to chaos theorists such as Katherine Hayles; the experience of reading *Greenvoe* justifies the comment.[4]

Yet the novel ends with survivors returning to perform an ancient ritual, most frightening and most hopeful – the ritual of death and resurrection. The dramatic dialogue of the village men as they enact traditional initiations says the same thing as The Skarf's tale of Vikings says: that memories are long in the Highlands and Islands, but that there are many ways of distilling them. Brown reaped rewards for this and his other fictions: an OBE, literary prizes, and warm and thoughtful reviews.

At first glance, Jane Duncan's work seems simpler in narrative method, to the point of naïveté. But the Jane Duncan story is not simple. First, 'Jane Duncan' is the nom de plume of Elizabeth Jane Cameron (1910-1976), who gossiped four times, and in four moods, about her own life and times. Elizabeth Cameron's memory is long too, though she did not grow up in the Highlands. She went to the home of a Highland grandmother for her summer holidays, but she grew up on the outskirts of Glasgow with her policeman father and her stepmother. From there to university, to the RAF in wartime, and then back to Scotland, where she fell in love with an engineer, and with him, she moved to Jamaica. Never did she tell him about her terrible, wonderful urge to write. But by the time he died, she had secretly written seven novels, most of them in the months when he was dying. Maybe going a long way from home had freed her from asking herself, 'What will people think?' (the anthem of women in a small society). His death freed her to contact a publisher. Swift acceptance, swift demand for more. When she sailed back to Britain in 1958 at the age of forty-eight, it was with a contract for three books and an assured interest in the other four on the part of Macmillan of London. They were published under the pseudonym Jane Duncan. (Publishers no longer bolt, wince, or shy away from a woman's name at the top of a manuscript. They have the reassuring memory of big sales for the mixed myriad of women writers who emerged in the twentieth century to carry away the sales records in every country.)

'This is the kind of person I am,' says Janet Sandison, the narrator in the first of Jane Duncan's 'My Friend' series, as if it were possible to explain the kind of person anyone is. But by the end of this series and its successors, we have a mysterious

sense of the writer's self, as well as of her masks. 'Yes, I am a
person like this: I am very keen on words,' says Janet Sandison
as she begins to gossip. She chats confidently about her friends
and acquaintances, always with the certainty that at core she is
a blithe being, a woman who was a treasured child in a warm
family. Grandparents, uncles and aunts, mother and father –
the circle readies Janet for a step out to the village school, to the
academy, to a first job as a nursemaid and a subsequent stint as
secretary, a turn in the intelligence office of wartime army,
secretarial and managerial work in an engineering plant, and
on and on, always finding friends who amuse, irritate, push,
tug, and absorb her. In the first book in the My Friends series,
My Friends the Miss Boyds (1959), she shifts, like a casual conver-
sationalist doubling back on herself, from stories that convey
her own assurance and competence to early memories of the
silliness and tragedy of unmarried women aging in the village
of Achcraggan, where marriage, the only career possible for
women, happens to be shut to them. She fuzzes the events of
the past with her own childish incomprehension, adding subtle
shadows to the village gossip. As memories weave inconse-
quentially through Janet Sandison's later stories, some grim,
some amusing, some frightening, Janet herself remains set on
telling her reader (and herself) 'the kind of person I am.' The
kind of writer she is is one who draws from gossip, speculation, dream recalls, memory dips, local history and legends;
one who adds ironic undercuttings; one who manipulates actuality to gain the fictional values of surprise and suspense; one
who seems to round off a story while still leaving puzzlement
and eagerness to hear 'what happened next.'

The early My Friends books (fifteen of them, from *My Friends
the Miss Boyds* and *My Friend Muriel*, both in 1959, to *My Friends
the Hungry Generation*, 1968) tell witty, friendly, self-amused,
reader-involving stories of a protected childhood and an introspective, wise, and generally happy adult experience. Jane
Duncan gave readers the portrait of a modern woman, without
acidity. She included everyone in the circle of friendship. Her
storytelling, though gossipy, is not reductive, exclusive, aggres-

sive, defensive. She offers anecdotes about people you would like to know (and some you are glad not to know), presented with the true sound of talk, self-interrupting, backward-glancing, guessing, interpreting; giving readers the feeling that the narrator is growing more familiar and yet more mysterious in the reticences, lacunae, overemphases. Scottish gossip about the Sandison home in 'Reachfar,' in this case, although the stories range also to London and to the West Indies.

All the My Friends stories are interwoven in a cat's cradle. The stories of the dead may open again with new insights or a flood of recovered memories. In spite of loss and change, the one binding thread in all the My Friends books is the affirmation of love – love for the elderly mentors who protect her childhood, amused affection for her weird clutch of co-workers, passion for Twice Alexander (who carries her away from Scotland when he accepts a job in the British West Indies), vulnerability to his domineering direction of her life, and openness to devastation at his death.

At this point in real life, Elizabeth Cameron, in a revulsion from the essentially upbeat quality of the Jane Duncan books, began composing her second series of four novels. A new narrator, named Jean Robertson, talks in two of these about another, darker childhood. The rest of Jean Robertson's story is told by male narrators, complicating the reader's comprehension of the girl who grows up in Glasgow suburbs and slums when her uprooted Highland father turns policeman and remarries. Against a gritty background, the four Jean Robertson stories unfold, with a fairy-tale cast of ogres, wicked stepmothers, cripples, and Cinderella. But these are stories without a conventional fairy-tale ending; the climax is brutal, the resolution an empty prosperity.

Elizabeth Cameron published these four books between 1969 and 1975, not as by 'Jane Duncan' but as by 'Janet Sandison.' Having begun to tell the story of another part of her life in another way, Cameron was free to return to her first persona. The next book by 'Jane Duncan' climaxes Janet Sandison's life story in *My Friend the Swallow* (1970), in which Twice Alexander dies, and Janet Sandison Alexander rises as author of books about her friends. Janet, like her true creator, Elizabeth Cameron, has always repressed the urge to write. Fear of failure, fear of mockery, repression because of her lover's need for her and his jealousy of her absorption in old stories, all have held her from writing. Now the narrator tells the story of her stories. The later My Friends books (from *My Friend the Swallow* in 1970 to *My Friends George and Tom* in 1976) face the fact of the death of Janet's mate and tell of her return to Scotland. These stories and the Jean Robertson ones are interlaced in publishing dates.

Late in life Elizabeth Cameron began weaving in another set of books: stories for children – 'the hungry generation.' In a short span of time she published eight of these children's books, fantasy adventures about 'the Camerons' (named for her nieces and nephews), drawn from earliest memories of a croft in northeast Scotland, near the Cromarty Firth. The Camerons reflect the life of the sensitive child who flickered in flashbacks in the Janet Sandison series. Their magic world braids in with the blunt realism of the late 'Reachfar' scenes and the depressing and repressing atmosphere created in the Jean Robertson books.

The series of pseudonyms masks the author's essential life, even though the old need to use a male-sounding nom de plume had disappeared. There was still a social and familial pressure against authorship, particularly for women. And maybe there is a particularly Scottish quality here, a desire for privacy, a feeling, like Sir Walter Scott's, that fiction has a frivolous connotation for dwellers in a serious country.

At any rate, in 1976 Elizabeth Cameron published *A Letter from Reachfar* in response to readers' requests for details of her 'real' life and working habits. It was published under the now highly marketable name of Jane Duncan. In it Cameron stripped off pompousness and pretensions, and revealed the mystery and inexplicable coincidences, spurts, stagnations, and loneliness of her life as a writer. This is an exceptionally convincing revelation of her late, troubled, and troubling development as a writer.

A Letter from Reachfar is a selective story still. For instance, there is little account of her warm and fostering connections with all sorts of younger writers. These included (of major interest to Canadians) the young Margaret Laurence. When Laurence was in England in the 1960s, working on her major novels, she went up north to Scotland in search of her roots. At the suggestion of Alan McLean, her editor at Macmillan's of London, she went to the Black Isle to visit Elizabeth Cameron, most successful of McLean's cadre of authors. *A Letter from Reachfar* leaves no record of how Cameron reacted to the Canadian novelist. But they shared literary roots. Margaret Laurence, in exile, found a colleague in the woman who had recreated her Scottish past while equally far from home.

Like other 'exiles and emigrés,' Elizabeth Cameron had found a way to voice her Scottish experiences while she was living abroad, in Jamaica in her case. Her complicated story illuminates the complexity of creating stories that will catch a national quality and yet suggest the multiplicity of nationalism, in account with a multi-layered perceiver. Lorena and Francis Hart, in their fine memoir and critique of Jane Duncan and her writing in *A History of Scottish Women's Writing*,[5] say, 'The problem was how to remain rooted in one's place and code and yet forge one's own identity, tell one's own story' (477).

Jane Duncan's popular success placed her, in her own time, like Sinclair and Oliphant and O. Douglas in theirs, somewhere on the outskirts of canonical literature. Yet as Jane Duncan, Jean Robertson, or Janet Sandison of Reachfar, Elizabeth Cameron had created fine books, serious, flippant, honest, enlightening, sad. At the time when Jane Duncan wrote, academics, especially narratologists, were evolving theories about the inner quality of stories. They paid little attention to the connection between popular kinds of storytelling and the lives of girls and women. Duncan, unconnected with the academy, went on practising the disregarded skill of gossip. And like all postmoderns, she destabilized the rigid assumptions which are like fixed grids in our minds. Psychoanalysis, linguistics, and transactional psychology all suggest that perception is a con-

structive, ongoing process, always subject to revision. Duncan's
stories, singly and as a series, approximate that reality of perception; they keep her readers moving, changing, never satisfied that the last word has been said.

Nevertheless, Jane Duncan was accorded none of the scholarly recognition, the reviewers' attention, that George Brown
Mackay attracted.[6] No OBE, no full-length critical study. Literary historians rarely name her when they tell the story of
literature in Scotland. The same fate has attended many a storyteller, weaving readable work for ordinary readers. They have
been sidestepped, however, not simply because of a chauvinist
attitude to their gender, but because their gender-based interests did not fit into 'the Great Tradition' as seen until recently
by intellectuals. Lately, however, feminist critics have dragged
them (and the male writers who shared their interest in the
details of home life) back into the light. We can retell the wom-
en's stories now, and so doing, finger again a plain but important strand in the fabric of Scotland and, by extension, of Canada.

Maybe academic disinterest was in the long run a freeing
influence. Too much puffery might endanger that tough and
forthright tone. At any rate, Scotland, like Canada, was and is a
place where 'we cut down the tall poppies' and ask anyone
getting above herself, 'Who do you think you are?'

Alice Laidlaw Munro was asked that same question when she
was a girl. 'Who do you think you are? – you mere girl, coming
from the poor edge of Wingham, a thin town, in a rough county,
noted mostly for its remoteness and its poverty?' She lived to
use the question as the title of one of her fine collections of
short stories. In them she would record moments in that world
at the outskirts, precisely but with the brilliance of magic realism. She would tell stories about eccentric people, living in
what to some eyes seems like a gothic environment, a 'scram-
bled, disarranged sort of country,' to quote from her story
'Friend of My Youth.'[7] Alice Munro stories also tell all of us
who we think we are and clarify the way we are, the kind of
people we verily are. They remind us of the way we collect

memories and wisps of understanding. They sound like the people we have known and talked to and lived with.

'Who do you think you are?' people out west asked Alice Laidlaw Munro when, having dropped out of the University of Western Ontario in 1951 to marry, she still tried to work outside the home, in a Victoria bookstore, and inside the home, at writing stories that began appearing in *Mayfair*, the *New Yorker*, *Chatelaine*, and other magazines. It was a life story not unlike Janet Sandison's up to this point: the move from a rural farming, fishing, and hunting village to university and then a long trip away from home – west, in Munro's case, to British Columbia. The point of comparison with Jane Duncan is in the drive to write.

Alice Munro always knew she was a storyteller, a person who simply – or not so simply – felt impelled to catch on paper her own insights into the lives of girls and women. She knew she had to go on writing, before and after the birth of three daughters, and while undergoing the breakup of marriage, and after returning to Ontario, and eventually after establishing a second marriage and a home in Clinton near the birthplace where it all began; meantime, and always, writing.

In all her fictions, from the early *Lives of Girls and Women* (1971) through the rich pile-up of short stories, Munro, like Jane Duncan, runs complex experience through a female narrator's memory and imagination. Duncan insists on the imperative of identity: 'You must know that this is the kind of person I am.' When Munro uses the phrase 'Something I've been meaning to tell you,' she is offering the same focus, on herself, on her memories, on the need to tell. Both writers provide the same quirky surprises as they shift meanings by recollecting and revising impressions. Since these two writers have worked in an era when they could take for granted the intrinsic interest in women's experience, they could delineate the emotions and ideas and puzzlements of women with ease and accuracy.

Munro works in somewhat the same way as Jane Duncan, twisting, shifting time, leaping through imperceptible connections; but she condenses her work into tight momentary readings, whereas Duncan ambles on, not just at book length but at series length, opening ever more complex vistas of herself. Jane Duncan did not break into print until she was forty-nine; Alice Munro began publishing in her twenties.

Unlike Jane Duncan, Alice Munro is not neglected by critics. On the contrary, the selective bibliography in Catherine Ross's monograph, for instance, illuminates the extent of her recognition by people who analyse and teach her work, as well as enjoy it.[8] With Munro, the enjoyment of literature and the study of literature at last coalesce again. Robert Burns was the people's poet and also the darling of the sophisticated salons; a paperback edition of the latest Alice Munro book nourishes the subway commuters and also furnishes grist for the small-grinding mills of the learned journals.

Like Jane Duncan, Munro is a writer who works in a world of memory, and her memories are of a Lake Huron village world as homely and as pungent as the croft and village that Janet Sandison grew up in, as salty as the community that Galbraith remembered in *The Scotch*. She tells the regional truth, as Galt and Galbraith once did, but with an intimacy unlike Galt and a sympathy unlike Galbraith. Hers is Lowland country, and her tone is ironic and reductive like theirs.

The short story 'Friend of My Youth' highlights the Scottish allusions and undertones that are part of Munro's Ontario background. At the same time it illustrates the narrative techniques that have brought her admiration from narratologists and postmoderns. The core of the story concerns two sisters, members of a rigid Presbyterian sub-sect, the Cameronians – 'some freak religion from Scotland,' the narrator's mother says (5). The direct reference to Scotland is just the first of the evocative Scottish details. One of the sisters is Flora, like Flora Macdonald, who loved and danced for Prince Charlie but never thought to marry him. The second sister is Ellie, conjuring memories of Scott's Ellen, the Lady of the Lake. The sisters' surname is Grieves, a Scottish dialect word for a farm manager. In Jane Duncan's novels, Janet's grandfather and father are presented as 'grieves,' managers of Sir Torquil's estate. The

Grieves sisters in Munro's tale manage an old farm and an old house, bleak and repressive, built to accord with the beliefs of their sect. This ultra-Calvinist group had flourished in Scotland (and less powerfully in Canada). The name has resonance as that of a Scottish clan proscribed like the rebels in *Rob Roy*. For Canadians, 'Cameron' suggests the Cameron regiment, going to war in life and in Margaret Laurence's *A Jest of God*. Both in that novel about barrenness and also in *The Fire-Dwellers*, Laurence gives her women, frustrated sisters, the name of Cameron.

Alice Munro presents this Scottish-tinged story in her characteristic tentative manner. She offers contradictory insights into the lives of the Grieves sisters. She begins with the story of a dream, leading to a recounting of memory – memory of her own mother enfolded in that mother's story of a remembered time of youth. Gossip is the next form of narrative that Munro uses, community talk about the threesome in the old house, blackened for lack of paint, in accord with Cameronian tenets. Ellie, the younger sister, has married the hired man, Robert Deal, who 'had come out from Scotland' (9) and had been engaged first to the older sister, Flora. Next, like a spoof of an old epistolary novel, Munro uses Flora's letters as a way of continuing the story. Then the narrator counters her mother's epistolary way of telling Flora's story by imagining two alternative ways of telling the same story, one (her mother's version) ennobling and dignifying her, the other (her own adolescent version) seeing Flora as martyr, a 'Presbyterian witch.' This play with alternative fictions constitutes the sort of metafiction now fashionable, as storytelling doubles back on itself, implodes, and redirects.

'Friend of My Youth' ends flatly: Ellie dies; Robert marries, not Flora but the coarse woman who nursed Ellie; and Flora leaves the farm, goes to town for a job in a store. The conclusion, however, brings a reversion to thoughts of the narrator's mother, who was Flora's friend. A final dry commentary returns to thoughts of the old Scottish Cameronian Presbyterians, self-righteous, fierce, hacking down the mighty, rejoicing at their own suffering, uncompromising. The final strange sentence is this: 'One of their ministers ... excommunicated all the other preachers in the world' (26).

Maybe this is an oblique comment on Scottishness in general, and the grotesque way in which the young Scot is absorbed into the Ottawa Valley community may be a parable on Canada and the Scottish tradition. Like most of Alice Munro's stories, this one dodges around meaning, tosses up a possible interpretation only to toss up an alternative one. This is a story about pride, guilt, preaching, joy. But the values or dangers of these attitudes, emotions, and activities are far from clear. Flora and Ellie are locked into each other's lives in something of the same relationship of dependency as the narrator and her illness-ravaged mother. The daughter's reaction against the 'dainty tyranny' (22) of her mother's sexual mores, epitomized in white gloves and tea parties, parodies the community's mockery of Cameronian puritanism. The significance of these antitheses loses its clarity in light of the narrator's conviction that most attitudes, even those that seem deep-rooted in principle, have come in 'as spores on the prevailing wind' (23).

The storyline is unorthodox. The narrator's dream is not a dream of love; her memory is not a memory of war or quest; her speculations are not about destiny. Her gossip is not about incest or abortion or sexual abuse. Her imaginings are not fantastic; her histories are not purposeful in any national sense. Yet here, at the outskirts of the 'supreme themes' of canonized literature, Alice Munro offers intense reading pleasure, a double pleasure, in the dramatic unfolding of event and in the author's delight in her own skill at unfolding.

Roland Barthes tell us that story essentially consists of beginning at one terminus, delineating possible paths to a conclusion, entering a black box in which decisions are made, experiencing transformations, and emerging at another terminus. This formula applies triply to 'Friend of My Youth.' Robert Deal comes from Scotland to a house in Canada that has turned black as it weathers. In this literal 'black box' he mates not with sturdy Flora but with tricksy Ellie and later with bossy Audrey, a 'terminus' far from his quiet coming into the story. For the narrator, Robert emerges as a figure of sexual force, transformed in the imagination of the adolescent narrator – her own 'black box' – into a being with power to separate her from her mother's mores. The total transformations in the story are obviously more complex. In the enveloping story the experiences of all varieties of storytelling – dream, memory, and so on – constitute the narrational black box within which the narrator's attitudes shift and change.

Such is the excitement of reading a Munro story. It is perturbing and astonishing to find the normal flow of narrative suddenly shift and reverse. It is stimulating to feel the force of juxtapositions, allusions, ambiguities, and dramatic doublings. Yet the Alice Munro method seems to me to continue a Scottish tradition of a special kind of storytelling, a kind that in its shifts in tone and focus resembles the rhythm of gossip. Gossip, like the chat in Duncan's novels, can be, and has been, derided as babble and tattle and giggle and tell. But it is traditionally the women's way of keying into society, keeping tabs on what is happening, and pushing the next happenings in a direction different from the expected, conventional path. Munro's stories perpetuate the old delight in gossip and also prove its serious function. In suburbs, in farm homes, in village stores, at the outskirts of official life, her women chat and confess, talking quietly in the shadow of power and pushing that shadow away for the reader. It takes great courage and discipline to do Munro's kind of work. Not the courage of warriors, mounting assault and facing armed ambush, but the courage of venture into the labyrinths of memory, gathering linked experience, and then writing experience and memory into a structure as complex and effective as any 'smart bomb.'

'Friend of My Youth' uses Scottish-Canadian materials; 'Hold Me Fast, Don't Let Me Pass,' another story in the 1990 volume, is set directly in Scotland proper. Munro had gone to Scotland on the exchange program that permits Scottish and Canadian writers to savour each other's homelands. In a 1992 interview, Munro discussed her interest in the Scottish influence on Canadian culture. She reminisced about family letters recording her ancestors' coming to Canada in a sailing ship in 1818. She recalled a childhood reading of Ralph Connor, whom she saw as a Canadian writer: 'his Scottishness didn't really penetrate to me I guess.'[9] She discussed her interest in finding that the Presbyterian Church in Canada derived from a radical, fundamentalist wing, like the Cameronians in 'Friend of My Youth,' rather than from the established church. For Munro, the trip into Scotland was a border crossing, into ancestral echoes, into memories of marriage, into literary traditions, into self. When Chris Gittings, the interviewer, asked about her visit to Scotland, 'going around, checking the records,' like Hazel in 'Hold Me Fast, Don't Let Me Pass,' Munro spoke of her surprise at finding that the poet James Hogg was 'a connection' (84). All this makes a revealing background to that most Scottish of her stories.

'Hold Me Fast, Don't Let Me Pass' begins with fragmentary impressions of the environs of a Scottish town: a ruined kirk where William Wallace is remembered, a courthouse where Walter Scott 'dispensed judgment'; mountains, woods, sun and wind and river; and '[o]ne gravestone sunk deep' (74). Hazel, middle-aged and widowed, has come here from Canada to retrace her husband's memories, of Air Force 'ops' during the Battle of Britain and of leaves in Scotland, fishing with a cousin, making love to a Scottish girl. Neither the past in Scotland nor the present turns out to be simple. Hazel finds a present-day tangle involving her husband's long-ago love, now harsh and unremembering, a personable man, and the young girl who loves him and wants to hold him fast in a re-enactment of the old Scottish ballad that re-echoes throughout the story. Neither of the two women can hold the man they love fast; 'I can't make two women happy,' he says (103). Beyond the modern drama, Hazel moves into an ancient world of spells and legends, and also into a refreshed memory of her aging, thinning, boring husband, whom she emotionally abandoned in the late days of his life. She knows now that she failed to 'hold him fast,' not 'striving toward him' either in the past or now, in memory (104). Her time in Scotland up, she will go back from legend-haunted Selkirk to the differently haunted village of Walley on Lake Huron.

Margaret Laurence and Hugh MacLennan, on their trips to Scotland, had rejected the Scottish connections as false bindings. Munro accepts Scottishness as part of the complexity she explores and is prescribed by in her own mind and in her art.

A fourth Canadian writer who went to Scotland to reassess the power of his heritage is Alistair MacLeod. He too was a participant in the Canadian-Scottish Writers' Exchange. He found kindred spirits and a supportive audience. An interviewer in 1992 reminded him, 'When you read in Edinburgh and Sorley MacLean was there, you could feel a real warmth in the room.'[10] MacLeod answered, 'I feel very close to those people. And I very much appreciate the fact that I was able to meet these people and that they have become to a certain extent friends. Sorley MacLean, and Iain Crichton Smith[;] and George Mackay Brown is a writer of whom I am very fond and I went to Orkney when I was in Scotland, and I liked him very much' (103). He added, 'This is not an influence or anything like that, but ... you have an affinity for certain writers, of course, who are somewhat like yourself' (103).

In his short stories, written both before and after his visit to Scotland, MacLeod uses the Scottish tradition as a symbol of intensity and integrity, qualities that he sees as eroding in modern Canada. 'A Tuning of Perfection' begins with a direct reference to the Clearances. An ancestor's house in Cape Breton is built high up on the mountain, 'because of the violence he had left in Scotland.'[11] The Scottish critic Colin Nicholson suggests that, as 'narratives of loss,' many of MacLeod's stories 'might well encode a displacement of the primal wounding which clan chieftains inflicted on their own kinsmen for the sake of personal enrichment.'[12] Specifically, in 'A Tuning of Perfection' the memory of old savagery leads to a story of a different kind of clearance – the sweeping away of the memory of Gaelic by old Archibald's descendants, who mouth the words of old songs without caring to learn their meanings. There is a clearance of traditional commitment, of loyalty and responsibility, as Archibald's family willingly debase their memories in deference to a television director's will. Such debasement is related in the story to the erosion of natural strength and sexuality, in eagles, in horses, as well as in humans. '*Mo Chridhe Trom,*' 'My Heart is Heavy,' the old man sings; but in the end he sings alone (123). In many ways this story sounds the same themes as 'Hold Me Fast, Don't Let Me Pass,' the Scottish memory tied to modern losses. Yet the ending of 'A Tuning of Perfection' – the moving, astonishing ending – is not a question but a confirmation. The old man stands straight on his mountain, smiling at the new men, fierce and reckless in their energy, who sing badly, but who nevertheless 'know ..., *really* know,' the value of the old singing (134).

MacLeod is not a folk singer. His style was formed in student days at St Francis Xavier and the University of New Brunswick, and honed in graduate work at Notre Dame and in teaching years at the University of Windsor. Yet just as in *Greenvoe* there is a 'speak,' a voicing quality like that in Gibbon's *A Scots Quair*, so in MacLeod's stories words form themselves in the rhythms of the Highlands, whether of Cape Breton or of Scotland. Alistair MacLeod reads his stories (I have heard him in Edinburgh and in Prince Edward Island) in a voice 'slow and markedly soft, lilting with an overtone of native Gaelic,' like the voice of Angus Murray in MacLennan's *Barometer Rising* (25). His reading takes me back to the long-ago memory of Cyrus Macmillan, chanting an ancient ballad to young people buffeted by dread of change and war.

Laurence and MacLennan, MacLeod and Munro – four Canadian writers responding to a shared heritage, not with a desire to imitate a model, but all with recognition of a strain that affects their art as well as their lives. They offer a range of gifts: clarity, savour, lightness, profundity, exhilaration, strength – gifts developed in the lands of vistas and memories. Northrop Frye said in his 'Conclusion' to the first edition of the *Literary*

History of Canada, 'I keep coming back to the feeling that there does seem to be such a thing as an imaginative continuum, and that writers are conditioned in their attitudes by their predecessors, or by the cultural climate of their predecessors, whether there is conscious influence or not.'[13]

Brought to Mind

I am retired now and in an empty nest. I rejoin a world of human friends, mostly women who have spent a lifetime reading books as I have, though most of them have not had the privilege of teaching and writing about the books they enjoy. We have been seen as a generation living between two waves of feminism: born too late to be suffragettes, too early to experience 'women's lib' demonstrations. We agree that we are feminists of a bookish kind. We chat on the phone; we go for walks around London, Ontario; we go for lunch together; we talk about books.

I no longer go to Edinburgh. I go to Bradenton, half-expecting to see Daisy Flett among the bridge players. My American friends and I walk the Florida beaches; we go to Florida libraries; we talk about books. We all anticipate the new Munro, new Findley, new Atwood. My new friends say they consider all these writers as part of the American tradition. They cite influences of Eudora Welty, Flannery O'Connor.

I come back home, via Montreal, and rejoice in having time to read at a friendly pace. I used to read Munro too slowly, in order to prepare lectures, or to organize notes for a review, or to mark student essays with informed judgment. At night I used to read Duncan too quickly, gobbling a draught in hope of blurring my workaday problems. Now I can sit in the parlour or the garden and enjoy my old book acquaintances, and sing the last of the verses by Burns:

And there's a hand, my trusty fiere!
And gie's a hand o' thine!
And we'll tak a right gude-willie-waugh,
For auld lang syne. (K 2:734–5)

Awareness and acceptance of affinity have continued up to the present time, between writers of Scotland and Canada (particularly but not exclusively women writers), based on similarities in geography, politics, economics, and the nature of discourse in the two countries. Our 'auld acquaintances,' the books by Scottish writers, well deserve to be cherished by Canadians. They refresh us, like a cup of tea (that cheers but does not inebriate). Or a dram of scotch (that inebriates *and* cheers). Like both tea and scotch, these books bring a revival of spirits, and a shift of consciousness.

We open the door, look down the vistas the stories reveal. Our memories are recharged by the narrative skill of the storytellers. We close the book and surface, still suffused with the feelings and ideas it stirred. Then we go on living our ever-changing life; and when we open the book again, we bring different eyes and nerves to it. The cycle goes on, living and reading, living affecting what and how we read, and reading becoming an ever more significant part of living. From literature to life, from life to literature, experience moves in a cycle, whether in Scotland or Canada or elsewhere, and whether in babyhood or grandparentdom or somewhere in between.

My notion of the function of literature appears in the titles of two books I read and reread when I was an undergraduate: *Through Literature to Life* by Ernest Raymond and *The Enjoyment of Literature* by John Cowper Powys. When I was a postgraduate student, preparing for a career in teaching and writing, I found two other books that reversed the story and told about the way that contemporary life flows into literary genres. *Poetry and the Modern World* and *The Novel and the Modern World* (though I did not know it at the time) were by a Scot, David

Daiches, whose work has set a standard for humanistic literary criticism ever since. Eventually, as a woman working in early days in a patriarchal profession, I found it helped to encounter other critics, women such as Janet Adam Smith and Hilda Neatby. (I also found it comforting to open the door, after hours, to funny, homey moments with O. Douglas or Sara Jeannette Duncan.) Over the years, many Canadians besides myself have enjoyed the fierce honesty muffled in quiet gossip in women's stories and the convoluted memories that lead through modern narratives to wisdom.

So much for the private benefits of reading Scottish and Canadian books. What about public advantages? These two sets of books fit into a current discussion of cultural and/or national identity. Robert Crawford, in *Devolving English Literature*, assesses the literature of his own country, Scotland, in the context of current opposition to the oppressive centrism of English and American literary pundits. Such chapter headings as 'Anthologizing America' and 'Modernism as Provincialism' suggest the relevance of his argument to the questions I have been examining.[1] As Professor Horst Drescher, a German scholar, said in reviewing Crawford's book, this 'thoroughly researched and seminal analysis ... compellingly demands a new reading and new interpretations of a large canon of "English" literary texts.'[2]

The devolution of Scottish tradition in Canadian literature also deserves a new reading. In transforming the Scottish part of their colonial inheritance, Canadians found a way of resisting cultural pressures from two imperializing nations, England and the United States of America. This is a story that complicates current dogma about the paths of post-colonialism.

The weavers of Canada's literary, educational, and social fabric still thread a Scottish colour into the Canadian plaid, twining it with the strong, unbending, unblending colours of other national strands, in spite of tensions, in spite of differences in language, dialect, point of view, religious stance, political colour, gender, class, and race. A singing strength, a romantic belief in ideals, an irony, a sentimentality, are all traceable in part at least to the power of Scottish traditions and authors. They deserve to be 'brought to mind' one last time.

Burns, Scott, Carlyle, Galt, all helped energize Canadian literature in early days. More recently, the dual focus of Stevenson – the pairing of Alan Breck Stewart and David Balfour, or Dr Jekyll and Mr Hyde – has brought reassurance of the normalcy of conflicting selves. Buchan's stories of fierce pursuit and endurance have toughened Canadians' refusal to merely slip and slide through existence. And Canadian women, emerging into modern potentiality, build on the assurances of compatible Scottish women writers.

As years go by, Scottish readers may take equal pleasure in the books of Munro and MacLeod, MacLennan and Montgomery, Lee and Laurence, Acorn and Ross – a long list of Scottish names to be worked into the longer, more multicultural roll-call of Canadian literature. By recording regional details, Canadian books can sharpen the Scots' sense of physical environment and extend imaginative environment to contain places unvisited, eras inaccessible, people and events not physically reachable. They can invade ethical and spiritual biases, perhaps by Canadian metaphors shifting long-cut channels of belief. They can help to slough off violent urges, release the sentimental tears that solace in a dry, rational, conventional world.

After we have brought these books, Scottish and Canadian, to mind, we should 'mind' them. Mind them, first, in the sense of obeying, accepting their directions, doing what they tell us to do. The long succession of women writers has warned us that the directions may slip obliquely from books, especially if the messages are anarchic and anti-establishment. Messages in books sometimes come from frank and pushy people like Janet Sandison's young relatives in *My Friends the Hungry Generation*; they more often come from secretive people like Hazel's reluctant hosts in 'Hold Me Fast.' Rarely do modern books preach with the clarity of Carlyle. But *The Vanishing Point* and *The Fire-Dwellers* tell us some of the things we can do to get out of the 'sour mud-swamp of existence.' Some writers still believe that solutions to problems can be obtained by self-control and self-sacrifice, and some writers are still ready to spin stories (not fairy tales) about acceptance and moderation and love. The messages do come, and we should mind them.

There is another sense of 'minding the books,' and that is, 'looking after them, guarding them.' I worry about who is going to mind the books in a day when parents are too busy to read to children, when librarians have become 'computer resource managers,' turning manuscripts into microfiche, and when publishers are so pushed by financial problems that they cannot foster new talent. I worry about the inroads of electronic technology. I worry about new clearances, like the destroying of Greenvoe by bulldozers, or the dismissal of authentic Gaelic folk song by television directors in 'A Tuning of Perfection.'

But the ending of those stories is affirmative. I do believe in the happy ending. Eventually, books will survive, even if many people neglect to mind them. They have such strength! They pull readers so powerfully across the border into a wonderful world of Highlands and Lowlands, mists and gardens and vistas – a world like Scotland, like Canada, like life.

So crouch, grandchildren, if you must, in front of your computer screen, not talking to each other or to it, but listening to its sound bites and responding by moving the wee mouse – so quickly! so admirably dexterously! I still don't believe you can turn without loss to those electronic substitutes for reading. Sure, you can escape, laugh, and romance on the strength of post-literate media, videos, interactive games, television, radio, film. But books, lyric, singable poetry, snappy, plot-clinching short stories, and nice, fat, readable novels, the true friends of youth, should surely never 'be forgot.'

I'll continue to augment those audio-visual joys by giving you books: *Holiday House* and *The Root Cellar*, *The Blue Castle* later, and later still *The Fire-Dwellers* and *The Vanishing Point*. They will channel the wisdom and the distress and the hopes of nations and of humanity to you, alone with your book. Soon you will find book friends of your own, to amuse and illuminate, entertain and enlarge, and enrage and inflame you. Some of those books may be Scottish or Canadian ones, even if Scotland and Canada become dimensionless specks on the information highway.

Some things will not change ...

The twenty-fifth of January 2011. The 'Thank God It's Friday' group will be polishing off their scotches and their beers; the barman will be hustling them a bit. He has to get set up for the Burns Night supper. The buffet is ready, all but the haggis – that is being delivered from the Wee Scotch Shop on Douglas Street. A piper from the Fergus band is here to pipe it in. The Burns people are beginning to drift in: the red-bearded master of ceremonies; Cathy from Glasgow, who will wittily respond to a barbed toast to the lassies; kilted archivist Hugh, who will propose 'the Immortal Memory.'

The TGIF-ers will drift away. The barman will set out his tidy row of shot glasses – fifty-six of them for the thirsty Scots, sentimental pseudo-Scots, married-to-Scots, and just plain party-minded January Canadians. Plus two ninety-ish women, once war brides from Glasgow. Burns Night can now begin.

There is love in the room – love in spite of the cold climate. A young woman with a shock of dark, curly hair is coming through the scotch into a moment of song:

O my Luve's like a red, red rose,
That's newly sprung in June;
O my Luve's like the melodie
That's sweetly play'd in tune ...

After the haggis, someone will put a chip in the microprocessor, and recorded voice will lead the song: 'Should auld acquaintance be forgot?'

Outside, in the chilly end of January, students will move across the campus, arms around each other, hands in each other's pockets. New music will blare from the graduate lounge, a three-note threnody with a triple lyric: 'Ah love yuh! Ah want yuh! Ah need yuh! Please don't go! Please don't go! Please don't go!'

Notes

Auld Lang Syne

1 The version of 'Edward, Edward' in Percy's *Reliques*, reprinted in *The Poetry of Scotland: Gaelic, Scots and English, 1380–1980*, 190–2, ed. Watson, runs, 'O I hae killed my fadir deir, Mither, mither.' Cyrus Macmillan (1882–1953) was later called to Ottawa to play a part in the wartime cabinet.
2 Leon Edel (1907–1997), as quoted in *The McGill You Knew*, ed. Collard, 118. For a fuller view of McGill in the 1920s, see the chapter 'McGill and the Moderns' in Compton, *A.J.M. Smith: Canadian Metaphysical*, 42–76. Tippett places the McGill Movement in a general modernist context in *The Making of English-Canadian Culture, 1900–1939*.
3 Published in 1922 under the pseudonym Alonié de Lestres.
4 Davey, *Post-National Arguments*, 266.
5 All quotations of Burns's poems are from *The Poems and Songs of Robert Burns*, ed. Kinsley; cited here as 'K.' 'Auld Lang Syne' (K 1:443–4) begins, 'Should auld acquaintance be forgot / And never brought to mind? / Should auld acquaintance be forgot, / And auld lang syne!'
6 First published in *Longman's Magazine*, November 1882. The essay begins, 'In anything fit to be called by the name of reading, the process itself should be absorbing and voluptuous; we should gloat over a book, be rapt clean out of ourselves' (69).

1: Burns, Acorn, and the Rivers of Song

1 These are the opening phrases of Burns's poems K 2:516; K 2:617; K 2:519.
2 McGuirk, in *Robert Burns and the Sentimental Era*, says, 'The Edinburgh public reacted to Burns as he had reacted to his mouse – with benevolent condescension' (71).
3 There are nine hundred biographical studies of Burns in the Mitchell Library in Glasgow. James A. Mackay, in *R.B.: A Biography of Robert Burns*, did an exhaustive job of re-examining all the primary records regarding Burns's life. His research did not, however, appreciably alter the standard biographies, such as Snyder, *The Life of Robert Burns*, and Fowler, *Robert Burns*. A controversial new study is Ian McIntyre, *Dirt and Deity*.
4 *Rabelais and His World*, first published in Russian in 1965. See Bittenbender, 'Bakhtinian Carnival in the Poetry of Robert Burns'; Morris, 'Burns' Heteroglossia'; and McGuirk, 'Burns and Bakhtin: The Opposition of Poetic and Novelistic Discourse.'
5 Valuable recent studies, including the essays in two volumes edited by Simpson, *Burns Now* and *Love and Liberty*, and in *Robert Burns and Cultural Authority*, ed. Crawford, add to stellar earlier evaluations such as Daiches, *Robert Burns and His World*; Crawford, *Burns: A Study of the Poems and Songs; Critical Essays on Robert Burns*, ed. Low; and *The Art of Robert Burns*, ed. Jack and Noble.
6 See Colley, *Britons*; Sher, *Church and University in the Scottish Enlightenment*; and Allan, *Virtue, Learning and the Scottish Enlightenment*, which all discuss this process of institutionalizing Presbyterian power.
7 According to Grant and Humes, 'The Scottish population was probably the best educated in the world for about three hundred years from the end of the 16th century'; see 'Scottish Education, 1700–2000,' 361. See also Lynch, *Scotland: A New History*. Rendall's *The Origins of the Scottish Enlightenment, 1707–1776* reproduces many of the legal and cultural documents which underlie the development of Scotland's distinctive society and gives a commentary on their significance.

8 McGuirk demonstrates in detail the way that Burns's work was written not in authentic dialect but in a 'designed and invented' language, 'a mixture of local dialect, archaic Middle Scots, dialect words of regions other than his own, sentimental idioms, and "high" English rhetoric' (McGuirk, *Robert Burns and the Sentimental Era*, xxii). See also Daiches, 'Robert Burns: The Tightrope Walker.'

9 Dorothy Wordsworth's *Recollections of a Tour Made in Scotland, A.D. 1803*, 41–5, shows the depth of her brother's feelings about Burns.

10 See Bumsted, *The People's Clearance*; Hunter, *A Dance Called America*; Cowan, *British Emigration to British North America*; see also local studies such as McLean, *The People of Glengarry*, and Doucette, *Cultural Retention and Demographic Change*.

11 See Duncan, 'Patterns of Settlement in the East,' 52. Duncan explains that when the Sots were defeated at Culloden by English forces in 1746, Highland chieftains dismissed the clansmen who had fought under their leadership. Many of these soldiers were absorbed into British Highland regiments, and when Quebec was conquered, they were given grants on the assumption that they would oppose any recurrence of French resistance to British rule. Again, at the end of the American Revolution, large grants were given to disbanded Highland regiments, most notably in Glengarry County and other areas north of Cornwall in eastern Upper Canada, in Chatham Township, Lower Canada, in Nova Scotia on the north side of Pictou Harbour, and along the St John River in New Brunswick. Again the assumption was that these troops would resist American assaults on the British colonies. 'Officers and men took up their land regiment by regiment, almost as if falling into line of battle' (55). All these military settlements · expanded in the 1780s and 1790s, as the veterans sent for friends and relatives in Scotland to join them. See also MacDonald, *Immigration and Settlement*, and *Canada: Immigration and Colonization, 1841–1903*; also Macnutt, *New Brunswick: A History, 1784–1867*.

12 Lynch, in 'Scottish Culture in Its Historical Perspective,' 39–40, says about the numbers of professional people who flowed out of

Scotland: 'A simple explanation for the size of the Scots' contribution to the imperial mission is difficult to find; it may be, as one
(non-Scottish) historian has speculated, that the Scots had centuries of practice working or fighting for a foreign culture behind
them. In some fields, however, it was clearly the distinctive
nature of Scottish education, as well as the numbers produced by
it which made the difference.' Lynch gives statistics: between
1750 and 1850 'Scotland's universities educated some 10,000
doctors, whereas Oxford and Cambridge produced 500' (40).

13 A much fuller list appears in Masters, 'The Scottish Tradition in
Higher Education,' 248–72.

14 Parker, *The Beginnings of the Book Trade in Canada*, chapters 1–3.
See also Gundy, 'Literary Publishing,' 188–202; and Gundy, *Book
Publishing and Publishers before 1900*.

15 See also my chapter on Lowland poetry in *The Scottish Tradition in
Canada*, 223–36, for other prominent Scots-Canadian poets of the
nineteenth century.

16 Cogswell, 'Literary Activity in the Maritime Provinces (1815–
1880),' 131.

17 For a discussion of attitudes to literary influence, see Bate, *The
Burden of the Past and the English Poet*; Bloom, *The Anxiety of
Influence*; and Said, *Culture and Imperialism*. I will return to the
question of 'anxiety of influence' at the conclusion of this section.

18 Collected edition, *The Poetical Works of Alexander McLachlan*, 185.
All citations from McLachlan, except for 'We Live in a Rickety
House,' are from the 1974 reprint edition.

19 Bentley, in his edition of *The Emigrant by Alexander McLachlan*, 86–
7, notes that when McLachlan writes about an indigenous species
such as the whippoorwill, he usually follows the lead of Isaac
Weld's *Travels* or Catharine Parr Traill's *Backwoods of Canada*.

20 Hughes gives full praise to this aspect of McLachlan's work in
'Poet Laureate of Labour,' 33–40.

21 From *The Emigrant and Other Poems* (1861), reprinted in *The
Blasted Pine*, ed. Scott and Smith, 81.

22 Quoted by Edwards in her entry for McLachlan in the *Dictionary
of Canadian Biography*.

23 Bentley, 'Introduction,' *The Emigrant by Alexander McLachlan*, il–l.

24 Matthews, *Tradition in Exile*, 140–7.
25 'Indian Summer,' W.W. Campbell, *The Poems of Wilfred Campbell* (1905), reprinted in *Literature in Canada*, ed. Daymond and Monkman, 1:311.
26 Dudek, *Selected Essays and Criticism*; quoted in Noonan, 'Drummond.'
27 Drummond, 'The Wreck of the Julie Plante,' *The Habitant and other French-Canadian Poems*, reprinted in *The Book of Canadian Poetry*, ed. Smith, 159.
28 Johnson, 'A Cry from an Indian Wife,' *Flint and Feather*, 17.
29 Carman, 'An Autumn Song,' *Songs from Vagabondia* (1894–1912), reprinted in *The Selected Poems of Bliss Carman*, ed. Pierce, 48. Other citations from Carman are from this edition.
30 Service, *Ploughman of the Moon*, 25, 16.
31 Service's biographers differ about the extent of his debt to Burns. Mackay, *Vagabond of Verse*, puts more emphasis on the childhood immersion in a Burns cult than do Klinck, *Robert Service*, or Lockhart, *On the Trail of Robert Service*, but even Mackay emphasizes later influences as most powerful. Service's own memoirs blur the references to Burns with a little self-mockery of his own youthful openness to the earlier poet's influence. Perhaps his lifelong habit of attending Burns dinners attests to a lingering affection. Service met John Buchan at one of these in the pre-war years. See also Burness, 'The Influence of Burns and Fergusson on the War Poetry of Robert Service.'
32 From Service, *Songs of a Sourdough*, reprinted in *Literature in Canada*, ed. Daymond and Monkman, 1:428–31.
33 Service, 'My Cross,' *Lyrics of a Lowbrow* (1951), reprinted in *Literature in Canada*, ed. Daymond and Monkman, 1:436.
34 Few of the critical works used in literature classes have included Service. Even Klinck, author of the excellent *Robert Service, a Biography*, omitted his work from the 1955–9 editions of the widely used *Canadian Anthology*, edited with Watters.
35 Mackay, *Vagabond of Verse*, 397.
36 From *Overture: Poems*, reprinted in *Poets between the Wars*, ed. Wilson, 85; the other phrases in this paragraph are from poems republished in the same anthology: Smith, 'The Lonely Land,'

106; Scott, 'Old Song,' 84; Klein, 'Portrait of the Poet as Land-scape,' 192.

37 Kenner's powerful essay on this topic, 'The Case of the Missing Face,' appears in *Our Sense of Identity*, ed. Ross. Kenner writes of the pathological dehumanizing in art, pictorial or poetic, as a Canadian phenomenon, 203–8.

38 Noonan, in 'The Importance of Poetry and the Power of the Phrase Mellifluous,' 7, writes of Margaret Atwood's astringent flatness, deliberately chipping away melody, as her reaction against the lyric mode endorsed by the schools.

39 From Klein, *The Rocking Chair and Other Poems*, reprinted in *Poets between the Wars*, ed. Wilson, 190.

40 Greenhill, *True Poetry*, ix. See also Greenhill's *Ethnicity in the Main Stream*.

41 Acorn, 'The Second World War,' *Dig Up My Heart*. There is no collected edition; quotations are, as designated, from this edition (*DUMH*), from *The Island Means Minago* (*IMM*), *I Shout Love and Other Poems* (*ISL*), and *More Poems for People* (*MPP*).

42 This is from a 1960 version of the poem, reprinted in *The Island Means Minago*, 65. There is a different version in *Whiskey Jack*, 14, with an introduction by Al Purdy, who quotes the earlier version (9).

43 Layton, 'Look, the Lambs Are All around Us!' *Collected Poems*, 79.

44 Cohen, 'Suzanne Takes You Down,' *Selected Poems, 1956–1968*, 209. Subsequent page references are to this collection.

45 A lively account of the poets' protest appears in Gudgeon, *Out of This World*, 103–8.

46 Lightfoot, *I Wish You Good Spaces*, 28.

47 Stompin' Tom Connors, 'Sudbury Saturday Night,' reprinted in *Listen: Songs and Poems of Canada*, ed. Hogan, 62.

2: Scott, Crawford, and the Highlands of Romance

1 See Youngson, *The Making of Classical Edinburgh, 1750–1840*. In *Virtue, Learning and the Scottish Enlightenment*, Allan renews discussion about the extent of the Enlightenment. See also Campbell and Skinner, *The Origins and Nature of the Scottish Enlightenment*.

2 'Memoir of the Early Life of Sir Walter Scott, Written by Himself. 1808,' in Lockhart, *Memoirs of the Life of Sir Walter Scott*, 1:40–1.

3 See Hart, *Lockhart as Romantic Biographer*, particularly chapter 5. New biographies that modify the Lockhart view include Johnson, *Sir Walter Scott, the Great Unknown*, and Mayhead, *Walter Scott*.

4 'Introduction' to the 1830 edition, *The Lady of the Lake* in *The Poetical Works of Sir Walter Scott*, (1896).

5 Crawford, in *Scott*, 39, writes of the belief that there was a connection between patriotism and the land beyond the Trossachs.

6 See Batho, 'Sir Walter Scott and the Sagas.' See also Cowan, 'Icelandic Studies in Eighteenth and Nineteenth Century Scotland.'

7 Interest in northern values was in part a response to the visits of Grimur Thorkelin. See 'Scott's Foreign Contacts,' in *Scott in Carnival*, eds. Alexander and Hewitt; see also Simpson, 'Scott and Old Norse Literature,' and my article on 'The Harp, the North, and Scott's Irony,' ibid.

8 The standard edition is *The Poetical Works of Sir Walter Scott*, ed. Robertson. Citations in the text relate to this edition. A paperback edition available in Canada is *The Lady of the Lake and Other Poems*, ed. Bennet (1967).

9 See Stewart, 'The Enchanted World of the Lady of the Lake,' 6.

10 *The Ecocriticism Reader*, ed. Glotfelty and Fromm.

11 Said, *The World, the Text, and the Critic*, 4; see also McDowell, 'The Bakhtinian Road to Ecological Insight,' 374.

12 The term 'Wizard of the North' was first used in the *Literary Gazette*, 14 July 1821; see Owen, *The Wizard of the North*, preface.

13 Frye sees romance of the kind that Scott produced as 'a vision of reality in terms of human concerns and hopes and anxieties' (*The Secular Scripture*, 14).

14 The major biography to date is Farmiloe, *Isabella Valancy Crawford*. A more recent biography has an even more telling title: Galvin, *Isabella Valancy Crawford: We Scarcely Knew Her*.

15 Farmiloe, *Isabella Valancy Crawford*, 28. See also Livesay, 'The Life of Isabella Valancy Crawford,' 8. Mrs Valancy Crawford Perry of Sault Ste Marie, niece of the poet, provided material on family history to Penny Petrone (editor of Crawford's *Fairy Tales*) and others (including myself).

16 See *Collected Poems of Isabella Valancy Crawford*, 304–5; Crawford's other pseudo-Scottish poems include 'The Rowan Tree' (301) and 'I'll Lauch to See the Year In' (303).

17 First published in *'Old Spookses' Pass,' 'Malcolm's Katie' and Other Poems* (Toronto: James Bain & Son, 1884), the poem was definitively reissued as *Malcolm's Katie: A Love Story*, fully annotated and edited by Bentley. Subsequent citations refer to the more widely available *Collected Poems*.

18 Hughes, 'Isabella Valancy Crawford: The Names in "Malcolm's Katie,"' 6.

19 The major study of Native materials in Canadian literature is Monkman, *A Native Heritage*. See also Yeoman, 'Towards a Native Mythology.'

20 'A Word from the Editor' [i.e., John W. Garvin], *The Collected Poems of Isabella Valancy Crawford*, 1.

21 The influence of Scott was still also perceptible in this work. L.M. Montgomery, by her son's testimony, could and did still recite reams of Scott's poetry when she was middle-aged. The icon of the lady of the lake – the young woman on an island – reappeared in *The Blue Castle*, where Valancy Stirling finds romance on the Isle of Mistawis.

22 See *The Crawford Symposium*, ed. Tierney; also Livesay's 'Tennyson's Daughter or Wilderness Child? and Reaney, 'Isabella Valancy Crawford.'

23 The quotations are from *The Lady of the Lake*, Browning's 'Home Thoughts, from Abroad,' Tennyson's *The Princess*, and Longfellow's *The Song of Hiawatha*.

24 *Selected Poems of Duncan Campbell Scott*, 96.

25 Johnston, 'The Significance of Scott's Minor Poems,' 15. Scott implies a hierarchic relationship between the 'white' – i.e., Scottish – and the Native heritage in 'The Half-Breed Girl,' when the young woman senses something 'behind her savage life': 'shadows in her soul' of 'the gleam of loch and shieling, / the mist on the moor, / Frail traces of kindred kindness, / Of feud by hill and strand, / The heritage of an age-long life / In a legendary land' (*Selected Poetry of Duncan Campbell Scott*, 43).

26 *E.J. Pratt on His Life and Poetry*, 145–6.

27 Pratt, *Towards the Last Spike*, 5.
28 Davey deflates Pratt's reputation in 'E.J. Pratt: Rationalist Technician.' See also Djwa, *E.J. Pratt: The Evolutionary Vision*.
29 See Jensen, *Love's Sweet Return*; Krentz, *Dangerous Men and Adventurous Women*.
30 Morton, 'The North in Canadian History,' 86, 87.

3: Scott, Findley, and the Borders of War

1 Since 1993, all of Scott's novels have been in the process of being reissued by the Edinburgh University Press, with modern editing and annotation, under the general editorship of David Hewitt. The new edition of *Waverley* not being available to me, I here use page references to the Cambridge University Press edition (1993).
2 The preface was written in 1829 for a reissue of the novel. Scott avowed that he hoped to do for his country what Maria Edgeworth had done for Ireland (xx).
3 See also MacQueen, *The Rise of the Historical Novel*, and Gordon, *Under Which King?*
4 The claim that *Waverley* is a 'landmark novel' is reiterated in the choice of this book for reissue in the World Literature Series (which also includes the Iliad, *Don Quixote*, and *Anna Karenina*), put out by Cambridge University Press in 1993.
5 Georg Lukács, *The Historical Novel*. See also MacQueen, *The Rise of the Historical Novel*.
6 The topic of borders is of crucial importance not only to historians and politicians but also to current environmentalists. Mollinson defines 'edge' as 'an interface between two mediums; it is the surface between the water and the air; the zone around a soil particle to which the water bonds; the shoreline between land and water; the area between forest and grassland ... Wherever species, climate, soils, slope, or any natural conditions or artificial boundaries meet, we have edges' (*Introduction to Permaculture*, 26).
7 See McLuhan, 'Canada: the Borderline Case,' 246–8.
8 See Campbell, 'Fiction and Experience in the Works of Sir Walter Scott,' 3.

9 Gerson says that the details of *Wacousta* prove that 'even a native-born Canadian found it impossible to divorce the romantic novel from its connection with Sir Walter Scott' (*A Purer Taste*, 86). Other studies of Scott's influences on *Wacousta* appear in articles by Ian MacLaren and Jay Macpherson in *Recovering Canada's First Novelist*, ed. Ross, 49–53, 69–72.

10 Hurley, *The Borders of Nightmare*. Hurley concentrates on the concept of borders political, aesthetic, and psychological. He writes of 'the border river and the surrounding wilderness, declaring themselves a realm of the unexplored,' cites Northrop Frye on 'the riddle of the unvisualized land' as creating 'an "obstructive blur" attending all border crossings' (47), and declares, 'The implosive character of the borderland ... compels commitment and participation in depth' (147).

11 Ballstadt, *Major John Richardson: A Selection of Reviews and Criticism*.

12 Lecker, 'Patterns of Deception in *Wacousta*.'

13 Duffy, *Sounding the Iceberg*, 3. Monkman, in 'Canadian Historical Fiction,' a review of Duffy's book, provides an excellent commentary on the genre.

14 Hurley, *The Borders of Nightmare*, 58.

15 See Lennox, '*Les anciens Canadiens*: Aubert de Gaspé and Scott,' 40. Aubert de Gaspé's debts to Scott are detailed in my article, 'The Politics of Conquest in Canadian Historical Fiction.'

16 *The Manor House of de Villerai* appeared first in the *Family Herald*, nos. 1–3 (16 Nov.–8 Feb. 1860). It has been republished as '*The Manor House of de Villerai*: A Tale of Canada under the French Dominion,' ed. Sorfleet, in *Journal of Canadian Fiction* 34 (1985).

17 See McMullen and Waterston, 'Rosanna Mullins Leprohon,' 331–6.

18 See Duffy, *Sounding the Iceberg*, 13–17; and Waterston, *Gilbert Parker*.

19 See the introduction to *The Seats of the Mighty*, ed. Waterston, New Canadian Library ed. (Toronto: McClelland & Stewart, 1971). The excised portion also contained a lyric imitative of Burns in such lines as 'Did ye hear the gay lilt o' the lark by the burn? / That's the voice of my bairnie, my dearie' (*The Seats of the Mighty*, Impe-

rial Edition [New York: Scribner's, 1913], 64). Controversy about editorial changes in Canadian historical novels also affects readings of *Wacousta*. See Cronk, 'The Editorial Destruction of Canadian Literature,' developed in his CEECT edition of *Wacousta*.

20 Raddall, *In My Time*, 11–21.

21 Buchan's appreciation appeared as a foreword to *The Pied Piper of Dipper Creek and Other Tales*, v.

22 See Young, *Thomas H. Raddall*; also his *Time and Place*, with particular emphasis on essays by Donna Smyth, Barry Moody, Chris Ferns, and my essay, 'Thomas Raddall, Historical Fiction, and the Canadian Romance,' 16–21.

23 For a range of comments on the use of Canadian history in children's fiction, see MacGillivray and Lynes, 'Paradise Ever Becoming,' and other articles in the 'History' issues, 23/24, 83, and 84, of *Canadian Children's Literature*.

24 Paul Fussell, in *The Great War and Modern Memory*, highlights the effect of ironic anti-war literature on young people, especially in the Vietnam War era.

25 Hutcheon, *The Canadian Postmodern*, 81.

26 Martel, 'Generals Die in Bed,' 12. This excellent double issue of *Journal of Canadian Studies/Revue d'études canadiennes* also contains an important essay by Kroller, 'The Exploding Frame: Uses of Photography in Timothy Findley's *The Wars*.' Martel's title refers to a Canadian war novel rediscovered and republished by Robert Neilson.

27 Page references are to the paperback edition of *The Wars* (London: Penguin, 1977). Other critics have noted parodic elements in the novel, suggesting that Findley is recognizing and playing with the Eurocentric tradition even when he sets himself against it. See Salutin, *Marginal Notes*.

28 Davey writes of the First World War as a 'national rite of passage' in *Post-National Arguments*; he sees Findley as portraying a Canada 'violent, patriarchal, misogynist,' in a war with 'all social and political considerations erased' (126).

29 Kerr has written on this topic in *Fiction against History*, as has White in 'The Burden of History.'

A Cup o' Kindness

1 Weinbrot, '"An Ambition to Excell."'
2 Table derived from McIntyre, 'The Scot as Farmer and Artisan,'
   166; source: *British Parliamentary Papers*, 1836, XL (76), 8; 1837,
   XLII (132), 9; 1839, XXXIII (613), 74; 1843, XXXIV (109), 11; 1854,
   XLVI (1763), 30; 1860, XLIV (606), 17.
3 Said, *Culture and Imperialism*, 336, 56.
4 Crosby, *Ecological Imperialism*; quoted by Said in 'Yeats and
   Decolonization,' in *Nationalism, Colonialism, and Literature*, ed.
   Eagleton, 77.
5 Said, *Culture and Imperialism*, and Ahmad, *Occidentosis*, are among
   seminal texts on colonialism and post-colonialism considered
   here.
6 Donoghue, *Ferocious Alphabets*, 144.
7 Frye, *The Educated Imagination*, 17 and passim.
8 *In Theory*, ed. Ahmad, 336. In the same collection of essays,
   Jameson raises what he considers 'true issues': 'periodization,
   production, politics, social and linguistic functions, political and
   ideological struggles, and multiple determinations of literary
   theory by conditions of production and location of its agents, in
   specific grids of class and institutions' (320).
9 New, *Articulating West*.

Signs of the Times

1 Arnold, 'Stanzas from the Grand Chartreuse,' in *Poems, 2nd Series*
   (1855), lines 85–6.
2 The twelfth of July, the anniversary of the Battle of the Boyne,
   was considered 'glorious' in small Protestant villages in Ontario. I
   understand that it is now referred to in Scotland simply as 'The
   Twelfth' – the term 'glorious' being reserved for 12 August, the
   start of the grouse-shooting season. Orange Day parades in
   Canada were without the terrorism now connected with comparable parades in modern Ireland.
3 Masters adds many more names of Scots in positions of power in
   the later part of the nineteenth century, in 'The Scottish Tradition
   in Higher Education.'

4 J.A. Irving and Johnson, 'Philosophical Literature to 1910,'
   451–60.

4: Galt, Ross, and the Lowlands of Irony

1 The *Statistical Account of Scotland*, compiled by Sir John Sinclair,
   was started in 1790 and completed by 1799, from data furnished
   by church ministers in local parishes.
2 Henry Mackenzie, the grand old man of fiction, author of *The
   Man of Feeling* (1771), praised Galt's handling of time – the way
   he used the narrator's own words to trace the little changes in
   society, and also the effect of those events on himself: 'those little
   changes which the course of his own years, as well as the course
   of events, produced in himself' ('Review of *Annals of the Parish*').
3 Frye, *The Anatomy of Criticism*, 34.
4 Hawthorne, 'The Custom-House: Introductory,' in *The Scarlet
   Letter*, 42–5. See also Costain, 'Theoretical History and the Novel.'
5 Galt, *Annals of the Parish*, 72. Galt's novel was first published by
   Blackwood in Edinburgh in 1821. Critically annotated editions of
   Galt novels are now appearing from the Scottish Academic Press,
   but none has yet superseded the 1967 edition by Kinsley in the
   Oxford English Novels series.
6 See MacQueen, 'John Galt and the Analysis of Social History,'
   335.
7 *Annals of the Parish* and other Galt novels attracted naive readers
   because of their apparent factuality. The mother of the editor of
   Blackwood's Edinburgh Magazine assumed that the novels were
   factual and allowed herself to enjoy them. (She disapproved of
   fiction such as Scott's.) Her son the editor liked to tell this story as
   a clarification of Galt's appeal. See Kinsley, 'Introduction,' *Annals
   of the Parish* (1967), ix.
8 Hutcheon, *Splitting Images*, 5–9.
9 See *The Tavern Sages*, ed. Alexander.
10 Whistler reprints nine versions of the founding of Guelph in
   'John Galt's Autobiography: Fact, Fiction and Truth,' 314–32.
11 The original edition (never republished) was *Bogle Corbet; or, The
   Emigrants*, 3 vols. (London: Colburn & Bentley, 1831). My edition
   for the New Canadian Library, *Bogle Corbet* (Toronto: McClelland

& Stewart, 1977), includes only the Canadian material, beginning with page 229 of volume 2 and continuing to the conclusion.

12 Quoted from the New Canadian Library edition of *Bogle Corbet*, 175.

13 *Tiger Dunlop's Upper Canada*, 92.

14 In 1832 John Wilson ('Christopher North') called Dunlop a 'Blackwoodian Backwoodsman, who can handle a quill as well as a hatchet' ('Review of Statistical Sketches,' *Blackwood's Magazine* 32 [July 1832]: 240). See Klinck, *William 'Tiger' Dunlop*, 143.

15 Although these authors, the Reverend S.J. Crockett and the Reverend John Watson ('Ian MacLaren'), cast a veil of sentiment over the 'Kailyard' (i.e., cabbage patch) parishes in their stories, the details beneath the veil were as sharply realized as in Galt's original work. See Campbell, *Kailyard*.

16 See *On Thomas Chandler Haliburton*, ed. Davies; *The Thomas Chandler Haliburton Symposium*, ed. Tierney; and Gwendolyn Davies, 'The Club Papers: Haliburton's Literary Apprenticeship,' and other papers in *Studies in Maritime Literary History, 1760–1930*, ed. Davies.

17 Waterston et al., *The Travellers: Canada to 1900*, an annotated bibliography, contains notes on the full range of travel books, from lively anecdotal reports such as John Howison's *Sketches of Upper Canada* (1821) to political-economic polemics such as Robert Gourlay's *Statistical Account of Upper Canada* (1822), followed by at least thirty other accounts in the same decade of regional fact-finding.

18 Mactaggart, *Three Years in Canada*, 2:290–1.

19 Strickland, *Twenty-Seven Years in Canada West*, 1:240.

20 Major Moodie, like his brother-in-law Samuel Strickland, had published a book of travels with Bentley, Galt's last publisher. (In 1832 Bentley had bought out Colburn, publisher of most other early travel accounts by Scots such as Mactaggart, McGregor, and Simpson.) Mrs Moodie turned from her earlier publisher (Smith, Elder), and *Roughing It* was published by Bentley. Her sister, Catharine Parr Traill, had also married a Scot, but for her Canadian work Traill chose a Toronto publisher, Maclear.

21 Moodie, *Roughing It in the Bush;* Ballstadt's edition in the Centre for Editing Early Canadian Texts series includes material by Major Moodie, omitted from many other editions.

22 See Whistler, 'Galt's Life and the Autobiography,' *John Galt: Reappraisals,* ed. Waterston, 52.

23 Dewdney, *Wind without Rain.* I use the term 'cultural history' in the sense of Jane Tompkins's *Sensational Designs: The Cultural Work of American Fiction, 1790–1860.*

24 The nature of Mrs Bentley's perception of the true state of affairs in the house and the village became the focus for several critical articles in *From the Heart of the Heartland,* ed. Moss.

25 McMullen, *Sinclair Ross,* ii.

5: Carlyle, Mitchell, Laurence, and the Storms of Rhetoric

1 The standard biography, Kaplan, *Thomas Carlyle* (1983), can be supplemented by a revisionist biography, Heffer, *Moral Desperado* (1995); brief but excellent is Campbell, *Thomas Carlyle* (1974).

2 Hanson and Hanson's *Necessary Evil* sheds interesting light on the marriage, as do Carlyle's *Collected Letters* and *Reminiscences.* See also *Thomas and Jane,* ed. Campbell.

3 Carlyle, 'Sir Walter Scott' (1838), 75–6.

4 The title is Latin for 'tailor re-tailored.' *Sartor Resartus* (1834) was reissued many times. Citations in this chapter are from Hudson's 1908 edition. A major modern study is Tennyson's *'Sartor' Called 'Resartus.'*

5 See Rosenberg, *Carlyle and the Burden of History.*

6 For comments on the Scottish influences on Laurence, see Thomas, *The Manawaka World of Margaret Laurence,* and also Thomas's '"The Chariot of Ossian." Essays in *Critical Approaches to the Fiction of Margaret Laurence,* edited in Edinburgh by Nicholson, are useful in this regard also.

7 Illuminating comments on Laurence's responses to Scottish writers and life appear in the collections of letters between her and Al Purdy, Wiseman, and other writers. See, for example, *Selected Letters of Margaret Laurence and Adele Wiseman,* ed. Lennox

and Panofsky, 193, 275, 279, for references to the 'black Celt' in Laurence's personality; 202, 243, 293, for references to trips to Scotland in 1963, 1965, 1968, and 1969.

8 In *Critical Approaches to the Fiction of Margaret Laurence*, ed. Nicholson, 163, 174.

9 Orm Mitchell, '"The Smell of Oatmeal,"' 114. On Mitchell's novels, other than *The Vanishing Point*, see Harrison, *W.O. Mitchell and His Works*; a biography of the novelist is being prepared by Orm and Barbara Mitchell.

10 In 'Planted Firmly in Some Soil,' Thomas generalizes about the Scottish influence on many writers: 'There is no other social mythology so pervasive in our literature as that of the Scots' (8).

11 Citations are from the first edition of *The Vanishing Point* (1973).

12 Citations are from the first edition of *The Fire-Dwellers* (1969).

13 Howe, in *Novels of Empire*, discusses the influence of Carlyle on the novelists of British India.

14 See also McLuhan's *The Gutenberg Galaxy* and *War and Peace in the Global Village*.

15 Frye, 'Third Essay: Archetypal Criticism: Theory of Myths,' *The Anatomy of Criticism*.

16 See McClung, *Sowing Seeds in Danny*, and Bruce, *The Channel Shore*. Margaret Laurence listed McClung among the writers who mattered to her, in a speech given to the Friends of the Bata Library, Trent University, in 1981.

Everlasting Yea?

1 *Scott Bicentenary Essays*, ed. Bell, presented fourteen papers by Scottish academics, five by Americans, and one by a Hungarian scholar – none by Canadians.

2 Of several celebratory volumes, the most important was *John Galt, 1779–1979*, ed. Whatley. Canadian Keith Costain and New Zealander Ian Gordon joined nine Scots, many more from new Scottish universities (Strathclyde, Dundee, and Stirling) than in the case of the Scott volume.

3 The spreading interest in the Scottish writers is marked by one of

the centenary publications, *Thomas Carlyle, 1981*, ed. Drescher. French, Canadian, American, Swedish, and of course Scottish scholars contributed essays.

4 MacDiarmid, *A Drunk Man Looks at the Thistle*, ed. Buthlay, 4.

5 Gibbon, *Sunset Song*, 9–10.

6 Gerson, *A Purer Taste*, 14.

7 Eagleton, *Exiles and Emigrés*, 22.

8 Professor Whalley made these comments in an informal address at a meeting of the Association of Canadian University Teachers of English at Queen's University, Kingston, in 1968.

Road to the Isles

1 See Wachowicz's article, 'L.M. Montgomery: At Home in Poland,' for explanation of the remarkable appeal of Montgomery's books to Polish people since 1912.

2 The topic of 'canons' and 'canonization' has been trenchantly covered in Lecker, *Making It Real*. Bloom, in *The Western Canon*, defines and defends a traditional list of 'books and schools of the ages.'

3 Parker, *The Beginnings of the Book Trade in Canada*, chapters 3–5. Parker's seminal study has been updated in biographies of some publishers in recent volumes of the *Dictionary of Canadian Biography*.

4 Van Loon, *The Structure and Membership of the Canadian Cabinet*, 44–8.

5 Porter, *The Vertical Mosaic*. See also the more recent study, Cairns, *The Politics of Gender, Ethnicity, and Language in Canada*.

6: Stevenson, Lee, and the Garden of Childhood

1 A recent biography is McLynn's *Robert Louis Stevenson* (1993). The standard biography is still Furnas, *Voyage to Windward* (1952).

2 Published as *An Inland Voyage* (1878) and *Travels with a Donkey in the Cevennes* (1879).

3 Fanny Van de Grift (Osbourne) had lost a third child before

meeting Stevenson. A controversial figure, she is best treated in Lapierre's *Fanny Stevenson: Entre passion et liberté*, trans. Cosman as *Fanny Stevenson: Muse, Adventuress and Romantic Enigma*.

4 *Treasure Island* was first published as 'The Sea Cook, or Treasure Island' by 'Captain George North' in *Young Folks* (Oct. 1881–Jan. 1882).

5 *A Child's Garden of Verses* (Edinburgh, 1885). Citations will be to the most popular edition, with illustrations by Jessie Wilcox Smith (New York: Scribner's, 1905). I have prepared a new annotated edition of *A Child's Garden of Verses*, to be published by Edinburgh University Press, as part of the centennial edition of all Stevenson's works, under the general editorship of Catherine Kerrigan (Edinburgh: University of Edinburgh Press, 1994–).

6 Issued serially in *Young Folks* (May–June 1886).

7 The first edition and others such as the Tusitala edition are being updated in the centennial edition cited above.

8 Eigner, *Robert Louis Stevenson and Romantic Tradition*, 93.

9 First published in the Toronto *Globe*, these essays were reprinted in 1979 by the University of Toronto Press.

10 These stories are from Scott, *The Witching of Elspie*.

11 Keith, in *Charles G.D. Roberts*, refers to 'Roberts' excessive praise of Stevenson' (64).

12 Mowat has written about his own first experiences in the north as a boy in *Born Naked* (1993), 215–41.

13 The Stevenson quotation appears in the Canadian edition (Toronto: Lester and Orpen Dennys, 1981) but not in the British edition (London: Heinemann, 1983).

14 Bettelheim, *The Uses of Enchantment*, 62–3. Bettelheim discusses the way that fairy tales and Mother Goose rhymes help children achieve autonomy (136) and find consolation (145).

15 Lee, *Jelly Belly*, 18.

16 'The Swing,' *Alligator Pie* (1974), 23. Further citations are from this volume.

17 Letter to the author dated 14 March 1991.

18 The lines appear in one of the Frank Neufeld illustrations in *Garbage Delight* (27). They are quoted in Grady, 'A Man's Garden of Verse.'

19 Lecker shows the process at work with respect to Milton Acorn in *Making It Real*, 45.

20 'Lee, Dennis,' *The Oxford Companion to Canadian Literature*, 1st ed., ed. William Toye (1983).

21 Daiches, *Robert Louis Stevenson and His World*, 60.

22 Eigner, *Robert Louis Stevenson and Romantic Tradition*.

23 Richler wrote several times about a school system in Montreal dominated by a Scottishness inappropriate for a multicultural group. He mocked the books and texts and songs still largely chosen on Scottish principles. The caricature of Mr MacPherson, the teacher in *Duddy Kravitz*, reflects this resentment. Mr MacPherson offends Duddy by his glorification of John Buchan, Lord Tweedsmuir. In a chapter titled 'Bond' in *Shovelling Trouble*, Richler offers a memory of Buchan's visit to a Junior Red Cross Prize Day at school as part of an indictment of Buchan's anti-Semitism, 61–2, 67, 83.

24 Little's 'bibliotherapy' books include *Mine for Keeps* and *Mama's Going to Buy You a Mockingbird*.

7: Barrie, Montgomery, and the Mists of Sentiment

1 Wright, *J.M. Barrie*, mixes biography and criticism. A new study, Jack, *The Road to the Never Land*, emphasizes Barrie's dramatic art, but includes valuable biographical material.

2 Birkin, in *J.M. Barrie and the Lost Boys* (which focuses on Barrie's relationship with the Llewelyn Davies family), suggests that Barrie's reminiscences about the poverty of his childhood were a late-developed affectation.

3 Barrie, *Auld Licht Idylls*, 81.

4 Barrie, *A Window in Thrums*, 236.

5 Barrie, *The Little Minister*. Citations that follow refer to a 1929 reprint in the New York World's Popular Classics series.

6 Bettelheim, *The Uses of Enchantment*, 125.

7 'Kilmeny' in Hogg, *Selected Poems and Songs*, 29.

8 *The Letters of Robert Louis Stevenson, to His Family and Friends*, 2:268, 1 Nov. 1892.

9 It is worth noting that these men were ministers of the new Free

Church, as differentiated from the Reverend Micah Balwhidder's old-style Presbyterianism.

10 See Blake, *Barrie and The Kailyard School.* The term was first used by J.H. Millar.
11 Leacock doused sentimental Scottish stories in 'Hannah of the Highlands; or, The Laird of Loch Aucherlocherty,' *Nonsense Novels*, 137–56.
12 Barrie's plays are collected in *The Plays of J.M. Barrie* (1928). Jack, in *The Road to Never Land*, suggests, for instance, that *Quality Street* includes a subtext critical of meekness as a controlling feminine force.
13 Manlove, 'Introduction,' *An Anthology of Scottish Fantasy Literature*, 11.
14 Montgomery, *Anne of Green Gables*, 414.
15 Montgomery, *Selected Journals*, 3:125.
16 See Campbell, *Kailyard.*
17 See Vipond, 'Best Sellers in English Canada.'
18 Montgomery carefully makes the Stirling family Anglican and gives its members 'English' first names such as Wellington and Georgiana, but the Scottish quality of her own remembered Cavendish, Prince Edward Island (or of Thrums in Barrie's *Tommy and Grizel*) is visible in the 'Deerwood, Ontario,' of *The Blue Castle.*

8: Buchan, MacLennan, and the Winds of Violence

1 A good analysis of Buchan's work is Daniell, *The Interpreter's House.*
2 Fromm, in *The Anatomy of Human Destructiveness*, provides a general thesis about human tendency to violence.
3 Buchan, *Memory Hold-the-Door*, 194.
4 Douglas, *Unforgettable, Unforgotten*, 143.
5 Webb, 'Introduction,' *A Buchan Companion*, xv.
6 One way of interpreting the political drive in Buchan's novels appears in Kruse, *John Buchan and the Idea of Empire.*
7 Smith, in *John Buchan*, 294–6, provides figures for Buchan's sales.
8 The clearest account of these men and their fictional equivalents

is in Swiggett's introduction to *Sick Heart River*. Clanroyden, for instance, is based on the character of Auberon Herbert, a college friend lost in the war, with added touches drawn from the character of T.E. Lawrence. See also Hart, *The Scottish Novel*, 169.

9 Scott's contribution to the myth of martial prowess is discussed in Gordon, 'Scott, Ferguson, and the Martial Spirit.'

10 Buchan, *The Three Hostages*, 13.

11 Dr Conan Doyle, a graduate of the University of Edinburgh, modelled the powers of observation and intuition of Sherlock Holmes on those of his old mentor in the college of medicine, Dr Joseph Bell, and of Dr Syme, his teacher in surgical diagnosis. See Edwards, *The Quest for Sherlock Holmes*.

12 In *Myself and Michael Innes*, Stewart provides a few clues about his literary persona as a mystery writer. He would turn later to another kind of fiction produced under his real name. Interestingly, the most subtle part of Stewart's *Staircase in Surrey* quintet, set in Oxford, focuses on the life of a tense and indubitably gifted young Scot.

13 Muir, *Scottish Journey*, 227. See Stegmaier, 'Edwin Muir's *Scottish Journey* and the Question of Violence.'

14 See Wallace and Stevenson, *The Scottish Novel since the Seventies*.

15 The standard biography is Cameron, *Hugh MacLennan*.

16 MacLennan, *Each Man's Son* (1951), x. Further citations are from this edition.

17 MacLennan gives to his imaginary Cape Breton town the name 'Broughton,' the same name as the Tweedside village where John Buchan spent his childhood.

18 Woodcock, in *Hugh MacLennan*, praises MacLennan's philosophy, craftsmanship, social perceptions, and spiritual insights. Most recent critics stop short of such praise.

19 MacLulich, *Hugh MacLennan*, 76–8.

20 The title, *Scotchman's Return,* of the American edition, available in Canada, was changed to *Scotsman's Return* in British editions.

Braggart's in My Step

1 *Anne of Green Gables* was converted into two early films, both

great box-office successes although disappointing to Montgomery herself. Like the more recent television versions, they expanded worldwide awareness of the novel. Public response to *The Selected Journals of L.M. Montgomery* has also expanded Montgomery's audience, bringing serious critics to the point of confronting the artistry and subtlety of her once-scorned 'girls' books.' In print form, her reach has long been astonishing. Millions of readers have responded fanatically to Anne, Emily, Sara, Valancy, Pat, and the others, in English or in translations. *Anne of Green Gables* had reached sixty-eight editions by 1985 and had been translated into Swedish, Japanese, Hebrew, Finnish, Spanish – dozens of languages, including Braille.

2 Davey, *Post-National Arguments*, 266.
3 My sense of place and space derives in part from *Geographies of the Mind*, ed. Lowenthal and Bowden, and *Philosophy in Geography*, ed. Gale and Olsson.

Open the Door!

1 Papers from the 1991 conference appear in a special edition of *British Journal of Canadian Studies*, ed. Williams. I contributed the keynote address, which appears in part in the chapter on Stevenson and Lee in the present volume.
2 Several books by historians widened the focus: Beard, *Woman as Force in History*; Armstrong and Armstrong, *The Double Ghetto*; Gillett, *A History of Education*; *The Proper Sphere*, ed. Cook and Mitchinson; *The Neglected Majority*, ed. Trofimenkoff and Prentice.
3 Spacks, *The Female Imagination*; Showalter, *A Literature of Their Own*; Gilbert and Gubar, *The Madwoman in the Attic*; Kolodny, *The Lay of the Land*; Pratt, *Archetypal Patterns in Women's Fiction*; Tompkins, *Sensational Designs*; DuPlessis, *Writing Beyond the Ending*.
4 See also Epperly, *The Fragrance of Sweet-Grass*; and Waterston, *Kindling Spirit*.
5 A good round-up of the major theorists of the 1960s to 1980s is Eagleton, *Literary Theory*. Culler, *Structuralist Poetics*, is a useful summary of theories of the European luminaries.

6 See *An Anthology of Scottish Women Poets*, ed. Kerrigan.

7 See also *Scotlands* I.2 (1994).

8 *Re(Dis)covering Our Foremothers*, ed. McMullen; MacMillan, McMullen, and Waterston, *Silenced Sextet*.

9 See, for example, the work on narratology by Mieke Bal, Carol Gilligan, Barbara Godard, Barbara Johnson, Evelyn Keller, Mary Nyquist, Jacqueline Rose, and Madan Sarup.

10 Spacks, *Gossip* (1985). Page references in the text are to this edition.

11 The idea of a 'double colonization of women' has been explored by post-colonial critics such as Helen Tiffin and Anna Rutherford. Historically, the break away from imperial repression, often unthinking and often probably kindly meant, both empowers and is empowered by the writing that women produced over the last century and a half.

12 Fielding studies the national rites of speech in *Writing and Orality.*

13 See Hutcheon's listing of postmodern qualities in *A Poetics of Postmodernism*; many of her terms are applicable to Scottish literature, past and present.

14 Hutcheon, *The Canadian Postmodern.*

9: Sinclair, Saunders, and the Outskirts of Story

1 See, for instance, *A Critical History of Children's Literature*, by the American scholar Cornelia Meigs, and *Written for Children*, by English critic John Rowe Townsend.

2 Compare the memories in *A Scottish Childhood*, ed. Kamm and Lean.

3 See Hart, *The Scottish Novel*, 93–7.

4 Williams says that Oliphant authored over a hundred works, including non-fiction. See Williams, *Margaret Oliphant*, and Colby and Colby, *The Equivocal Virtue*. A fine recent study is Jay, *Mrs Oliphant: 'A Fiction to Herself.'*

5 See Gray, 'Religion, Culture and Social Class in Late Nineteenth and Early Twentieth Century Edinburgh.'

6 The quotation is from *We Travel Home* (1934), 258. Quoted by Dickson in 'Annie S. Swan and O. Douglas,' 332.

7 See also DuPlessis, *Writing Beyond the Ending*.
8 See Smith, 'And Woman Created Woman,' 41–3; also Elphinstone, 'Willa Muir: Crossing the Genres.'
9 The extent of influence is suggested in Murray's title: 'Selves, Names and Roles: Willa Muir's *Imagined Corners* Offers Some Inspiration for *A Scots Quair*.'
10 See John Carswell, 'Introduction' to Virago edition of Catherine Carswell, *Open the Door!* Norquay's 'Catherine Carswell, *Open the Door!*' cites only a negative comment in Morris, *Literature and Feminism*, 142–3.
11 See DuPlessis, *Writing Beyond the Ending*.
12 Angus MacDonald, 'Modern Scots Novelists,' in *Edinburgh Essays on Scots Literature*, ed. Wood (1933); quoted by Dickson in 'Annie S. Swan and O. Douglas,' 341.
13 *Silenced Sextet*, by MacMillan, McMullen, and Waterston, deals with six of these underestimated women writers of the nineteenth century: Rosanna Mullins Leprohon, May Agnes Fleming, Margaret Murray Robertson, Susan Frances Harrison ('Seranus'), Margaret Marshall Saunders, and Joanna E. Wood.
14 Robertson's life is covered in a one-column entry by Demers in the *Oxford Companion to Canadian Literature* (1997, unchanged from 1983). There is no entry on her in the 1967 edition.
15 Tausky, in his entry in the *Oxford Companion to Canadian Literature* (1997), notes, 'Nearly thirty articles have been written in the same number of years about *The Imperialist*.' Early and late I have contributed to the total, from 'Canadian Cabbage, Canadian Rose' in 1973 to '*The Imperialist* and the Politics of Presbyterian Ministry' in 1995. There have also been three full-length studies of Duncan, by Misao Dean, Marian Fowler, and Thomas E. Tausky.
16 A brief account of Saunders' life appears in 'Margaret Marshall Saunders,' an MA thesis written at Acadia University (1978) by her niece Karen Saunders.
17 See McMullen, 'Marshall Saunders' Mid-Victorian Cinderella'; see also Waterston, 'Marshall Saunders: A Voice for the Silent,' *Silenced Sextet*, by MacMillan, McMullen, and Waterston, 137–68.
18 *Beautiful Joe*, published first in the United States, was reprinted in

a hundredth anniversary edition in 1994 by the Ginger Press in Owen Sound, near the small town of Meaford where the original of Joe lived.

19 This novel, like L.M. Montgomery's early novels, was published by L.C. Page and Company of Boston. Page had a bad reputation for exploiting the women who wrote the very popular books he published. See *The Selected Journals of L.M. Montgomery*, 3:136–7, for a late typical conversation between Saunders and Montgomery about the conditions of publishing that oppressed ·women writers.

20 Red-haired, impulsive, and voluble, Bidiane anticipates and perhaps is a model for Montgomery's Anne.

21 Saunders had written more sentimentally about orphans in *'Tilda Jane: an Orphan in Search of a Home* in 1901 and in other works, again antedating Montgomery.

22 Munro, 'Afterword,' L.M. Montgomery, *Emily of New Moon*, New Canadian Library (1989).

23 See the impressive bibliographies in *A History of Scottish Women's Writing*, ed. Gifford and MacMillan, 676–707.

10: Duncan, Munro, and the Vistas of Memory

1 See Stanford, *Muriel Spark*, 37–40.

2 Stanford's *Muriel Spark* (1963) and Massie's *Muriel Spark* (1979) were published in Edinburgh. Bold, *Muriel Spark* (1986), Hynes, *Critical Essays on Muriel Spark* (1992), and Whittaker, *The Faith and Fiction of Muriel Spark* (1982) are among other valuable critics of Spark.

3 For a commentary on the full complexity of the novel, see Robb, *'Greenvoe*: A Poet's Novel.' Bold, in *George Mackay Brown*, surveys Brown's full range of work in short stories, essays, and novels. See also Murray and Tait, 'George Mackay Brown: *Greenvoe*.'

4 Hayles, *Chaos Bound*.

5 Hart and Hart, 'Jane Duncan: The Homecoming of Imagination.'

6 The only major study I know is the half-chapter on Duncan in Hart, *The Scottish Novel*, 385–93, and the article by Lorena and Francis Hart, cited in the previous note.

7 Munro, 'Friend of My Youth,' *Friend of My Youth*, 4–5. Subsequent references are to this volume.
8 Ross, *Alice Munro: A Double Life*.
9 Gittings, 'The Scottish Ancestor,' 89.
10 Gittings, 'A Conversation with Alistair MacLeod,' 98.
11 MacLeod, 'A Tuning of Perfection,' *As Birds Bring Forth the Sun and Other Stories*, 102.
12 Nicholson, 'Regions of Memory,' 131. See also Nicholson, 'Footprints on the Soul.'
13 *Literary History of Canada*, ed. Klinck (1st ed., 1965), 849. The 'Conclusion' is the same in both first and second editions, Canadian version.

Brought to Mind

1 Crawford, *Devolving English Literature*, 3.
2 Drescher, 'Identity,' 7–8.

Books Cited

Primary Texts

Acorn, Milton. *Dig Up My Heart: Selected Poems, 1952–1983*. Toronto: McClelland & Stewart, 1983.

– *I Shout Love and Other Poems*. Toronto: AYA Press, 1987.

– *The Island Means Minago*. Toronto: NC Press, 1975.

– *More Poems for People*. Toronto: NC Press, 1972.

– *Whiskey Jack*. Ed. James Deahl. Scarborough: HMS Press, 1986.

Alexander, William. *Johnny Gibb of Gushetneuk*. Introd. William Donaldson. East Linton: Tuckwell, 1995.

Atwood, Margaret. *Alias Grace*. Toronto: McClelland & Stewart, 1996.

– *Bodily Harm*. Toronto: McClelland & Stewart, 1981.

– *Surfacing*. Toronto: Anansi, 1972.

– *Survival*. Toronto: Anansi, 1972.

Aubert de Gaspé, Philippe. *Canadians of Old*. 1863. Trans. C.G.D. Roberts. New York: Appleton, 1890.

Barker, Elspeth. *O Caledonia*. London: Penguin, 1991.

Barrie, J.M. *Auld Licht Idylls*. London: Hodder and Stoughton, 1888.

– *The Little Minister*. 1891. Repr. New York World's Popular Classics, 1929.

– *Peter Pan; or, The Boy Who Would Not Grow Up*. In *The Plays of J.M. Barrie*.

– *The Plays of J.M. Barrie*. London: Hodder and Stoughton, 1911.

– *A Window in Thrums*. London: Hodder and Stoughton, 1889.

Brown, George Mackay. *Greenvoe*. London: Hogarth, 1972.

Bruce, Charles. *The Channel Shore*. Toronto: Macmillan, 1954.

Buchan, John. *Memory Hold-the-Door*. London: Nelson, 1940.

– *Sick Heart River*. 1941. Ed. Howard Swiggett. Toronto: Musson, 1944.

– *The Thirty-Nine Steps*. London: Hodder and Stoughton, 1915.

– *The Three Hostages*. London: Hodder and Stoughton, 1926.

– *Witch Wood*. London: Hodder and Stoughton, 1927.

Burns, Robert. *The Poems and Songs of Robert Burns*. Ed. James Kinsley. 3 vols. Oxford: Clarendon, 1968.

Campbell, W.W. *The Poems of Wilfred Campbell*. Toronto: Briggs, 1905.

Carlyle, Thomas. *The Collected Letters of Thomas and Jane Welsh Carlyle*. 28 vols. Ed. C.R. Sanders, C. Ryals, K.J. Fielding, W. Bell, I. Campbell, A. Christianson, J. Clubbe, and H. Smith. Durham: Duke University Press, 1970–99.

– *Reminiscences*. 1881. Introd. Ian Campbell. London: Dent, 1972.

– *Sartor Resartus*. 1834. Introd. W.H. Hudson. London: Dent, 1908.

– 'Sir Walter Scott.' *Critical and Miscellaneous Essays, 4, The Works of Thomas Carlyle*, 29. Ed. H.D. Traill. Centenary ed. London: Chapman and Hall, 1896–9.

Carman, Bliss. *The Selected Poems of Bliss Carman*. Ed. Lorne Pierce. Toronto: McClelland & Stewart, 1954.

Carswell, Catherine. *Open the Door!* 1920. Repr. London: Virago, 1986.

Cohen, Leonard. *Selected Poems, 1956–1968*. Toronto: McClelland & Stewart, 1968.

Crawford, Isabella Valancy. *The Collected Poems of Isabella Valancy Crawford*. Ed. J.W. Garvin; with an introd. by Ethelwyn Wetherald. 1905. Repr., ed. James Reaney, Toronto: University of Toronto Press, 1972.

– *Malcolm's Katie: A Love Story*. Ed. D.M.R. Bentley. London, Ont: Canadian Poetry Press, 1987.

Crockett, S.R. *The Stickit Minister*. London: Bliss Sands, 1896.

Dewdney, Selwyn. *Wind without Rain*. Toronto: Copp Clark, 1946.

Douglas, O. *Penny Plain*. London: Hodder and Stoughton, 1922.

– *Pink Sugar*. London: Hodder and Stoughton, 1924.

– *Unforgettable, Unforgotten*. London: Hodder and Stoughton, 1945.

Drummond, W.H. *The Habitant and Other French-Canadian Poems.*
New York: Putnam, 1907.

Duncan, Jane. *Letter from Reachfar.* London: Macmillan, 1975.

– *My Friends George and Tom.* London: Macmillan, 1976.

– *My Friend Muriel.* London: Macmillan, 1959.

– *My Friends the Hungry Generation.* London: Macmillan, 1968.

– *My Friends the Miss Boyds.* London: Macmillan, 1957.

– *My Friend the Swallow.* London: Macmillan, 1970.

– (as Janet Sandison). *Jean in the Morning.* London: Macmillan, 1969.

– *Jean at Twilight.* London: Macmillan, 1972.

Duncan, Sara Jeannette. *The Imperialist.* 1904. Repr. Toronto:
McClelland & Stewart, 1961.

Dunlop, William. *Statistical Sketches of Upper Canada.* 1832. Repr. as
Tiger Dunlop's Upper Canada. Ed. Carl Klinck. Toronto: McClelland
& Stewart, 1967.

Findley, Timothy. *The Wars.* London: Penguin, 1977.

Galt, John. *Annals of the Parish, or, The Chronicle of Dalmailing during
the Ministry of the Rev. Micah Balwhidder ...* 1821. Repr., ed. James
Kingsley, Oxford English Novels, London: Oxford University
Press, 1967.

– *Autobiography.* London: Cochrane and McCrone, 1833.

– *Bogle Corbet; or, The Emigrants.* London: Colburn & Bentley, 1831.
Vol. 3 repr. Toronto: McClelland & Stewart, 1977.

– 'Statistical Account of Upper Canada.' *Philosophical Magazine,*
October 1807.

Galbraith, J.K. *The Scotch.* Toronto: Macmillan, 1964.

Gibbon, Lewis Grassic. *Sunset Song.* London: Jarrolds, 1932.

Hogg, James. *The Private Memoirs and Confessions of a Justified Sinner.*
1824. London: Cressett, 1947.

– *Selected Poems and Songs.* Ed. David Groves. Edinburgh: Scottish
Academic Press, 1986.

Innes, Michael. *Lament for a Maker.* London: Penguin, 1938.

Johnson, Pauline. *Flint and Feather.* Toronto: Musson, 1912.

Klein, A.M. *The Rocking Chair and Other Poems.* Toronto: Ryerson,
1948.

Laurence, Margaret. *The Diviners.* Toronto: McClelland & Stewart,
1974.

– *The Fire-Dwellers*. Toronto: McClelland & Stewart, 1969.
– *Heart of a Stranger*. Toronto: Macmillan, 1976.
– *Selected Letters of Margaret Laurence and Adele Wiseman*. Ed. John Lennox and Ruth Panofsky. Toronto: University of Toronto Press, 1997.
Layton, Irving. *Collected Poems*. Toronto: McClelland & Stewart, 1965.
Leacock, Stephen. *Nonsense Novels*. London: John Lane, 1911.
Lee, Dennis. *Alligator Pie*. Toronto: Macmillan, 1974.
– *Garbage Delight*. Toronto: Macmillan, 1977.
– *Jelly Belly*. Toronto: Macmillan, 1983.
Leprohon, Rosanna. *The Manor House of de Villerai: A Tale of Canada under the French Dominion*. Ed. J.R. Sorfleet. *Journal of Canadian Fiction* 34 (1985).
Lightfoot, Gordon. *I Wish You Good Spaces: Poetic Selections from the Songs of Gordon Lightfoot*. Ed. S.P. Schutz. Boulder: Blue Mountain, 1977.
Little, Jean. *Mama's Going to Buy You a Mockingbird*. New York: Viking, 1984.
– *Mine for Keeps*. Boston: Little, Brown, 1962.
Lunn, Janet. *The Root Cellar*. Toronto: Lester and Orpen Dennys, 1981.
McClung, Nellie. *Sowing Seeds in Danny*. New York: Doubleday, 1908.
MacDiarmid, Hugh. *A Drunk Man Looks at the Thistle*. 1926. Ed. Kenneth Buthlay. Edinburgh: Scottish Academic Press, 1987.
McLachlan, Alexander. *The Emigrant*. 1861. Ed. D.M.R. Bentley. London: Canadian Poetry Press, 1991.
– *The Poetical Works of Alexander McLachlan*. Ed. E.M. Fulton. Toronto: University of Toronto Press, 1974.
Maclaren, Ian. *Beside the Bonnie Brier Bush*. New York: Dodd Mead, 1895.
MacLennan, Hugh. *Barometer Rising*. New York: Duell Sloan & Pierce, 1941.
– *Each Man's Son*. Boston: Little, Brown, 1951.
– *The Precipice*. Toronto: Collins, 1949.
– *Return of the Sphinx*. Toronto: Macmillan, 1967.
– *Scotchman's Return and Other Essays*. New York: Scribner, 1960. Title in UK is *Scotsman's Return*.
– *Two Solitudes*. New York: Duell Sloan, 1945.

– *The Watch that Ends the Night*. Toronto: Macmillan, 1959.

MacLeod, Alistair. *As Birds Bring Forth the Sun and Other Stories*. 1986. Repr. with afterword by Jane Urquhart. Toronto: McClelland & Stewart, 1992.

– *The Last Salt Gift of Blood*. 1976. Repr. with afterword by Joyce Carol Oates. Toronto: McClelland & Stewart, 1989.

Macmillan, Cyrus. *Canadian Fairy Tales*. Toronto: Gundy, 1922.

– *Canadian Wonder Tales*. Toronto: Gundy, 1918.

Mactaggart, John. *Three Years in Canada: An Account of the Actual State of the Country in 1826–7–8 ...* London: Colburn, 1829.

Mitchell, W.O. *The Vanishing Point*. Toronto: Macmillan, 1973.

Montgomery, L.M. *Anne of Green Gables*. Boston: L.C. Page, 1908.

– *The Blue Castle*. Toronto: McClelland & Stewart, 1926.

– *Kilmeny of the Orchard*. Boston: Page, 1911.

– *The Selected Journals of L.M. Montgomery*. Ed. Mary Rubio and Elizabeth Waterston. 4 vols. Toronto: Oxford University Press, 1985–98.

Moodie, Susanna. *Roughing It in the Bush*. 1852. Repr., ed. Carl Ballstadt. Ottawa: Carleton University Press, 1988.

Mowat, Farley. *Born Naked*. Toronto: Key Porter, 1991.

– *Lost in the Barrens*. Boston: Little, Brown, 1956.

Muir, Edwin. *Scottish Journey*. 1935. Repr., ed. T.C. Smout. Edinburgh: Scottish Academic Press, 1980.

Muir, Willa. *Imagined Corners*. 1931. Repr. Edinburgh: Canongate, 1987.

Munro, Alice. 'Afterword.' *Emily of New Moon*, by L.M. Montgomery. Toronto: McClelland & Stewart, 1989.

– *Friend of My Youth: Stories*. New York: Knopf, 1990.

Oliphant, Margaret. *Some Passages in the Life of Mrs. Margaret Maitland*. London: Colburn, 1849.

Pratt, E.J. *E.J. Pratt on His Life and Poetry*. Ed. Susan Gingell. Toronto: University of Toronto Press, 1983.

– *Towards the Last Spike*. Toronto: Macmillan, 1952.

Raddall, Thomas. *Hangman's Beach*. Toronto: Doubleday, 1966.

– *In My Time: A Memoir*. Toronto: McClelland and Stewart, 1976.

– *The Pied Piper of Dipper Creek and Other Tales*. Introd. John Buchan. Edinburgh: Blackwood, 1939.

Reaney, James. *The Boy with an R in His Hand*. Toronto: Macmillan, 1965.

– *Twelve Letters to a Small Town*. Toronto: Ryerson, 1962.

Richardson, John. *Wacousta; or, The Prophecy: a Tale of the Canadas*. 1832. Repr., ed. D.R. Cronk. Ottawa: Carleton University Press, 1987.

Richler, Mordecai. *The Apprenticeship of Duddy Kravitz*. London: Andre Deutsch, 1959.

– *Shovelling Trouble*. Toronto: McClelland & Stewart, 1972.

Robertson, Margaret. *Shenac's Work at Home*. 1866. Repr., ed. Gwendolyn Guth. Ottawa: Tecumseh, 1993.

Saunders, Margaret Marshall. *Beautiful Joe: An Autobiography*. Philadelphia: American Baptist Publishing Society, 1894.

– *Bonnie Prince Fetlar: The Story of a Pony and His Friends*. Toronto: McClelland & Stewart, 1920.

– *The Girl from Vermont: The Story of a Vacation School Teacher*. Boston: Griffin & Rowland, 1910.

– *My Spanish Sailor*. London: Ward, 1889.

– *Rose à Charlitte: An Acadien Romance*. Boston: L.C. Page, 1898.

– *The Story of the Graveleys: A Tale for Girls*. Toronto: Briggs, 1903.

– *'Tilda Jane: An Orphan in Search of a Home*. Boston: Page, 1901.

Scott, Duncan Campbell. *Selected Poems of Duncan Campbell Scott*. Ed. Glen Clever. Ottawa: Tecumseh, 1974.

– *The Witching of Elspie*. Toronto: McClelland& Stewart, 1923.

Scott, Frank. *Overture: Poems*. Toronto: Ryerson, 1945.

Scott, Walter. *The Lady of the Lake*. 1810. *The Poetical Works of Sir Walter Scott*. Ed. J. Logie Robertson. London: Henry Froude, 1896. Repr., ed. C.L. Bennet. New York: Airmont, 1967.

– *Waverley, or, 'Tis Sixty Years Since*. 1814. Repr., ed. Richard Humphrey. Cambridge: Cambridge University Press, 1993.

Sellar, Robert. *Hemlock: A Tale of the War of 1812*. Montreal: Grafton, 1890.

– *Morven: A Legend of Glengarry*. 1910. Repr. Toronto: Britnell's, 1917.

Service, Robert. *Ploughman of the Moon: An Adventure in Memory*. New York: Dodd, Mead, 1945.

– *Songs of a Sourdough*. Toronto: Briggs, 1907.

Sinclair, Catherine. *Beatrice; or, The Unknown Relatives*. Edinburgh: Whyte, 1852.

– *Holiday House*. 1839. Repr. Edinburgh: Hamish Hamilton, 1972.

– *Jane Bouverie; or, Prosperity and Adversity*. Edinburgh: Whyte, 1846.

– *Modern Accomplishments; or, The March of Intellect*. Edinburgh: Whyte, 1836.

Stevenson, Robert Louis. *A Child's Garden of Verses*. 1885. Repr., illus. Jessie Wilcox Smith. New York: Scribner's, 1905.

– 'A Gossip on Romance.' *Longman's Magazine*, Nov. 1882.

– *Kidnapped*. 1886. London: Oxford University Press, 1964.

Stewart, J.I.M. *Myself and Michael Innes: A Memoir*. London: Gollancz, 1987.

Strickland, Samuel. *Twenty-Seven Years in Canada West; or, the Experiences of an Early Settler*. London: Bentley, 1853.

Walker, David Harry. *Ash*. Boston: Houghton Mifflin, 1976.

– *Black Dougal*. London: Collins, 1978.

– *Geordie*. London: Collins, 1950.

– *Harry Black: A Novel*. London: Collins, 1956.

– *Lean, Wind, Lean: A Few Times Remembered*. London: Collins, 1984.

– *The Storm and the Silence*. Boston: Houghton Mifflin, 1949.

– *Where the High Winds Blow*. London: Collins, 1960.

Secondary Sources

Ahmad, Aijaz, ed. *In Theory: Classes, Nations, Literatures*. London: Verso, 1992.

– *Occidentosis: A Plague from the West*. Berkeley: Mizan, 1984.

Åhmansson, Gabriella. *A Life and Its Mirrors: A Feminist Reading of L.M. Montgomery's Fiction*. Uppsala: University of Uppsala, 1991.

Alexander, J.H., ed. *The Tavern Sages*. Aberdeen: Association for Scottish Literary Studies, 1992.

– and David Hewitt, eds. *Scott in Carnival: Selected Papers from the 4th International Scott Conference, Edinburgh, 1991*. Aberdeen: Association for Scottish Literary Studies, 1993.

Allan, David. *Virtue, Learning and the Scottish Enlightenment: Ideas of Scholarship in Early Modern History*. Edinburgh: Edinburgh University Press, 1993.

Armstrong, Pat, and Hugh Armstrong. *The Double Ghetto: Canadian Women and Their Segregated Work*. Toronto: McGraw-Hill, 1966.

Bachelard, Gaston. *The Poetics of Space*. Trans. Maria Jolas. New York: Orion, 1964.

Bakhtin, Mikhail. *The Formal Method in Literary Scholarship*. Trans. A.J. Wehrle. Cambridge: Harvard University Press, 1985.
– *Rabelais and His World*. Trans. Hélène Iswolsky. Blomington: Indiana University Press, 1984.
Bal, Mieke. *Narratology: Introduction to the Theory of Narrative*. Trans. Christine van Boheemen. Toronto: University of Toronto Press, 1985.
– *On Storytelling: Essays in Narratology*. Sonoma: Polebridge, 1991.
Ballstadt, Carl. *Major John Richardson: A Selection of Reviews and Criticism*. Montreal: Lande Foundation, 1972.
Barthes, Roland. *Mythologies*. Trans. Annette Lavers. London: Cape, 1972.
Bate, W.J. *The Burden of the Past and the English Poet*. Cambridge: Belknap, 1970.
Batho, Edith. 'Sir Walter Scott and the Sagas: Some Notes.' *Modern Language Review* 24 (1929): 409–15.
Beard, Mary R. *Woman as Force in History: A Study of Transitions and Realities*. New York: Macmillan, 1946.
Bell, Alan, ed. *Scott Bicentenary Essays: Selected Papers Read at the Sir Walter Scott Bicentenary Conference*. Edinburgh: Scottish Academic Press, 1973.
Benson, Eugene, and William Toye, eds. *The Oxford Companion to Canadian Literature*. 2nd ed. Toronto: Oxford University Press, 1997.
Bettelheim, Bruno. *The Uses of Enchantment: The Meaning and Importance of Fairy Tales*. New York: Knopf, 1976.
Birkerts, Sven. *The Gutenberg Elegies: The Fate of Reading in an Electronic Age*. New York: Faber & Faber, 1996.
Birkin, Andrew. *J.M. Barrie and the Lost Boys*. London: Constable, 1979.
Bittenbender, J.C. 'Bakhtinian Carnival in the Poetry of Robert Burns.' *Scottish Literary Journal* 21 (1994): 23–38.
Blake, George. *Barrie and the Kailyard School*. London: Arthur Barker, 1951.
Bloom, Harold. *The Anxiety of Influence: A Theory of Poetry*. 1973. 2nd ed. New York: Oxford University Press, 1997.
– *The Western Canon: The Books and School of the Ages*. New York: Harcourt Brace, 1994.

Bold, Alan. *George Mackay Brown*. Edinburgh: Oliver and Boyd, 1978.
– *Muriel Spark*. London: Methuen, 1986.
Brooks, Cleanth, and R.P. Warren. *Understanding Poetry*. New York: Holt, 1938.
Bumsted, J.M. *The People's Clearance: Highland Emigration to British North America, 1770–1815*. Edinburgh: Edinburgh University Press, 1982.
Burness, Edwina. 'The Influence of Burns and Fergusson on the War Poetry of Robert Service.' *Studies in Scottish Literature* 21 (1986): 135–46.
Cairns, Alan. *The Politics of Gender, Ethnicity, and Language in Canada*. Toronto: University of Toronto Press, 1986.
Calder, Jenni. *RLS: A Life Study*. London: Hamish Hamilton, 1980.
Cameron, Elspeth. *Hugh MacLennan: A Writer's Life*. Toronto: University of Toronto Press, 1981.
Campbell, Ian. 'Fiction and Experience in the Works of Sir Walter Scott.' *Scottish Tradition* 1 (winter 1971): 1–13.
– *Kailyard*. Edinburgh: Ramsay Head, 1981.
– ed. *Thomas and Jane: Selected Letters from the Edinburgh University Library Collection*. Edinburgh: Friends of the Edinburgh University Library, 1980.
– *Thomas Carlyle*. London: Hamish Hamilton, 1974.
Campbell, Roy, and Andrew Skinner, eds. *The Origins and Nature of the Scottish Enlightenment* Edinburgh: John Donald, 1982.
Carswell, John. 'Introduction.' *Open the Door!* by Catherine Carswell. London: Virago, 1986.
Clever, Glenn, ed. *The E.J. Pratt Symposium*. Ottawa: University of Ottawa Press, 1977.
Cogswell, Fred. 'Literary Activity in the Maritime Provinces (1815–1880).' *Literary History of Canada*, ed. C.F. Klinck. 2nd ed. 1:116–38. Toronto, University of Toronto Press, 1976.
Colby, Vineta, and Robert Colby. *The Equivocal Virtue: Mrs Oliphant and the Victorian Literary Market Place*. Hamden: Archon, 1966.
Collard, Edgar, ed., *The McGill You Knew*. Montreal: McGill University Press, 1975.
Colley, Linda. *Britons: Forging the Nation, 1707–1837*. New Haven: Yale University Press, 1992.

Compton, Anne. *A.J.M. Smith: Canadian Metaphysical*. Toronto: ECW
  Press, 1994.
Cook, Ramsay, and Wendy Mitchinson, eds. *The Proper Sphere:*
  Women's Place in Canadian Society. Toronto: Oxford University
  Press, 1976.
Costain, Keith. 'Theoretical History and the Novel: The Scottish
  Fiction of John Galt,' *Essays on Literary History* 43 (1976): 342–65.
Cowan, E.J. 'Icelandic Studies in Eighteenth and Nineteenth Scot-
  land.' *Studia Islandica*, ed. S.J. Korsteinsson. Reyjavik: University of
  Iceland, 1972.
Cowan, Helen I. *British Emigration to British North America: The First*
  Hundred Years. Toronto: University of Toronto Press, 1961.
Craig, David. *Scottish Literature and the Scottish People, 1680–1830*.
  London: Chatto and Windus, 1961.
Crawford, Robert. *Devolving English Literature*. Oxford: Clarendon,
  1992.
– ed. *Robert Burns and Cultural Authority*. Edinburgh: Edinburgh
  University Press, 1997.
Crawford, Thomas. *Burns: A Study of the Poems and Songs*. 1965. Repr.
  Edinburgh: Canongate, 1994.
– *Scott*. Edinburgh: Oliver and Boyd, 1965.
Cronk, Douglas. 'The Editorial Destruction of Canadian Literature: A
  Textual Study of Major John Richardson's *Wacousta; or, the Proph-*
  ecy.' MA dissertation, Simon Fraser University, 1977.
Crosby, Alfred. *Ecological Imperialism: The Biological Expansion of*
  Europe, 900–1900. Cambridge: Cambridge University Press, 1986.
Crosland, T.W.H. *The Unspeakable Scot*. London: Grant Richards,
  1902.
Culler, Jonathan. *Structuralist Poetics: Structuralism, Linguistics, and*
  the Study of Literature. Ithaca: Cornell University Press, 1975.
Daiches, David. *The Novel and the Modern World*. Chicago: University
  of Chicago Press, 1939.
– *The Paradox of Scottish Culture: The Eighteenth-Century Experience*.
  London: Oxford University Press, 1964.
– *Poetry and the Modern World*. Chicago: University of Chicago Press,
  1940.
– *Robert Burns and His World*. 1966. Repr. New York: Viking, 1971.

– 'Robert Burns: The Tightrope Walker.' *Love and Liberty: Bicentennial Essays on Robert Burns*, ed. Kenneth Simpson. East Linton: Tuckwell, 1997.

– *Robert Louis Stevenson and His World*. London: Thames and Hudson, 1973.

Daniell, David. *The Interpreter's House: A Critical Assessment of John Buchan*. London: Nelson, 1975.

Davey, Frank. 'E.J. Pratt: Rationalist Technician,' *Canadian Literature* 61 (summer 1974): 65–78.

– *Post-National Arguments: The Politics of the Anglophone-Canadian Novel since 1967*. Toronto: University of Toronto Press, 1993.

Davies, Gwendolyn. 'Capturing the British Literary Market: Marshall Saunders and Late Nineteenth-Century Canadian Writing.' *Imperial Canada, 1867–1917*, ed. Colin M. Coates. Edinburgh: Centre of Canadian Studies, 1997.

– ed. *Studies in Maritime Literary History, 1760–1930*. Fredericton: Acadiensis, 1991.

Davies, R.A., ed. *On Thomas Chandler Haliburton: Selected Criticism*. Ottawa: Tecumseh, 1979.

Daymond, Douglas, and Leslie Monkman, eds. *Literature in Canada*. Toronto: Gage, 1978.

Dean, Misao. *A Different Point of View: Sara Jeannette Duncan*. Montreal: McGill-Queen's University Press, 1991.

Derrida, Jacques. *Of Grammatology*. Trans. G.C. Spivak. Baltimore: Johns Hopkins University Press, 1976.

Dickson, Beth. 'Annie S. Swan and O. Douglas: Legacies of the Kailyard.' *A History of Scottish Women's Writing*, ed. Douglas Gifford and Dorothy McMillan. Edinburgh: Edinburgh University Press, 1997.

Djwa, Sandra. *E.J. Pratt: The Evolutionary Vision*. Vancouver: Copp Clark, 1974.

Donaldson, G. *The Scots Overseas*. London: Robert Hale, 1966.

Donoghue, Denis. *Ferocious Alphabets*. Boston: Little, Brown, 1987.

Doucette, Laurel. *Cultural Retention and Demographic Change: Studies of the Hebridean Scots in the Eastern Townships of Quebec*. Ottawa: National Museums of Canada, 1980.

Drescher, Horst. 'Identity,' *Scottish Literary Journal* 21 (1994): 7–8.

– ed. *Thomas Carlyle, 1981*. Frankfurt am Main: Verlag Peter Lang, 1983.

Drolet, Gilbert. '"Prayers against Despair"': A Retrospective Note on Findley's *The Wars.' Journal of Canadian Fiction* 33 (1981–2): 142–55.

Dudek, Louis. *Selected Essays and Criticism*. Ottawa: Tecumseh, 1978.

Duffy, Dennis. *Sounding the Iceberg: An Essay on Canadian Historical Novels*. Toronto: ECW Press, 1986.

Duncan, K.J. 'Patterns of Settlement in the East.' *The Scottish Tradition in Canada*, ed. W. Stanford Reid. Toronto: McClelland & Stewart, 1976.

DuPlessis, Rachel Blau. *Writing beyond the Ending: Narrative Strategies of Twentieth-Century Women Writers*. Bloomington: Indiana University Press, 1985.

Eagleton, Terry. *Exiles and Emigrés: Studies in Modern Literature*. New York: Oxford University Press, 1973.

– *Literary Theory: An Introduction*. Minneapolis: University of Minnesota Press, 1983.

– ed. *Nationalism, Colonialism and Literature*. Minneapolis: University of Minnesota Press, 1990.

Edwards, Mary Jane. 'McLachlan, Alexander.' *Dictionary of Canadian Biography*. 12:622. Toronto: University of Toronto Press, 1990.

Edwards, Owen Dudley. *The Quest for Sherlock Holmes: A Biographic Study of Arthur Conan Doyle*. Edinburgh: Mainstream, 1983.

Eigner, Edwin. *Robert Louis Stevenson and Romantic Tradition*. Princeton: Princeton University Press, 1966.

Elphinstone, Margaret. 'Willa Muir: Crossing the Genres.' *A History of Scottish Women's Writting*, ed. Douglas Gifford and Dorothy McMillan. Edinburgh: Edinburgh University Press, 1997.

Epperly, Elizabeth Rollins. *The Fragrance of Sweet-Grass: L.M. Montgomery's Heroines and the Pursuit of Romance*. Toronto: University of Toronto Press, 1992.

Farmiloe, Dorothy. *Isabella Valancy Crawford: The Life and Legends*. Ottawa: Tecumseh, 1983.

Ferguson, De Lancy. *Pride and Passion: Robert Burns, 1759–1796*. New York: Oxford University Press, 1929.

Fielding, Penny. *Writing and Orality: Nationality, Culture, and Nineteenth-Century Scottish Fiction*. Oxford: Clarendon, 1996.

Fowler, Marian. *Redney: A Life of Sara Jeannette Duncan*. Toronto: Anansi, 1983.

Fowler, R.H. *Robert Burns*. London: Routledge, 1988.

Fromm, Erich. *The Anatomy of Human Destructiveness*. New York: Holt, Rinehart and Winston, 1973.

Frye, Northrop. *The Anatomy of Criticism: Four Essays*. Toronto: University of Toronto Press, 1957.

– *The Educated Imagination*. Toronto: Canadian Broadcasting Company, 1963.

– *The Secular Scripture: A Study of the Structure of Romance*. Cambridge: Harvard University Press, 1976.

Frykman, Erik. *John Galt's Scottish Stories, 1820–1823*. Uppsala: Lundequistka, 1959.

Furnas, J.C. *Voyage to Windward: The Life of Robert Louis Stevenson*. New York: Sloane, 1951.

Fussell, Paul. *The Great War and Modern Memory*. London: Oxford University Press, 1975.

Gale, Stephen, and Gunner Olsson, eds. *Philosophy in Geography*. Boston: Reidel, 1979.

Galvin, Elizabeth McNeill. *Isabella Valancy Crawford: We Scarcely Knew Her*. Toronto: Natural Heritage/Natural History, 1994.

Gerson, Carole. *A Purer Taste: The Writing and Reading of Fiction in Nineteenth-Century Canada*. Toronto: University of Toronto Press, 1989.

Gifford, Douglas, and Dorothy McMillan, eds. *A History of Scottish Women's Writing*. Edinburgh: Edinburgh University Press, 1997.

Gilbert, Sandra M., and Susan Gubar. *The Madwoman in the Attic: The Woman Writer and the Nineteenth Century Literary Imagination*. New Haven: Yale University Press, 1979.

Gillett, Margaret. *A History of Education: Thought and Practice*. Toronto: McGraw-Hill, 1966.

Gittings, Chris. 'A Conversation with Alistair MacLeod.' *Scotlands* (1995): 88–106.

– 'The Scottish Ancestor: A Conversation with Alice Munro,' *Scotlands* (1994): 83–96.

Glotfelty, Cheryl, and Harold Fromm, eds. *The Ecocriticism Reader*. Athens: University of Georgia Press, 1996.

Godard, Barbara, ed. *Gynocritics/ La gynocritique: Feminist Approaches to Canadian and Quebec Women's Writing.* Toronto: ECW Press, 1987.

Gordon, Ian. *John Galt: The Life of a Writer.* Edinburgh: Oliver and Boyd, 1972.

Gordon, R.C. 'Scott, Ferguson, and the Martial Spirit.' *Scottish Tradition* 6 (1976): 66–82.

– *Under Which King? A Study of the Scottish Waverley Novels.* Edinburgh: Oliver and Boyd, 1969.

Grady, Wayne. 'A Man's Garden of Verse.' *Saturday Night,* November 1983, 73.

Grant, Nigel, and Robert Humes. 'Scottish Education, 1700–2000.' *Scotland: A Concise Cultural History,* ed. P.H. Scott. Edinburgh: Mainstream, 1993.

Gray, R.Q. 'Religion, Culture and Social Class in Late Nineteenth and Early Twentieth Century Edinburgh.' *The Lower Middle Class in Britain, 1870–1914,* ed. Geoffrey Crossick. London: Croom Helm, 1977.

Greenhill, Pauline. *Ethnicity in the Main Stream: Three Studies in English Canadian Culture in Ontario.* Montreal: McGill-Queen's University Press, 1994.

– *True Poetry: Traditional and Popular Verse in Ontario.* Montreal: McGill-Queen's University Press, 1989.

Groulx, Lionel. *L'appel de la race.* 1922. Repr. Montreal: Fides, 1980.

Gudgeon, Chris. *Out of This World: The Natural History of Milton Acorn.* Vancouver: Arsenal, 1996.

Gundy, H. Pearson. *Book Publishing and Publishers before 1900.* Toronto: Bibliographical Society of Canada, 1965.

– 'Literary Publishing.' *Literary History of Canada,* ed. C.F. Klinck. 2nd ed. Vol. 1. Toronto: University of Toronto Press, 1976.

Hanson, Lawrence, and Elisabeth Hanson. *Necessary Evil: The Life of Jane Welsh Carlyle.* Edinburgh: Constable, 1952.

Harrison, Dick. *W.O. Mitchell and His Works.* Toronto: ECW Press, 1991.

Hart, Francis. *Lockhart as Romantic Biographer.* Edinburgh: Edinburgh University Press, 1971.

– *The Scottish Novel: From Smollett to Spark.* Cambridge: Harvard University Press, 1978.

Hart, Lorena Laing, and Francis Hart. 'Jane Duncan: The Homecoming of Imagination.' *A History of Scottish Women's Writing*, ed. Douglas Gifford and Dorothy McMillan. Edinburgh: Edinburgh University Press, 1997.

Hawthorne, Nathaniel. *The Scarlet Letter*. 1850. Repr. New York: Norton, 1988.

Hayles, Katherine. *Chaos Bound: Orderly Disorder in Contemporary Literature and Science*. Ithaca: Cornell University Press, 1990.

Heffer, Simon. *Moral Desperado: A Life of Thomas Carlyle*. London: Weidenfeld and Nicolson, 1995.

Hewitt, David, ed. *Scott and His Times*. Aberdeen: University of Aberdeen Press, 1984.

Hogan, Homer, ed. *Listen: Songs and Poems of Canada*. Toronto: Methuen, 1972.

Holland, Norman. *The Dynamics of Literary Response*. New York: Oxford University Press, 1968.

Howe, Susanne. *Novels of Empire*. New York: Columbia University Press, 1949.

Howells, Coral Ann. *Private and Fictional Worlds: Canadian Women Novelists of the 1970s and 1980s*. London: Methuen, 1987.

Hughes, Kenneth. 'Isabella Valancy Crawford: The Names in "Malcolm's Katie."' *Canadian Notes and Queries* 14 (November 1974): 6.

– 'Poet Laureate of Labour.' *Canadian Dimension* 11 (March 1976): 33–40.

Humes, Walter, and Hamish Paterson. *Scottish Culture and Scottish Education, 1800–1980*. Edinburgh: John Donald, 1983.

Hunter, James. *The Dance Called America: The Scottish Highlands, the United States and Canada*. Edinburgh: Mainstream, 1994.

Hurley, Michael. *The Borders of Nightmare: The Fiction of John Richardson*. Toronto: University of Toronto Press, 1992.

Hutcheon, Linda. *The Canadian Postmodern: A Study of Contemporary English-Canadian Fiction*. Toronto: Oxford University Press, 1988.

– 'Eruptions of Postmodernity: The Postcolonial and the Ecological.' *Essays in Canadian Writing* 51–2 (1993–4): 146–53.

– *A Poetics of Postmodernism: History, Theory, Fiction*. London: Routledge, 1989.

– *Splitting Images: Contemporary Canadian Ironies*. Toronto: Oxford University Press, 1991.

Hynes, Joseph, ed. *Critical Essays on Muriel Spark*. New York: Macmillan, 1992.

Irving, J.A., and A.H. Johnson. 'Philosophical Literature to 1910.' *Literary History of Canada*, ed. C.F. Klinck. 2nd ed., 1: 447–60. Toronto: University of Toronto Press, 1976.

Iser, Wolfgang. *The Act of Reading*. Baltimore: Johns Hopkins University Press, 1978.

Jack, R.D.S. *The Road to the Never Land: A Reassessment of J.M. Barrie's Dramatic Art*. Aberdeen: Aberdeen University Press, 1991.

– and Andrew Noble, eds. *The Art of Robert Burns*. Totowa: Barnes and Noble, 1982.

Jameson, Frederic. *Marxism and Form: Twentieth-Century Dialectic Theories of Literature*. Princeton: Princeton University Press, 1971.

Jay, Elizabeth. *Mrs Oliphant: 'A Fiction to Herself.'* Oxford: Clarendon, 1995.

Jensen, Margaret Ann. *Love's Sweet Return: The Harlequin Story*. Toronto: Women's Educational Press, 1984.

Jessop, Ralph. *Carlyle and Scottish Thought*. Basingstoke: Macmillan, 1997.

Johnson, Edgar. *Sir Walter Scott, the Great Unknown*. London: Hamish Hamilton, 1970.

Johnston, Gordon. 'The Significance of Scott's Minor Poems.' *The Duncan Campbell Scott Symposium*. Ottawa: University of Ottawa Press, 1980.

Kamm, Antony, and Anne Lean, eds. *A Scottish Childhood: 70 Famous Scots Remember*. Glasgow: Collins, 1985.

Kaplan, Fred. *Thomas Carlyle: A Biography*. Cambridge: Cambridge University Press, 1983.

Keith, W.J. *Charles G.D. Roberts*. Toronto: Copp Clark, 1969.

Kenner, Hugh. 'The Case of the Missing Face.' *Our Canadian Identity*, ed. Malcolm Ross. Toronto: Ryerson, 1954.

Kerr, James. *Fiction against History: Scott as Storyteller*. Cambridge: Harvard University Press, 1989.

Kerrigan, Catherine, ed. *An Anthology of Scottish Women Poets*. Edinburgh: Edinburgh University Press, 1991.

Kertzer, J.M. *Margaret Laurence and Her Works.* Toronto: McClelland & Stewart, 1987.

Kinsley, James. *Burns and the Peasantry.* London: Oxford University Press, 1975.

Klinck, C.F., ed. *Literary History of Canada.* Toronto: University of Toronto Press, 1965. 2nd ed., 1976.

– *Robert Service: A Biography.* Toronto: McGraw-Hill Ryerson, 1976.

– *William 'Tiger' Dunlop: Blackwoodian Backwoodsman, Essays by and about Dunlop.* Toronto: Ryerson, 1958.

– and R.E. Watters, eds. *A Canadian Anthology.* Toronto: Gage, 1955.

Kolodny, Annette. *The Lay of the Land: Metaphors as Experience and History in American Life and Letters.* Chapel Hill: University of North Carolina Press, 1984.

Krentz, Jayne Ann. *Dangerous Men and Adventurous Women: Romance Writers on the Appeal of Romance.* Philadelphia: University of Pennsylvania Press, 1992.

Kristeva, Julia. *Desire in Language: A Semiotic Approach to Literature and Art.* Ed. Leon S. Raudiez. Oxford: Blackwell, 1980.

Kroller, Eva-Marie. 'The Exploding Frame: Uses of Photography in Timothy Findley's *The Wars.' Journal of Canadian Studies/Revue d'études canadiennes.* 16 (fall/winter 1981): 68–74.

Kruse, Juanita. *John Buchan and the Idea of Empire: Popular Literature and Political Ideology.* Lewiston: E. Mellen, 1989.

Lapierre, Alexandra. *Fanny Stevenson: Muse, Adventuress and Romantic Enigma.* Trans. Carol Cosman. London: Fourth Estate, 1995.

Lecker, Robert. *Making It Real: The Canonization of English-Canadian Literature.* Concord, Ont.: Anansi, 1995.

– 'Patterns of Deception in *Wacousta.' The Canadian Novel: Beginnings* II, ed. John Moss. Toronto: NC Press, 1989.

Lee, Dennis. 'Cadence, Country, Silence: Writing in Colonial Space.' *boundary* 2 (1974): 151–68.

Lennox, John. *'Les anciens Canadiens*: Aubert de Gaspé and Scott.' *British Journal of Canadian Studies* 7 (1992): 39–48.

Livesay, Dorothy. 'The Life of Isabella Valancy Crawford.' *The Crawford Symposium,* ed. Frank Tierney. Ottawa: University of Ottawa Press, 1979.

– 'Tennyson's Daughter or Wilderness Child? The Factual and

Literary Background of Isabella Valancy Crawford.' *Journal of Canadian Fiction* 2 (summer 1973): 161–7.

Lockhart, G.W. *On the Trail of Robert Service*. Barr: Luath, 1991.

Lockhart, J.G. *Memoirs of the Life of Sir Walter Scott, Bart*. Edinburgh: Murray, 1843–6.

Low, Donald A, ed. *Critical Essays on Robert Burns*. London: Routledge and Kegan Paul, 1975.

Lowenthal, David, and M.J. Bowden, eds. *Geographies of the Mind: Essays in Historical Geosophy in Honor of John Kirtland Wright*. New York: Oxford University Press, 1975.

Lownie, Andrew. *John Buchan: The Presbyterian Cavalier*. London: Constable, 1995.

Lukács, Georg. *The Historical Novel*. 1938. Trans. Hannah Stanley Mitchell. London: Merlin, 1962.

Lynch, Michael. *Scotland: A New History*. 1991. Repr. Pimlico, 1997.

– 'Scottish Culture in Its Historical Perspective.' *Scotland: A Concise History*, ed. P.H. Scott. Edinburgh: Mainstream, 1993.

Macdonald, Norman. *Canada: Immigration and Colonization, 1841–1903*. Toronto: Macmillan, 1966.

– *Immigration and Settlement: The Administration of Imperial Land Regulations*. Toronto: Longmans Green, 1939.

McDowell, Michael. 'The Bahktinian Road to Ecological Insight.' *The Ecocriticism Reader*, ed. Cheryl Glotfelty and Harold Fromm. Athens: University of Georgia Press, 1996.

MacGillivray, S.R., and J. Lynes. 'Paradise Ever Becoming: War of 1812 Narratives for Young Readers.' *Canadian Children's Literature/ Littérature canadienne pour la jeunesse* 84 (winter 1996): 6–16.

McGuirk, Carol. 'Burns and Bahktin: The Opposition of Poetic and Novelistic Discourse.' *The Eighteenth Century: Theory and Interpretation* 32 (1991): 58–72.

– *Robert Burns and the Sentimental Era*. Athens: Georgia University Press, 1985.

McIntyre, J.A. 'The Scot as Farmer and Artisan.' *The Scottish Tradition in Canada*, ed. W. Stanford Reid. Toronto: McClelland & Stewart, 1976.

McIntyre, Ian. *Dirt and Deity: A Life of Robert Burns*. London: Harper Collins, 1995.

Mackay, James A. *R.B.: A Biography of Robert Burns*. Edinburgh: Mainstream, 1992.

– *Vagabond of Verse: Robert Service: A Biography*. Edinburgh: Mainstream, 1995.

Mackenzie, Henry. 'Review of *Annals of the Parish*.' *Blackwood's Edinburgh Magazine*, May 1821, 203.

McLean, Marianne. *The People of Glengarry: Highlanders in Transition, 1745–1820*. Montreal: McGill-Queen's University Press, 1991.

McLuhan, Marshall. 'Canada: The Borderline Case.' *The Canadian Imagination*, ed. David Staines. Cambridge : Harvard University Press, 1977.

– *The Gutenberg Galaxy: The Making of Typographic Man*. Toronto: University of Toronto Press, 1962.

– *The Mechanical Bride: Folklore of Industrial Man*. New York: Vanguard, 1951.

– *Understanding Media: The Extensions of Man*. New York: McGraw-Hill, 1964.

– *War and Peace in the Global Village*. New York: McGraw-Hill, 1968.

MacLulich, T.D. *Hugh MacLennan*. Boston: Twayne, 1983.

McLynn, Frank. *Robert Louis Stevenson: A Biography*. London: Hutchison, 1993.

Macmillan, Carrie, Lorraine McMullen, and Elizabeth Waterston. *Silenced Sextet: Six Nineteenth-Century Canadian Women Novelists*. Montreal: McGill-Queen's University Press, 1992.

McMullen, Lorraine. 'Marshall Saunders' Mid-Victorian Cinderella; or, The Mating Game in Victorian Scotland.' *Canadian Children's literature / La littérature canadienne pour la jeunesse* 34 (1984): 31–40.

– ed. *Re(Dis)covering Our Foremothers: Nineteenth Century Canadian Women Writers*. Ottawa: University of Ottawa Press, 1990.

– *Sinclair Ross*. Boston: Twayne, 1979.

– and Elizabeth Waterston. 'Rosanna Leprohon: At Home in Many Worlds.' *Silenced Sextet: Six Nineteenth-Century Canadian Women Novelists*. Montreal: McGill-Queen's University Press, 1992.

Macnutt, W.S. *New Brunswick: A History, 1784–1867*. Toronto: Macmillan, 1963.

MacQueen, John. 'John Galt and the Analysis of Social History.' *Scott*

Bicentenary Essays, ed. Alan Bell. Edinburgh: Edinburgh University Press, 1973.

– *The Rise of the Historical Novel*. Edinburgh: Scottish Academic Press, 1989.

Manlove, Colin. *An Anthology of Scottish Fantasy Literature*. Edinburgh: Canongate, 1996.

Manning, Susan. *The Puritan-Provincial Vision: Scottish and American Literature in the Nineteenth Century*. Cambridge: Cambridge University Press, 1990.

Martel, Gordon. 'Generals Die in Bed: Modern Warfare and the Origins of Modernist Culture': Canada and the Wars. *Journal of Canadian Studies / Revue d'études canadiennes* (fall/winter 1981): 2–13.

Massey, Vincent, ed. *Report of the Royal Commission on National Development in the Arts, Letters & Sciences*. Ottawa: King's Printer, 1951.

Massie, Allan. *Muriel Spark*. Edinburgh: Ramsay Head, 1979.

Masters, D.C. 'The Scottish Tradition in Higher Education.' *The Scottish Tradition in Canada*, ed. W. Stanford Reid. Toronto: McClelland & Stewart, 1976.

Mathews, Robin. *Canadian Literature: Surrender or Revolution*. Ottawa: Steel Rail, 1978.

– *Canadian Identity: Major Forces Shaping the Life of a People*. Ottawa: Steel Rail, 1988.

Matthews, J.P. *Tradition in Exile: A Comparative Study of Social Influences on the Development of Australian and Canadian Poetry in the Nineteenth Century*. Toronto: University of Toronto Press, 1962.

Mayhead, Robin. *Walter Scott*. London: Routledge & Kegan Paul, 1968.

Meigs, Cornelia. *A Critical History of Children's Literature from Earliest Times to the Present*. New York: Macmillan, 1953.

Miller, Casey, and Kate Swift. *Words & Women: New Language in New Times*. 1976. Updated, New York: HarperCollins, 1991.

Mitchell, Orm. '"The Smell of Oatmeal": W.O. Mitchell's Battle with Presbyterianism.' *British Journal of Canadian Studies* 7 (1992): 102–16.

Mollinson, Bill. *Introduction to Permaculture*. Tayalgum: Tagari, 1994.

Monkman, Leslie. 'Canadian Historical Fiction.' *Queen's Quarterly* 94 (1987): 630–40.

– *A Native Heritage: Images of the Indian in English-Canadian Literature.*
Toronto: University of Toronto Press, 1981.

Morris, David, 'Burns' Heteroglossia.' *The Eighteenth Century: Theory and Interpretation* 28 (1987): 3–27.

Morris, Pam. *Literature and Feminism: An Introduction.* Cambridge: Blackwell, 1993.

Morton, W.L. *The Canadian Identity.* Toronto: University of Toronto Press, 1972.

– *Manitoba: A History.* Toronto: University of Toronto Press, 1957.

– 'The North in Canadian History.' *Canada's Changing North*, ed. W.C. Wonders. Toronto: McClelland & Stewart, 1971.

Moss, John, ed. *The Canadian Novel: Beginnings II.* Toronto: NC Press, 1980.

– ed. *From the Heart of the Heartland: The Fiction of Sinclair Ross.* Ottawa: University of Ottawa Press, 1992.

Mott, F.L. *Golden Multitudes: The Story of Best Sellers in the United States.* New York: Bowker, 1947.

Murray, Isobel. 'Selves, Names and Roles: Willa Muir's *Imagined Corners* Offers Some Inspiration for *A Scots Quair*.' *Scottish Literary Journal* 21 (May 1994): 56–64.

– and Robert Tait. 'George Mackay Brown: *Greenvoe*.' *Ten Modern Scottish Novels.* Aberdeen: Aberdeen University Press, 1984.

New, W.H. *Articulating West: Essays on Purpose and Form in Modern Canadian Literature.* Toronto: New Press, 1972.

Nicholson, Colin, ed. *Critical Approaches to the Fiction of Margaret Laurence.* London: Macmillan, 1990.

– 'Footprints on the Soul: A Scots-Canadian Connection in the Work of Sorley MacLean and Alistair MacLeod.' *A Shaping of Connections: Commonwealth Literature Studies – Then and Now*, ed. Maes Jelinek, Kirsten Petersen, and Anna Rutherford. Aarhus: AKA, 1989.

– 'Regions of Memory: Alistair MacLeod's Fiction.' *British Journal of Canadian Studies* 7 (1992): 128–37.

– 'There and Not There: Aspects of Scotland in Laurence's Writing.' *Critical Approaches to the Fiction of Margaret Laurence*, ed. Colin Nicholson. London: Macmillan, 1990.

Noble, Andrew. *Robert Louis Stevenson.* Totowa: Barnes and Noble, 1983.

Noonan, Gerald. 'Drummond, William Henry.' *The Oxford Companion to Canadian Literature*, ed. Eugene Benson and William Toye. Toronto: Oxford University Press, 1997.

– 'The Importance of Poetry and the Power of the Phrase Mellifluous.' *Canadian Children's Literature / Littérature canadienne pour la jeunesse* 42 (1986): 6–8.

Norquay, Glenda. 'Catherine Carswell, *Open the Door!' A History of Scottish Women's Writing*, ed. Douglas Gifford and Dorothy McMillan. Edinburgh: Edinburgh University Press, 1997.

O'Brien, Susie. 'Nature's Nation, National Natures? Reading Ecocriticism: A Canadian Context.' *Canadian Poetry* 42 (spring/ summer 1998): 17–41.

Ormond, Leonee. *J.M. Barrie*. Edinburgh: Scottish Academic Press, 1987.

Owen, Carola. *The Wizard of the North: The Life of Sir Walter Scott*. London: Hodder & Stoughton, 1973.

Parker, George. *The Beginnings of the Book Trade in Canada*. Toronto: University of Toronto Press, 1985.

Petrone, Penny. 'In Search of Isabella Valancy Crawford.' *The Isabella Valancy Crawford Symposium*, ed. Frank Tierney. Ottawa: University of Ottawa Press, 1979.

Phillipson, N.T. 'Nationalism and Ideology.' *Government and Nationalism in Scotland*, ed. J.N. Wolfe. Edinburgh: University of Edinburgh Press, 1968.

Pitlock, Norman. *The Invention of Scotland: The Stuart Myth and the Scottish Identity*. London: Routledge, 1991.

Porter, John. *The Vertical Mosaic: An Analysis of Social Class and Power in Canada*. Toronto: University of Toronto Press, 1965.

Powys, John Cowper. *The Enjoyment of Literature*. New York: Simon and Schuster, 1938.

Pratt, Annis. *Archetypal Patterns in Women's Fiction*. Bloomington: Indiana University Press, 1981.

Rattray. W.J. *The Scot in British North America*. Toronto: MacLear, 1880.

Raymond, Ernest. *Through Literature to Life*. London: Cassell, 1928.

Reaney, James. 'Isabella Valancy Crawford.' *Our Living Tradition*. 2nd and 3rd series. Toronto: University of Toronto Press, 1959.

Reid, W. Stanford, ed. *The Scottish Tradition in Canada*. Toronto: McClelland & Stewart, 1976.

Rendall, Jane. *The Origins of the Scottish Enlightenment, 1707–1776*. London: Macmillan, 1978.

Ricou, Laurie. *Vertical Man, Horizontal World*. Vancouver: University of British Columbia Press, 1973.

Rose, Jacqueline. *The Case of Peter Pan, or, the Impossibility of Children's Fiction*. 1984. Basingstoke: Macmillan, 1994.

Robb, David. '*Greenvoe*: A Poet's Novel.' *Scottish Literary Journal* 19 (May 1992): 47–60.

Rosenberg, John D. *Carlyle and the Burden of History*. Oxford: Clarendon, 1985.

Ross, Catherine. *Alice Munro: A Double Life*. Toronto: ECW Press, 1992.

– ed. *Recovering Canada's First Novelist*. Erin, Ont.: Porcupine's Quill, 1984.

Ross, Malcolm, ed. *Our Sense of Identity: A Book of Canadian Essays*. Toronto: Ryerson, 1954.

Rubio, Mary, ed. *Harvesting Thistles: The Textual Garden of L.M. Montgomery*. Guelph: Canadian Children's Press, 1994.

Rutherford, Anna, ed. *From Commonwealth to Post-Colonial*. Sydney: Dangaroo, 1992.

– ed. *Post-Colonial Women's Writing*. Armidale: Dangaroo, 1994.

Said, Edward. *Culture and Imperialism*. New York: Knopf, 1993.

– *The World, the Text, and the Critic*. Cambridge: Harvard University Press, 1983.

Salutin, Rick. *Marginal Notes: Challenge to the Main Stream*. Toronto: Lester and Orpen Dennys, 1984.

Saunders, Karen. 'Margaret Marshall Saunders: Children's Literature as an Expression of Early 20th Century Reform.' MA dissertation, Acadia University, 1978.

Scott, Frank, and A.J.M. Smith, eds. *The Blasted Pine*. Toronto: Macmillan, 1960.

Scott, P.H. *John Galt*. Edinburgh: Scottish Academic Press, 1985.

– ed. *Scotland: A Concise Cultural History*. Edinburgh: Mainstream, 1993.

Shaw, H.E. *The Forms of Historical Fiction: Sir Walter Scott and His Successors*. Ithaca: Cornell University Press, 1983.

Sher, Richard. *Church and University in the Scottish Enlightenment: The Modern Literati of Edinburgh*. Princeton: Princeton University Press, 1985.

Showalter, Elaine. *A Literature of Their Own: British Women Authors from Brontë to Lessing*. Princeton: Princeton University Press, 1977.

Simpson, John. 'Scott and Old Norse Literature.' *Scott Bicentenary Essays*, ed. Alan Bell. Edinburgh: Scottish Academic Press, 1973.

Simpson, Kenneth, ed. *Burns Now*. Edinburgh: Cannongate Academic Press, 1994.

– ed. *Love and Liberty: Robert Burns, a Bicentenary Celebration*. East Linton: Tuckwell, 1997.

Smith, A.J.M., ed. *The Book of Canadian Poetry*. Toronto: Gage, 1943.

Smith, Alison. 'And Woman Created Woman: Carswell, Shepherd and Muir, and the Self-Made Woman.' *Gendering the Nation*, ed. Christopher Whyte. Edinburgh: Edinburgh University Press, 1995.

Smith, Janet Adam. *John Buchan: A Biography*. 1965. Repr. Oxford: Oxford University Press, 1985.

Snyder, Franklyn B. *The Life of Robert Burns*. New York: Macmillan, 1932.

Spacks, Patricia M. *The Female Imagination*. New York: Knopf, 1972.

– *Gossip*. New York: Knopf, 1985.

Speirs, John. *The Scots Literary Tradition*. London: Chatto and Windus, 1940.

Stanford, Derek. *Muriel Spark: A Biographical and Critical Study*. Edinburgh: Centaur, 1963.

Steffler, Margaret. 'The Canadian Romantic Child: Travelling the Border Country, Exploring the "Edge."' *Canadian Children's Literature* 89 (spring 1998): 5–17.

Stegmaier, Edmund, 'Edwin Muir's *Scottish Journey* and the Question of Violence.' *Scottish Literary Journal* 19 (November 1992): 50–60.

Stewart, Ralph. 'The Enchanted World of the Lady of the Lake.' *Scottish Literary Journal* 22 (November 1995): 6.

Strong-Boag, Veronica, and Anita C. Fellman, eds. *Rethinking Canada: The Promise of Women's History*. Toronto: Copp Clark Pitman, 1986.

Swiggett, Howard. 'Introduction.' *Sick Heart River*, by John Buchan. Toronto: Musson, 1941.

Tausky, Thomas E. *Sara Jeannette Duncan: Novelist of Empire.* Port
Credit: P.D. Meany, 1980.

Tennyson, G.B. *'Sartor' Called 'Resartus.'* Princeton: Princeton University Press, 1965.

Thomas, Clara. '"The Chariot of Ossian": Myth and Manitoba in *The
Diviners.'* *Journal of Canadian Studies* 13 (fall 1978): 55–63.

– *Love and Work Enough: The Life of Anna Jameson.* Toronto: University
of Toronto Press, 1967.

– *The Manawaka World of Margaret Laurence.* Toronto: McClelland &
Stewart, 1975.

– 'Margaret, Morag, and the Scottish Ancestors.' *Scottish Influences
on Canadian Literature: A Selection of Papers Delivered at the University of Edinburgh, May 9–12, 1991,* ed. Michael Williams. *British
Journal of Canadian Studies* (1992).

– '"Planted Firmly in Some Soil": Margaret Laurence and the Canadian Tradition in Fiction.' *Critical Approaches to the Fiction of
Margaret Laurence,* ed. Colin Nicholson. London: Macmillan, 1990.

Tierney, Frank, ed. *The Crawford Symposium.* Ottawa: University of
Ottawa Press, 1979.

– ed. *The Thomas Chandler Haliburton Symposium.* Ottawa: University
of Ottawa Press, 1979.

Tiffin, Helen, Bill Ashcroft, and Gareth Griffiths, eds. *Key Concepts in
Post-Colonial Studies.* London: Routledge, 1998.

Tippett, Maria. *The Making of English-Canadian Culture, 1900–1939:
The External Influences.* Toronto: ECW Press, 1987.

Tompkins, Jane. *Sensational Designs: The Cultural Work of American
Fiction, 1790–1860.* New York: Oxford University Press, 1985.

Townsend, John Rowe. *Written for Children: An Outline of English
Children's Literature.* New York: Lippincott, 1983.

Susan Mann, and Alison Prentice. *The Neglected Majority: Essays in
Canadian Women's History.* Toronto: McClelland & Stewart, 1977.

Van Loon, Richard. *The Structure and Membership of the Canadian
Cabinet.* Report no. 8. Ottawa: Royal Commission on Bilingualism
and Biculturalism, 1966.

Vipond, Mary. 'Best Sellers in English Canada, 1889–1918: An Over-
view.' *Journal of Canadian Fiction* 24 (1979): 96–119.

Wachowicz, Barbara. 'L.M. Montgomery: At Home in Poland.' *Canadian Children's Literature/Littérature canadienne pour la jeunesse* 46 (1987): 7–36.

Wallace, Gavin, and Randall Stevenson. *The Scottish Novel since the Seventies*. Edinburgh: Edinburgh University Press, 1993.

Waterston, Elizabeth. *Gilbert Parker*. Canadian Writers and Their Works, Fiction Series 2. Toronto: ECW, 1989.

– 'The Harp, the North, and Scott's Irony.' *Scott and His Times*, ed. David Hewitt. Aberdeen: University of Aberdeen Press, 1984.

– ed. *John Galt: Reappraisals*. Guelph: University of Guelph, 1985.

– *Kindling Spirit: L.M. Montgomery's Anne of Green Gables*. Canadian Fiction Studies, 19. Toronto: ECW Press, 1993.

– 'The Lowland Tradition in Canadian Literature.' *The Scottish Tradition in Canada*, ed. W. Stanford Reid. Toronto: McClellland & Stewart, 1976.

– 'The Politics of Conquest in Canadian Historical Fiction.' *Mosaic* 3 (fall 1969): 116–24.

– et al. *The Travellers: Canada to 1900*. Guelph, University of Guelph, 1989.

Watson, Robert. *The Poetry of Scotland: Gaelic, Scots and English, 1380– 1980*. Edinburgh: Edinburgh University Press, 1995.

Watson, Roderick. *The Literature of Scotland*. Basingstoke: Macmillan, 1984.

Watters, R.E. *A Checklist of Canadian Literature and Background Materials, 1628–1950*. Toronto: University of Toronto Press, 1959.

Webb, Paul. *A Buchan Companion: A Guide to the Novels and Short Stories*. Stroud: Alan Sutton, 1994.

Weinbrot, Howard D. '"An Ambition to Excell": The Aesthetics of Emulation in the Seventeenth and Eighteenth Centuries.' *Huntington Library Quarterly* 48 (1985): 121–39.

Whatley, Christopher, ed. *John Galt, 1779–1979*. Edinburgh: Ramsay Head, 1979.

Whistler, Nick. 'John Galt's Autobiography: Fact, Fiction and Truth.' MA dissertation, University of Guelph, 1984.

White, Hayden. 'The Burden of History.' *Topics of Discourse: Essays in Cultural Criticism*. Baltimore: Johns Hopkins University Press, 1978.

– *The Content of the Form*. Baltimore: Johns Hopkins University Press, 1987.

Whittaker, Ruth. *The Faith and Fiction of Muriel Spark*. London: Macmillan, 1982.

Whyte, Christopher, ed. *Gendering the Nation*. Edinburgh: Edinburgh University Press, 1995.

Williams, Merryn. *Margaret Oliphant: A Critical Biography*. London: Macmillan, 1986.

Williams, Michael, ed. *Scottish Influences on Canadian Literature: A Selection of Papers Delivered at the University of Edinburgh, May 9–12, 1991. British Journal of Canadian Studies* 7 (1992).

Wilson, Milton, ed. *Poets between the Wars*. Toronto: McClelland & Stewart, 1967.

Wittig, Kurt. *The Scottish Tradition in Literature*. Edinburgh: Oliver and Boyd, 1958.

Woodcock, George. *Hugh MacLennan*. Toronto: Copp Clark, 1969.

Wordsworth, Dorothy. *Recollections of a Tour Made in Scotland, A.D. 1803*. Repr. New Haven: Yale University Press, 1997.

Wright, Allen. *J.M. Barrie: Glamour of Twilight*. Edinburgh: Ramsay Head Press, 1976.

Yeoman, Ann. 'Towards a Native Mythology.' *Canadian Literature* 52 (spring 1972): 39–47.

Young, Alan. *Thomas H. Raddall*. Boston: Twayne, 1983.

– ed. *Time and Place: The Life and Works of Thomas Raddall*. Fredericton: Acadiensis, 1991.

Young, Douglas. *Scotland*. London: Cassell, 1971.

Youngson, A.J. *The Making of Classical Edinburgh, 1750–1840*. 1966. Edinburgh: Edinburgh University Press, 1993.

Zipes, Jack. *Breaking the Magic Spell: Radical Theories of Folk and Fairy Tales*. New York: Routledge and Chapman Hall, 1982.

Index